Strategic Marketing Management:
Planning and Control
2001–2002

The Chartered Institute of Marketing/Butterworth-Heinemann Marketing Series is the most comprehensive, widely used and important collection of books in marketing and sales currently available worldwide.

As the CIM's official publisher, Butterworth-Heinemann develops, produces and publishes the complete series in association with the CIM. We aim to provide definitive marketing books for students and practitioners that promote excellence in marketing education and practice.

The series titles are written by CIM senior examiners and leading marketing educators for professionals, students and those studying the CIM's Certificate, Advanced Certificate and Postgraduate Diploma courses. Now firmly established, these titles provide practical study support to CIM and other marketing students and to practitioners at all levels.

 The Chartered
Institute of Marketing

Formed in 1911, the Chartered Institute of Marketing is now the largest professional marketing management body in the world with over 60,000 members located worldwide. Its primary objectives are focused on the development of awareness and understanding of marketing throughout UK industry and commerce and in the raising of standards of professionalism in the education, training and practice of this key business discipline.

Strategic Marketing Management: Planning and Control

2001–2002

Helen Meek, Richard Meek
and John Ensor

Published on behalf of
The Chartered Institute of Marketing

OXFORD AUCKLAND BOSTON JOHANNESBURG MELBOURNE NEW DELHI

Butterworth-Heinemann
Linacre House, Jordan Hill, Oxford OX2 8DP
225 Wildwood Avenue, Woburn, MA 01801-2041
A division of Reed Educational and Professional Publishing Ltd

℞ A member of the Reed Elsevier plc group

First published 2001

British Library Cataloguing in Publication Data
A catalogue record for this book is available from the British Library

ISBN 0 7506 53132

For information on all Butterworth-Heinemann
publications visit our website at www.bh.com

Typeset by Avocet Typeset, Brill, Aylesbury, Bucks
Printed and bound in Italy

FOR EVERY TITLE THAT WE PUBLISH, BUTTERWORTH-HEINEMANN
WILL PAY FOR BTCV TO PLANT AND CARE FOR A TREE.

Contents

A message from the author

This workbook is designed specifically to meet the needs of students studying for the Chartered Institute of Marketing Strategic Marketing Management: Planning and Control exam. The structure of the workbook mirrors the Planning and Control syllabus and reflects the relative weighting given to each aspect of the syllabus. The Planning and Control module acts as a foundation on which the other Diploma subjects are based. This module builds on the operational aspects of marketing that have already been covered at Certificate and Advanced Certificate level. However, this module is firmly focused on the strategic rather than the operational aspects of marketing. It is expected that students will already be competent in all areas covered in the Certificate and Advanced Certificate modules.

The syllabus reflects the importance of strategy development, and in particular the critical areas of implementation and control of plans. There is now slightly less emphasis placed on planning and the planning process. The following are key themes of the syllabus:

- Developing a view of the future through various forecasting techniques.
- Innovation and creativity.
- Branding.
- Implementation and control of plans which now equates to 15% of the syllabus.
- The use and evaluation of marketing tools and techniques.

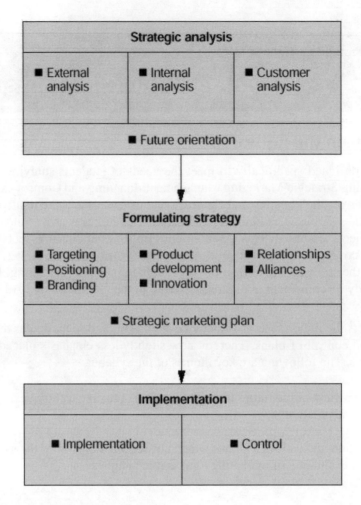

Figure 1
Process of strategic marketing (Drummond and Eusor, 2001)

The process of strategic marketing is shown in the figure above. The workbook is structured around this framework. The syllabus is broken down into five distinct areas:

- Market-led approach to planning (10%).
- Analysis (25%).
- Techniques for analysis and strategy development (20%).
- Strategy formulation and selection (30%).
- Implementation and control (15%).

The following figure provides a diagrammatical overview of the book and how it relates to the various components of the syllabus.

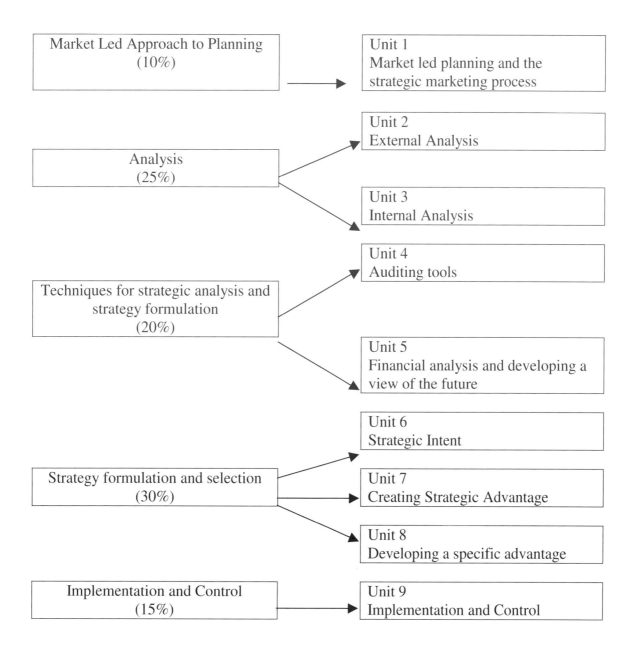

Figure 2
Overview of the book

This workbook is designed to bridge the gap between the theory of strategic marketing and its practical application, this is achieved by providing students with practical examples and encouraging them to reflect on their own knowledge and understanding by the inclusion of relevant exam questions and mini-cases. The case examples have been sourced using www.Lexis-Nexis.com

Strategic marketing is a vast subject and there is a wealth of books, articles and on-line materials available for students studying the Planning and Control module. The recommended reading for the Planning and Control module is extensive and many students feel overwhelmed by the number of recommended and additional texts on the reading list. This workbook is designed to act as a 'map' for students to lead them through the syllabus and to refer them to relevant further reading where necessary. The text is designed to complement the texts on the reading list, not to replace them. It is essential that students demonstrate both 'depth' and 'breadth' of knowledge of strategic marketing, and this can only be achieved by reference to other core and supporting texts. A key role of this book is to provide students with signposts to further reading.

The examiners are looking for evidence that you have the ability to apply the theoretical concepts of strategic marketing to practical situations. Therefore it is suggested that you develop a portfolio of examples that will demonstrate key aspects of the syllabus. There are numerous sources of materials – such as *The Financial Times* and other quality newspapers, websites and other on-line resources and marketing journals such as *Marketing, Marketing Week* and *Campaign*. By building a portfolio of articles you will arm yourself with relevant examples that you will be able to use in the Planning and Control exam.

An introduction from the academic development advisor

Over the past few years there have been a series of syllabus changes initiated by the Chartered Institute of Marketing to ensure that their qualifications continue to be relevant and of significant consequence in the world of marketing, both within industry and academia. As a result Butterworth-Heinemann and I have rigorously revised and updated the Coursebook series to make sure that every title is the best possible study aid and accurately reflects the latest CIM syllabus.

The revisions to the series this year include both restructuring and the inclusion of many new mini cases and examples. There are a number of new and accomplished authors in the series commissioned both for their CIM course teaching and examining experience, and their wide general knowledge of the latest marketing thinking.

We are certain that you will find the new look-books a highly beneficial study tool as you prepare for the CIM examinations. They will guide you in a structured and logical way through the detail of the syllabus, providing you with the required underpinning knowledge, understanding and application of theory.

The editorial team and authors wish you every success as you embark upon your studies.

Karen Beamish

Academic Development Advisor

How to use these workbooks

Everyone who has contributed to this series has been careful to structure the books with the exams in mind. Each unit, therefore, covers an essential part of the syllabus. You need to work through the complete workbook systematically to ensure that you have covered everything you need to know.

This workbook is divided into units each containing a selection of the following standard elements:

- **Objectives** tell you what part of the syllabus you will be covering and what you will be expected to know, having read the unit.
- **Study guides** tell you how long the unit is and how long its activities take to do.
- **Questions** are designed to give you practice – they will be similar to those you get in the exam.
- **Answers** (at the end of the book) give you a suggest format for answering exam questions. *Remember* there is no such thing as a model answer – you should use these examples only as guidelines.
- **Activities** give you a chance to put what you have learned into practice.
- **Debriefings** (at the end of the book) shed light on the methodologies involved in the activities.
- **Exam hints** are tips from the senior examiner or examiner which are designed to help you avoid common mistakes made by previous candidates.
- **Study tips** give you guidance on improving your knowledge base.
- **Insights** encourage you to contextualize your academic knowledge by reference to real-life experience.

- **Definitions** may be used for words you must know to pass the exam.
- **Summaries** cover what you should have picked up from reading the unit.

While you will find that each section of the syllabus has been covered within this text, you might find that the order of some of the topics has been changed. This is because it sometimes makes more sense to put certain topics together when you are studying, even though they might appear in different sections of the syllabus itself. If you are following the reading and other activities, your coverage of the syllabus will be just fine, but don't forget to follow up with trade press reading!

Objectives

By the end of this unit you will:

- Understand what is meant by 'market orientation'
- Understand and be able to discuss the contribution marketing makes to 'market-led strategic management'
- Be able to discuss, and give examples of, drivers of change
- Understand the relationship between corporate and marketing strategy
- Understand the basis of planning and control, the structure of planning and the cycle of control
- Know the differences between objectives, strategy, tactics and contingency planning
- Appreciate the impact that organizational culture and structures have on marketing planning
- To know the process and structure of marketing planning and to be able to discuss the differences between strategic and tactical planning

Study guide

- This unit will take you about 3 hours to work through
- We suggest that you take a further 3 hours to do the various activities and questions in this unit.

Introduction

The marketing concept is inherently simple – satisfying customers whilst at the same time achieving organizational goals. Few people would disagree with this principle, however many organizations find it very difficult to put the concept into practice. Marketing planning is highly challenging because it takes place against a backdrop of continuous environmental change, increasing competition, changing customer needs and limited resources. Marketing strategy has therefore become a vital component of organizational success. This unit will provide an overview of strategic marketing planning, discuss marketing's relationship with corporate strategy and in particular introduce the concept of market-led strategic change. The components of a strategic marketing plan will also outlined.

Marketing revisited

There are numerous definitions of marketing and it is not the purpose of this study text to provide a definitive list. Instead it will highlight the key issues in relation to the many and varied definitions of marketing that exist. Crosier (1975) reviewed more than 50 definitions of marketing and concluded that definitions of marketing could be classified into three distinct groups:

1. The *marketing process*, which is concerned with connecting the supplier and the customer.
2. The *marketing concept*, (philosophy) which suggests that marketing is concerned with exchange between willing parties.

3. The *marketing orientation*, which is the phenomenon that makes the marketing process and the marketing concept achievable.

Despite the numerous definitions of marketing it is clear that marketing can be discussed from two different perspectives. Firstly, it can be seen as a functional activity concerned with operational aspects such as promotion, pricing, product development, distribution or market research. It can also be seen in the wider context as a business philosophy that seeks to put the customer at the centre of an organization's activities. This philosophy is often referred to as the *marketing concept*.

There is now generally universal agreement that marketing is a way of doing business – i.e. a philosophy that is driven by the customer rather than a purely functional activity. Most definitions of marketing include two dimensions; the need to identify and satisfy customer needs (more effectively than competitors) and to achieve organizational goals. These goals do not necessarily have to be related to profitability. For many organizations, in particular not-for-profit organizations, there will be other types of goals that are just as important such as environmental or employee goals. It has been argued that an organization's primary (and only) responsibility is to its stakeholders in terms of maximizing their return. However, others argue that organizations have a responsibility not only to their customers and stakeholders but also to society in general. Kotler (2000) pp25 states that:

> Some people have questioned whether the marketing concept is an appropriate organizational philosophy in an age of environmental deterioration, resource shortages, explosive population growth, world hunger and poverty, and neglected social services. Are companies that do an excellent job of satisfying consumer wants necessarily acting in the best long-run interest of consumers and society? The marketing concept sidesteps the potential conflicts between consumer wants, consumer interest and long-run societal welfare.

He goes on to suggest that, due to these potential conflicts, companies should adopt the societal marketing concept, which:

> Holds that the organization's task is to determine the needs, wants and interests of target markets and to deliver the desired satisfactions more effectively and efficiently than competitors in a way that preserves or enhances the consumer's and the society's well-being

There are many examples of organizations, such as the Body Shop, Iceland, Cafédirect (a fairtrade product) and the Co-operative Bank (see below), that are seemingly keen to adopt this societal marketing concept. However, many other organizations have failed to acknowledge their responsibilities to wider society, an indeed still struggle to satisfy their customers. The extent to which organizations are internally or externally focused can be illustrated in Figure 1.1. This matrix highlights the importance of being not only customer-focused but also competitor focused.

The degree of competitor focus

	Low	High
Low	Myopic and inwardly focused	Transfixed by one or more competitors
High	Preoccupied by one or more customer groups	Market-driven

The degree of customer focus

Figure 1.1
The management team's customer and competitor orientation

It is clear that those companies who adopt an 'outside in' approach to business (as opposed to an 'inside out' approach) are more likely to be aware, not only of changing customer needs, but also of activities of established and potential competitors, and will therefore be more able to anticipate and adapt to environmental change. The characteristics of these 'market-oriented' organizations will be explored in the next section.

Case history

The Co-operative Bank – The importance of being ethical

The Co-operative Bank uses its ethical banking policy as a major means of differentiation. It has recognized the increasing interest of customers in ethical issues. MORI were commissioned by the Bank in 2000 to undertake a survey of customer attitudes to ethical products. The results suggest that across all consumer markets as many as 30% of consumers will demand ethical products and services. The Bank has recognized the increasing importance of the societal marketing concept and has therefore adopted an ethical investment policy, based on extensive consultation with its customers. Through its website the Bank actively encourages customer participation and feedback. The Bank demonstrates its commitment to the societal marketing concept in its ecological mission statement:

'We, The Co-operative Bank, will continue to develop our business, taking into account the impact our activities have on the environment and society at large. The nature of our activities are such that our indirect impact by being selective in terms of the provision of finance and banking arrangements is more ecologically significant than the direct impact of our trading operations. However, we undertake to continually assess all our activities and implement a programme of ecological improvement based on the pursuit of the following four scientific principles:

- Nature cannot withstand a progressive build-up of waste derived from the Earth's crust.
- Nature cannot withstand a progressive build-up of society's waste, particularly artificial persistent substances which it cannot degrade into harmless materials.
- The productive area of nature must not be diminished in quality (diversity) or quantity (volume) and must be enabled to grow.
- Society must utilize energy and resources in a sustainable, equitable and efficient manner.

We consider that the pursuit of these principles constitutes a path of ecological excellence and will secure future prosperity for society by sustainable economic activity. The Co-operative Bank will not only pursue the above path itself, but also endeavour to help and encourage all its stakeholders to do likewise.

We will aim to achieve this by:

Financial Services

Encouraging business customers to take a pro-active stance on the environmental impact of their n activities, and investing in companies and organizations that avoid repeated damage of the environment.

Management Systems

Assessing our ecological impact, setting ourselves clear targets, formulating an action plan and monitoring how we meet them, and publishing the results.

Purchasing and Outsourcing

Welcoming suppliers whose activities are compatible with both our Ethical Policy and Ecological Mission Statement, and working in partnership with them to improve our collective performance.

Support

Supporting ecological projects and developing partnerships with businesses and organizations whose direct and indirect output contributes to a sustainable society.

Legislation

Adhering to environmental laws, directives and guidelines while continually improving upon our own contribution to a sustainable society.'

The Co-operative Bank has a developed a detailed ethical policy that outlines how customers money should or should not be invested. Their position includes a their stance on investments in relation to human rights, the arms trade, trade and social involvement, ecological impact and animal welfare. For example, their stance in relation to human rights and the arms trade is as follows:

Market orientation

In a company that is market-oriented, all departments (not just the marketing department) would be customer-focused, and the aim of providing superior customer value would be seen as everybody's responsibility (that everybody is seen as a part-time marketer). Some authors refer to this as the market orientation; others as the marketing orientation. Often the two terms are used interchangeably. However, Piercy (2000) argues that *markets* are what are important, not *marketing* and therefore more emphasis should be placed on 'market orientation'. Many studies have attempted to identify the key characteristics of market-oriented companies. Kohli & Jawaroski (1990) identified that:

A market orientation entails:

1. one or more departments engaging in activities geared towards developing an understanding of customers' current and future needs and the factors affecting them
2. sharing of this understanding across departments and
3. the various departments engaging in activities designed to meet select customer needs.

In other words, a market orientation refers to the organization wide generation, dissemination and responsiveness to market intelligence.

Narver and Slater (1990) developed the following model that highlights the key components of a market orientation.

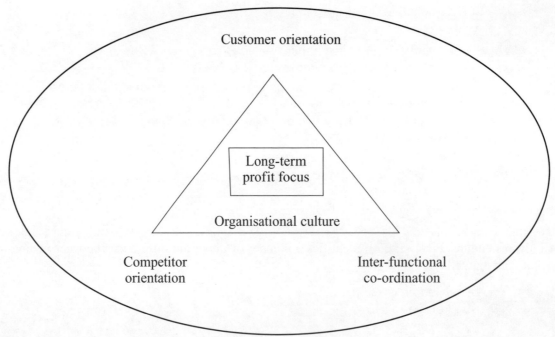

Figure 1.2
A Model of Market Orientation (Adapted from Narver and Slater (1990).)

- Customer orientation – concerned with understanding customers so that you can better meet their needs.
- Competitor orientation – having an awareness of competitors' capabilities.
- Interfunctional co-ordination – all aspects of the business striving to create value.
- Organizational culture – a culture that facilities organizational learning.
- Long-term profit focus – as opposed to a short-term perspective.

Activity 1.2

How market-oriented is your organization?

Hooley et al (1998) in their text *Marketing Strategy and Competitive Positioning* have developed a framework for evaluating market orientation. Complete the assessment presented on pp.11-13 of their book, by applying it to your own organization. To what extent do you think your organization is market-oriented, and how helpful is this framework in understanding the key components of market orientation?

When considering an organization's market orientation it is also essential that the external environment be taken into consideration because this is continually changing and will impact on the development and implementation of market orientation.

Extended knowledge

The *Financial Times* ran an excellent Marketing series, entitled 'Mastering Marketing' in 1998. Find and read the following articles that provide a useful discussion of market orientation.

Meehan S. & Barwise P. (1998) *Do you Value Customer Value?*

Carpenter G. (1998). *Changing the rules of the marketing game.* Financial Times Mastering Marketing Series, 14 September.

Market-led Strategic Change (MLSC)

A key theme throughout the Planning and Control syllabus is that of market-led strategic change. Piercy (2000) developed this phrase and places much emphasis on 'going to market' rather than marketing. Marketing can be regarded as belonging to specialists, whereas 'going to market' is what companies do and should be the responsibility of all employees. It may be argued that marketing departments could disappear in a truly market-oriented organization but going to market will always endure. Piercy (2000) identifies a number of important differences between 'going to market' and marketing.

- Strategies are based on customers and markets.
- Internal processes or change and external actions are driven by those strategies.
- Focus is on delivering a customer-focused strategy.
- Relationships are fundamental (customers, competitors, intermediaries).
- Information technology underpins new ways of doing business.

Many successful companies have succeeded, not because of their structured marketing programmes but because of their understanding of the *customer* and their ability to sense the market. Marketing functions such as promotion, marketing research and NPD are all important aspects of the process of marketing.

Piercy (2000) suggests that managers need to concentrate on three key issues:

- Customers – understanding customers.
- Market strategy – segmenting the market, selecting target markets and developing a strong competitive position.
- Implementation – getting the strategy to the marketplace.

Too often these important issues are not given priority because immediate problems get in the way. Managers should be concentrating on these strategic issues rather than getting involved in the tactics. Many strategies fail, not because they are poor strategies but because they have been poorly implemented. Managers need to focus as much on the implementation as they do on the contents of the strategy. This issue will be discussed in the unit 'Implementation and Control'.

Piercy (2000) acknowledges that the process of going to market is not easy, may require substantial change in the way organizations are run and that a key role of marketing is to encourage and facilitate change so that employees are more likely to accept and embrace it willingly. Piercy acknowledges that the market is dynamic and that for companies to maintain their competitive advantage they will have to respond to the following new challenges:

- New customer demands and expectations – Customer expectations are increasing and they are less willing to accept second-class service.
- New competitors – competition is coming not just from established competitors but also from new entrants, such as the entrance of Virgin into financial services and easyJet into car rental.
- New types of organizations being established – many organizations are downsizing and becoming more narrowly focused. Others (such as Time Warner and AOL) are entering strategic alliances and collaborative partnerships.

- Whole new ways of doing business are being developed – for example, electronic marketing.

It is imperative that marketers continually adapt and respond to these new challenges in order to gain/maintain competitive advantage.

Extended knowledge

Market-led Strategic Change by Nigel Piercy (2000) is essential, and entertaining, reading for this topic. Read at least Chapter 1 – Whatever happened to marketing?

Chapter 1 of Hooley et al. (1998) also provides a comprehensive discussion of this topic.

Question 1.1

Market-led strategic change

Answer the question 5 from the June 1999 paper and compare your answer with the outline answer in the CIM specimen answers.

> Your Managing Director has returned from a conference at which reference was made to market-led strategic change. Prepare a briefing paper explaining what market-led strategic change entails.

Drivers of change

Change is inevitable and companies that wish to maintain a market-led approach must take into consideration both cyclical and evolutionary change when developing their marketing strategies. The rate at which the external environment changes varies according to the nature of the business but increasingly all organizations are facing escalating levels of change. Therefore, according to Drummond & Ensor (2001),

'it is important to see the concept of change as an integral part of strategy'

Drummond & Ensor (2001) suggest that the concept of change can be evaluated in terms of the following questions:

1. What drives change? The continually evolving environment in terms of political, economic, social and technological developments (PEST) is driving change.
2. How does change impact on our markets/ business environment?
3. What is the result of change on the organization's strategy? The change may result in either opportunities in terms of changing customer needs or conversely organizations may become complacent and drift away from the needs of the marketplace.

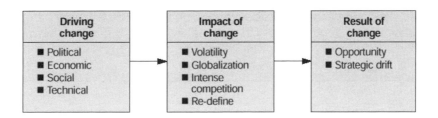

Driving change	Impact of change	Result of change
■ Political ■ Economic ■ Social ■ Technical	■ Volatility ■ Globalization ■ Intense competition ■ Re-define	■ Opportunity ■ Strategic drift

Figure 1.3
This figure summarizes the three questions posed by Drummond & Ensor (2001)

Change is inevitable. To survive companies need to adapt and to convert the threats created by the changing environment into opportunities in order to avoid 'strategic drift'. Marks and Spencer is a prime example of a company that did not adapt to the changing customer demands and as a result has lost many of its loyal customer base.

Case history

The Internet – new opportunities for Direct Line with jamjar.com venture

Direct Line, an established direct insurer and financial services provider, has entered into the Internet car retailing sector. There has been much publicity surrounding inflated UK car prices. Direct Line saw the opportunity to capitalize on this, and the increased interest in buying on-line, by launching their jamjar.com venture.

Jamjar.com is an Internet based car retailing operation that claims to provide 15-30% discounts on UK sourced cars as well as on imports from continental Europe. Customers can view and select from a wide range of both new and used cars and may trade in their existing car. Cars are delivered to the customer's home and there is a 7-day 'no questions asked' return policy, if customers are not satisfied. Customers are even emailed a digital photograph of their car once it is loaded on to the car transporter to reassure them of their purchase!

Internet car sales are revolutionizing the way in which people buy cars and many car manufacturers are having to re-evaluate their distribution strategies and their relationships with their dealers. The Internet is the source of many new opportunities but it is also it is also a threat to traditional ways of doing business.

Source: Griffiths (2000) www.Lexis-Nexis.com *and* www.jamjar.com

Exam hint

The Planning and Control examiner is looking for evidence that you can discuss the impact of changes on marketing strategy and provide applied examples. The following exam question was included on the June 1997 exam paper.

Societies are changing in a wide variety of ways. Identify the nature and significance of two such changes that are taking place within your own society and discuss their implications for the marketing planning and control process.

In the *FT Mastering Marketing* (1998) series Kotler predicted that the following trends will be shaping marketing by the year 2005:

- Disintermediation of wholesalers and retailers owing to electronic commerce. B2B purchasing over the Internet has increased even faster than consumer on-line buying.
- Reduction in the number of customers visiting traditional shop-based retailers. Retailers will offer customers an 'experience' in addition to a product assortment in the form of entertainment, coffee shops, etc.
- Customer databases containing rich information of individual customer preferences will be used to mass-customize products.
- Companies will develop strategies to retain customers to a greater extent, and attracting customers from competitors will become more difficult. Companies will concentrate on increasing the value of existing customers.
- Companies will develop ways of accounting that can measure individual customer profitability so that they will be able to target customers.
- Many companies will have moved towards a loyalty building strategy and away from a transactional approach.
- Companies will become much leaner by outsourcing their non-core activities.
- Field salespeople will become franchisees rather than company employees.
- Importance of mass TV advertising will diminish, as there is a proliferation of specialized on-line magazine and TV channels.
- Companies will find it difficult to sustain competitive advantages and the only sustainable advantage lies in an ability to learn and change faster than competitors.

It is apparent that monitoring the external environment and developing a view of the future is a key element in developing successful future strategy.

The strategic marketing process

Up to this point we have focused primarily on marketing strategy. However, it is impossible to discuss marketing strategy without looking at it in the context of overall corporate strategy. There is often much confusion as to the similarities and differences of marketing and corporate strategy. This may partly be due to the fact that in a market-oriented organization, where the customer is at the heart of the organization, it is likely that marketing is the largest contributor to corporate planning. This section will highlight the relationship between marketing and corporate strategy, discuss the planning framework and clarify the different types of planning.

What is strategy?

The term strategy is probably one of the most used and often misunderstood terms in business. There is no universal definition of strategy and yet it is used extensively. Strategy has the same meaning, whether we are discussing corporate, marketing, promotional or even advertising strategy: it is concerned with how we might achieve our objectives. The difference between each type of strategy relates to the level at which the strategy is being developed. *Corporate strategy* according to Johnson and Scholes (1999), is:

> concerned with what types of business the company as a whole should be in and is therefore concerned with decisions of scope

whereas *marketing strategy* aims to transform corporate objectives into a competitive market position.

The main role of marketing strategy is to differentiate products/services from those of competitors by meeting the needs of customers more effectively. Therefore, marketing strategy addresses three key areas :

- Assessing the external environment and identifying customer needs.
- Matching customer needs with internal resources and competencies.
- Implementing programmes that achieve a superior competitive advantage.

In the 1970s and 1980s a great deal of emphasis was placed on strategic planning and developing corporation-wide plans, often in a centralized manner. This produced detailed plans but often problems occurred at implementation because insufficient attention was given to how the plans were going to be executed. Today in business more attention is being given to strategic management (as opposed to strategic planning). This concerns both the formulation of strategy and how the strategy may be implemented. It is increasingly recognized that organizations need to be able to manage change in light of a dynamic environment. Figure 1.4 illustrates the elements of strategic management.

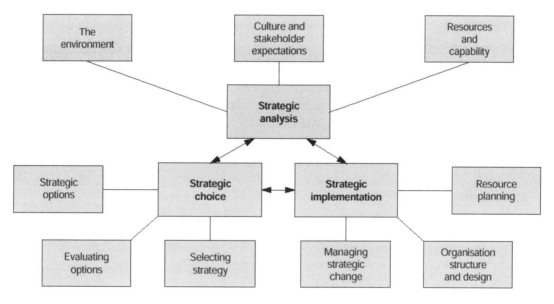

Figure 1.4
Elements of strategic management (Johnson & Scholes, 1999)

It can be seen that strategic management consists of three elements:

- *Strategic analysis* – concerned with answering the question 'where are we now?' This involves analysing the external environment, internal resources and capabilities and stakeholder expectations.
- *Strategic choice* – what are the options available and which is the most attractive?
- *Strategic implementation* – often the most overlooked of strategy. It is concerned with allocating resources and turning the plans into action.

This process can be as well applied to marketing strategy.

The corporate strategy/ marketing interface

It is impossible to discuss marketing strategy without first putting it into the context of corporate planning. The relationship between corporate planning and marketing planning can best be

11

explained by Figure 1.5. It is helpful to think of these decisions sitting in a hierarchy with corporate planning at the top and marketing planning below it. The diagram also illustrates that, alongside marketing planning, plans should be developed for other functional areas of the business such as human resources management (HRM), logistics, operations. The vision and mission will drive the overall direction of the company and the functional areas of business will all work towards achieving the corporate objectives. The vision and mission will be discussed in unit 'Strategic intent'.

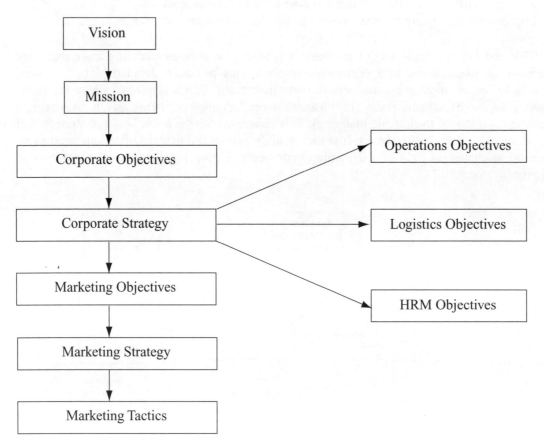

Figure 1.5
Corporate and Marketing Planning Hierarchy

According to Drummond & Ensor (2001) marketing strategy can be characterized by:

1. Analysing the business environment and defining customer needs.
2. Matching activities to customer needs.
3. Implementing programmes to achieve a competitive position relative to competitors.

Marketing strategy is therefore concerned with three elements – customers, competitors and internal corporate issues as illustrated in Figure 1.6. Strategic marketing management has three major phases: firstly, strategic analysis in order to answer the question where are we now? This will include external analysis of customers, competitors and the macroenvironment and internal analysis of corporate capabilities; secondly formulation of strategy in terms of creating and evaluating alternative options and thirdly implementation where the strategies are translated into action. The three stages are not mutually exclusive and are not necessarily linear in fact it is expected that there will be some feedback and amendments as the process progresses.

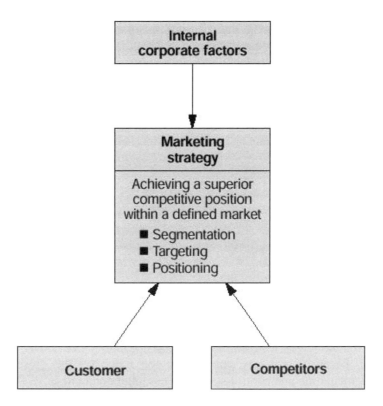

Figure 1.6
The basis of marketing strategy (Drummond & Ensor, 2001)

Extended knowledge

Chapter 1 of Drummond & Ensor's text *Strategic Marketing Planning and Control* provides a useful discussion of strategic marketing management.

In order to develop a successful marketing strategy many organizations adopt a structured approach to planning and control.

The basis of planning and control

Planning is a fundamental part of a manager's role. The purpose of planning is to allocate and co-ordinate resources to help achieve predetermined objectives. In a continually changing environment planning encourages managers to consider the future, to try to anticipate the likely outcomes and develop strategies that will capitalize on these changes. The plan itself also acts as a means of communicating the plan to others. Figure 1.7 illustrates the typical planning and control cycle that organizations may use to develop plans. This framework can be applied at both a corporate and a marketing level. The process will be similar although the focus of the plan will differ.

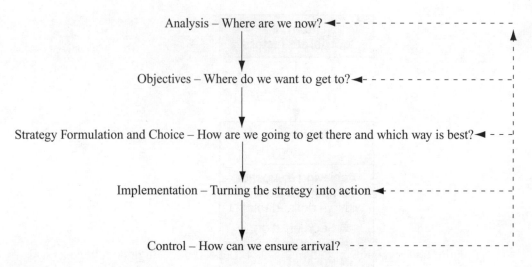

Figure 1.7
The Basis of Planning and Control

This planning framework encourages managers to develop quantified goals and then identify alternative strategies that might lead to these objectives being met. Plans force managers to consider the future, because they may concentrate too much on the present and ignore the important. The implementation and control stages are essential components of the planning process but are often not given the attention they deserve. Too often plans are developed with little thought as to how they may actually be put into practice. Relevant control mechanisms need to be developed to measure the success of the plan against the initial objectives. Control measures are often bolted on at the end but this may be too late. It may be necessary to develop intermediary control measures to act as early warning signals so that corrective action can be taken if necessary. The information generated from the control measures is then fed back into the planning and control cycle to inform future plans.

Types of planning

There is often much confusion regarding the terminology associated with strategy – objectives, strategy, tactics, contingency planning. Objectives, corporate, marketing or advertising, are concerned with what is to be achieved and should be SMART (Specific, Measurable, Actionable, Realistic and Time bound). Strategy and tactics are both concerned with how to achieve the objectives and the difference between them depends on the level from which you are looking. For example, what is regarded as a tactic by the marketing director (such as a money-off coupon) may be regarded as a strategy by a marketing assistant. The difference between a strategy and a tactic is not clear cut and will vary from organization to organization. Table 1.1 highlights some of the differences between strategy and tactics

	Strategy	Tactics
	Table 1.1: Differences Between Strategy and Tactics (Weitz & Wensley 1988)	
Importance	More important	Less important
Level at which conducted	Senior managers	Junior management
Time horizons	Long	Short
Regularity	Continuous	Periodic
Nature of problem	Unstructured and often unique, involving considerable risk and uncertainty	More structured and repetitive, with risks easier to assess
Information needed	Require large amounts of external information, much of which is subjective and futuristic	Depend more on internally generated accounting and marketing research information
Detail	Broad	Narrow and specific
Ease of evaluation	Decisions are more difficult to make and evaluate	Decisions are easier to make and evaluate

Exam hint

At the Diploma level the CIM is expecting students to be concerned with strategic rather than tactical issues. Too many candidates confuse strategy and tactics and provide detailed discussion of tactical marketing programmes rather than focusing on the strategic issues. Make sure you understand the differences between strategy and tactics and that you reflect this understanding in your answers.

Contingency planning is concerned with developing plans to deal with events that may occur but that are not addressed in the main plan. For example, companies involved in exporting their goods may develop contingency plans to deal with fluctuations in exchange rates.

Definition

Objective

A statement of what an organization is trying to achieve. Ideally objectives should be SMART (Specific, Measurable, Actionable, Realistic and Time bound).

Definition

Strategy

A broad statement of the way in which objectives are to be met.

Activity 1.3

Planning in Action

Consider your own organization and its planning and control cycle. What types of planning are evident? How effective are the plans? How are they controlled? To what extent do you think the planning process could be improved?

Planning in the real world

Strategic planning was once heralded as the only way to devise and implement strategies that would gain competitive advantage. A great deal of time and energy was put into developing frameworks that facilitated planning. The planning function was often separated from the rest of the organization and staffed by specialists. Planning models such as the one illustrated in Figure 1.7 continue to provide a useful framework; however, it is increasingly being recognized that strategic planning is not strategic thinking, and in some cases strategic planning actually gets in the way of strategic thinking. Many organizations have rigid planning cycles that have to be adhered to, whereas creative strategies do not necessarily conform to these timescales.

Extended knowledge

Henry Mintzberg provides an excellent discussion of the difference between strategic planning and strategic thinking. Refer to Mintzberg's article 'The Fall and Rise of Strategic Planning' in *The Harvard Business Review* January-February 1994, pp.107-114.

Barriers to Planning

Many plans fail, not because they are based on inappropriate strategies but for other reasons that often relate to the human aspects of organizations. Drummond & Ensor (2001) identify the following barriers to successful planning:

- *Culture* – if organizations are not market-oriented staff may receive plans with much resistance and be reluctant to change their work practices.
- *Power and politics* – all organizations are subject to internal politics. Far too often people have their own agendas that can lead to internal conflict.
- *Analysis, not action* – much time can be wasted by analysing vast amounts of data without actually taking any action. This is a criticism often directed at students sitting the Analysis and Decision case study; they spend far too long analysing the data and fail to give adequate attention to the key issue of developing a future strategy.
- *Resource issues* – there may be insufficient resources available to implement the plan.
- *Skills* – in some cases managers do not have the skills necessary to make best use of the planning process. Too often planning becomes a ritualistic task that often results in an extrapolation of the previous year's activities.

Other barriers to successful planning include perceived lack of time, resentment of imposed plans, a reluctance to commit to targets and in some cases lack of knowledge or interest. Many plans fail at the implementation stage, and it is therefore suggested that the planning process must focus on this critical stage. Implementation will be discussed further in the unit 'Implementation and control'. Piercy (2000) advocates a multi-dimensional model of planning, which is illustrated in Figure 1.8. This model emphasizes that the planning process is concerned not only with the techniques associated with planning but also with the behavioural aspects and organizational dimension of the planning process.

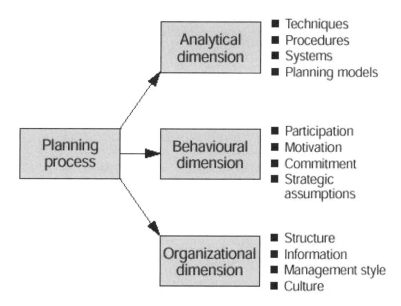

Figure 1.8
A multi-dimensional model of marketing planning (Piercy, 2000)

It is clear that, for successful planning, not only has the plan got to be appropriate but also commitment from staff must be gained, and the structure and culture of the organization must facilitate and encourage change.

Organizational structures and culture

The way in which an organization is structured and the style of culture it exhibits will influence organizational effectiveness and efficiency. This study text is not going to discuss in detail the various alternatives in term of how organizations may be structured, but will provide a brief discussion of the alternatives and highlight the implications for marketing planning. Figure 1.9 identifies the three main approaches to organization structure.

Organization by:		
	Advantages	*Disadvantages*
1 *Function*	Logical	Poor communication
	Allows for a clear division of work on the basis of specialisms	Tends to inhibit creativity
		Limits the development of cross-functional teams
2 *Product/brand*	Direct accountability for the performance of individual products and brands	Costs tend to be higher than for 1
	Cross-functional activities can be integrated	Levels of complexity increase
	Levels of specialism can be increased	
3 *Territory or market sector*	More focused market decision making	Higher overheads
	Better local knowledge	Possible duplication of effort
	Stronger links and relationships with customers	

Figure 1.9
The advantages and disadvantages of different organizational structures

Some organizations have developed matrix structures to overcome some of the shortfalls of these various structures. Matrix structures are designed to encourage a multidisciplinary approach, a higher degree of flexibility, better teamwork and to facilitate organizational learning and innovation. Figure 1.10 illustrates an example of a matrix structure for a manufacturing company.

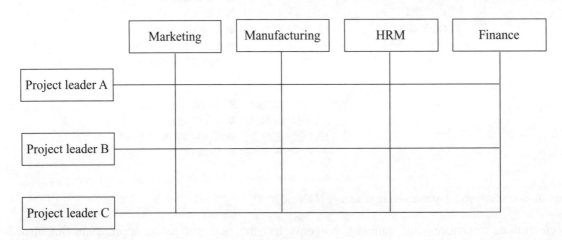

Figure 1.10
Matrix organization for a manufacturing company

Within organizations there is also an informal structure that exists alongside the formal one. This consists of social networks and relationships that have developed and may cut across department boundaries. The informal network should not be ignored when considering how to implement plans because it can often be a powerful means of getting thinks done (however, it can also create obstacles).

Activity 1.4

Organizational structure

Draw an outline of your organization/ SBU structure

What impact does the structure have on:

- planning
- communication
- culture

within your organization?

The culture of an organization has a major influence over the planning process and must be considered when developing plans. Culture relates to the 'way we do things around here'. It is often very difficult to change and can be a long and painful process.

Definition

Culture

Aaker (1998) suggested that organizational culture involves three elements: (1) A set of shared values or dominant beliefs that define an organization's priorities; (2) A set of norms of behaviour; (3) Symbols and symbolic activities used to develop and nurture those shared values and norms.

The culture of an organization often develops over many years and is influenced by a whole range of factors such as management style, organizational structure, the organization's history, chief executive leadership style, type of market, number and intensity of competition, location, PEST factors, union involvement and the nature of the business (i.e. traditional or based on new technologies). All of these factors will develop a culture that is unique to a particular organization. However, it is possible to identify various different organizational cultures. Deal & Kennedy (Deal and Kennedy, 2000.) identify four different cultures according to their attitude to risk (see Figure 1.11).

| | Speed of feedback | |
	Slow feedback	Fast feedback
Hard risk	"Bet your company culture"	"Hard Macho culture"
Attitude to risk		
Low risk	"Process culture"	"Work hard/play hard culture"

Figure 1.11
Corporate Cultures

The company's corporate culture will have a major impact on the successful implementation of plans. It will influence the extent to which staff are prepared to change, adapt and accept new ways of working, will have an impact on staff motivation and will affect the image of the organization.

Case history

A clash of two cultures

Mergers, partnerships and strategic alliances are becoming commonplace in the industrial landscape and yet research has shown that many of these relationships do not reap the promised benefits. According to a KPMG study, just 17% of cross-border mergers and acquisitions from 1996 to the end of 1998 added to shareholder value. What so many acquirers forget is that while finance might propel the deal, it's lack of marketing synergy that will undo it. 'The hard stuff is relatively easy to calculate. But they usually haven't done their homework on the soft stuff, and so the integration fails because of a culture clash' says Anita Hoffman, business development director at management consultancy Accenture. 'There is little discussion about how the two cultures will fit together in terms of how they go to market, how they sell and how they treat the customer' says Helena Rubenstein, managing director of branding consultancy *The Lab*.

The potential for a culture clash was enormous when Unilever acquired Ben and Jerry's ice cream. Ben and Jerry's distinctive ethically oriented culture and brand values are in stark contrast to the vast conglomerate's culture. There was a danger that Ben and Jerry's would be submerged in Unilever's culture and lose its uniqueness. In an attempt to retain its unique culture and the brand's ethical stance a clause that stated that 8% of pre-tax profits should continue to go to charity was incorporated into the buyout agreement.

A major challenge for all parties involved in mergers, acquisitions or partnerships is how to effectively integrate disparate cultures. The importance of culture cannot be over emphasized and companies should seek out partners that they believe will prove to be complementary and synergistic.

Source: Mazur (2001), www.Lexis-Nexis.com

Strategic Marketing Plans

The final section of this unit will focus on the structure of the strategic marketing plan. Planning and plans are two very different concepts. Planning is concerned with the process of developing a coherent plan whilst the plan relates to the output (often the physical plan). The plan is the means by which the strategy is communicated within the organization. The structure and content of a strategic marketing plan will vary considerably between organizations. Numerous books written on marketing planning propose slightly different formats. However, many contain common components, including:

- Current situation – external and internal analysis.
- Objective setting.
- Strategy formulation.
- Marketing programmes.
- Implementation issues.
- Control measures.

There is no one best format for a marketing plan and organizations will develop their own frameworks that match the needs of their company.

Despite the varying formats and structures of marketing plans they should all have one thing in common – they should generate *action*. It has been known for marketing executives to slave over the development of a marketing plan only to find that it never sees the light of day and is shelved because it is no longer appropriate. Marketing plans should be sufficiently flexible to take into account the changing environment.

Drummond & Ensor (2001). Chapter 12

McDonald (1999).

Kotler P (2000). Chapter 3

Marketing plans were covered in the CIM Advanced Certificate module Marketing Operations. It may be worthwhile revisiting this module to refresh your memory.

Chapter end material

Summary

- Marketing is not only concerned with functional activities such as promotion, pricing and market research. It is a business philosophy that seeks to put the customer at the centre of an organization's activities.
- The importance of the societal marketing concept is increasingly being recognised by many companies. This concept suggests that organizations not only have a responsibility to their customers and stakeholders, but they also have a responsibility to society in general.
- The key components of a market orientation include having a customer orientation, a competitor orientation, interfunctional co-ordination, a supportive organizational culture and a long-term perspective.
- Market-led strategic change refers to the process of 'going to market' where firms should concentrate on understanding customers, segmentation, targeting and positioning and importantly the means by which strategies are implemented.
- Organizations operate in a dynamic environment and therefore they have take into considerations those external influences that will impact on their business. These influences are often referred to as drivers of change.
- In market-oriented organizations it is likely that marketing will be the largest contributor to corporate strategy. Corporate strategy is concerned with what types of business the company as a whole should be in i.e. the scope of the business. Marketing strategy is concerned with transforming corporate objectives into a competitive market position.
- Planning is a fundamental part of a manager's role. It is concerned with the allocation and coordination of resources to help achieve predetermined objectives. The planning framework encourages managers to develop a systematic approach to developing objectives and then developing strategies to achieve these objectives.
- Strategy and tactics are often confused. They are both concerned with achieving objectives but the difference depends on the level within an organization from which you are looking.
- There are many barriers to planning within organizations that marketers must learn to overcome, such as power and politics, lack of skills, lack of time and an organizational culture that resists change.
- Organizational structures and culture can have a major impact on organizational effectiveness and efficiency.
- A strategic marketing plan is the vehicle by which the marketing strategy is communicated within the organization. The structure and format of a strategic marketing plan will vary considerably between organizations. There is no one 'best' structure.

Further study

Extending knowledge

Bibliography and links

Aaker D (1998), *Strategic Market Management*, 5th Ed, John Wiley & Sons.

Crosier K (1975), *What Exactly is Marketing?*, Quarterly Review of Marketing, Winter.

Deal T and Kennedy A (2000), *The New Corporate Cultures*, Texere Publishing.

Drummond G & Ensor J (2001), *Strategic Marketing Planning and Control*, Butterworth-Heinemann.

Griffiths J (2000), *Direct Line enters market*, Financial Times, 12 July p.4.

Hooley G J, Saunders J A & Piercy N F (1998), *Marketing Strategy and Competitive positioning*, 2nd Ed, Prentice-Hall.

Johnson G & Scholes K (1999), *Exploring Corporate Strategy*, 5th Ed, Prentice-Hall

Kohli A K & Jaworski B J (1990), cited in Hooley G J, Saunders J A & Piercy N F (1998), *Marketing Strategy and Competitive positioning*, 2nd Ed, Prentice-Hall.

Kotler P (2000), *Marketing Management: The Millennium Edition*, Prentice-Hall.

Narver J C Slater S F (1990), cited in Hooley G J , Saunders J A & Piercy N F (1998), *Marketing Strategy and Competitive positioning*, 2nd Ed, Prentice-Hall.

Mason T (2000), *The Importance of Being Ethical – a new breed of caring consumerism means companies need to consider ethical issues*, Marketing, 26 October, p.27

Mazur L (2001), *Acquisition activity is on a high, but in most cases the deals fail to deliver*, Marketing, 8 February p.26

McDonald M (1999), *Marketing Plans: How to Prepare Them, How to Use Them*, 4th Ed, Butterworth-Heinemann.

Mintzberg H (1994), *The Fall and Rise of Strategic Planning*, Harvard Business Review, January – February 1994, pp.107-114.

Piercy N (2000), *Market-Led Strategic Change*, 2nd Ed, Butterworth-Heinemann.

Weitz B A & Wensley R (1988), *Readings in Strategic Marketing*, Dryden.

www.co-operativebank.co.uk

www.jamjar.com

Objectives

By the end of this unit you will:

- Be aware of and understand the importance of the external environment in developing strategy.
- Be able to discuss various factors that are acting as drivers of change, and be able to provide examples of them.
- Understand the dimensions of an environmental monitoring system.
- Be able to describe, apply and critically evaluate Porter's model of industry analysis.
- Understand the importance of competitor analysis and be able to undertake a detailed analysis of competitors.
- Know the components of a market analysis.
- Appreciate the importance of customer analysis and be able to undertake a detailed analysis of both organizational and consumer customers.

Study guide

- This unit will take you about 4 hours to work through
- We suggest that you take a further 3 hours to do the various activities and questions in this Unit.

Introduction

An important part of the strategy development process is that of strategic analysis – i.e. answering the question 'Where are we now?'. Without first understanding this question it is impossible for organizations to decide where they want to go. Strategic analysis consists of undertaking an audit of both the external environment and the internal corporate environment. This unit is concerned with the external environment in the form of the macroenvironment (PEST) and microenvironment (industry, market, competitors and customers). The next unit will address the issues relating to internal corporate analysis. Organizations do not exist in a vacuum and when developing their marketing strategy is it essential they take into account the changing external environment. Undertaking a strategic analysis will enable organizations to identify potential opportunities and threats that may be arise from the changing environment and allow them to exploit potential opportunities and reduce the impact of threats.

Porter (1985) stressed the importance of analysing the external environment:

> The essence of formulating strategy is relating a company to its environment ... Every industry has an underlying structure or set of fundamental economic and technical characteristics. The strategist must learn what makes the environment tick.

Environmental Scanning

The environment is dynamic and it is often commented that the speed of change is increasing. This creates problems of uncertainty for managers and therefore, the need to monitor these changes is of paramount importance to all organizations. The means by which information is gathered about the environment is often referred to as environmental scanning.

Definition

Environmental scanning

The process of monitoring and analysing the marketing environment of a company (Jobber, 1998 p.125)

Fahey & Narayanan (1986) identify three basic goals for environmental analysis:

1. The analysis should provide an understanding of current and potential changes taking place in the environment.
2. Environmental analysis should provide important intelligence for strategic decision makers.
3. Environmental analysis should facilitate and foster strategic thinking in organizations.

Many organizations find it difficult to develop effective methods for scanning the environment. Probably more challenging is the task of converting this information into action. Information is basically a tool to reduce risk in decision-making. Too many organizations collect information religiously without actually using it to help make decisions. organizations must develop scanning processes that not only collect the data but also convert this data into useful information that can aid decision-making. Information must then be transmitted to the right people, at the right time, and in the right format. Scanning includes both directed and undirected searching as well as informal and formal processes. On the one hand scanning may involve formal analysis of the economic environment including interviews with industry experts; on the other hand it may include browsing the national newspapers at the weekend. Both forms of scanning can be of equal value.

Environmental monitoring system

For environmental scanning to be effective it is important that organizations develop effective systems for managing the information generated from the process. Johnson & Scholes (1999) propose a framework for undertaking an environmental analysis (Figure 2.1). This model provides companies with a more formal approach to monitoring the environment.

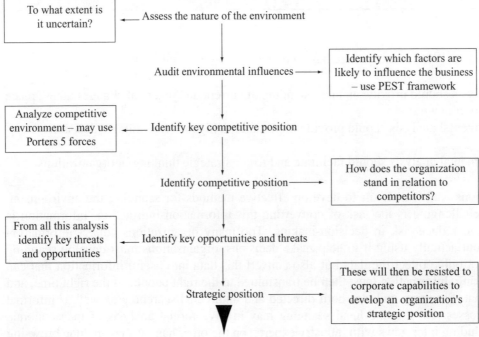

Figure 2.1
Steps in Environmental Analysis (Johnson & Scholes, 1999, p.99)

There is almost unlimited information available, and organizations cannot hope to scan all of it. Therefore, organizations have to look at the return on investment of their efforts in terms of the contribution the information makes to the marketing decision-making process. Aguilar (1967) suggest that managers search for information in five broad categories:

1. Market intelligence (market potential, competitors, customers, etc.).
2. Technical intelligence (licensing and patents, new products and processes, etc.).
3. Acquisition intelligence (information on mergers, partnerships and acquisitions).
4. Broad issues (PEST factors).
5. Other intelligence (resource availability, miscellaneous).

Extending knowledge

Read p.20–21of Drummond & Ensor (2001), which provides a good summary of Aguilar's five categories of information.

See chapter 5 (p. 128) of Jobber (1998) for an interesting discussion of environmental scanning.

The process of environmental scanning is of paramount importance when organizations are trying to identify the 'drivers of change' for their industry. Too often, companies fail to even identify major 'drivers of change' because they are looking backwards instead of forwards.

Activity 2.2

Environmental Scanning

With reference to your own organization identify types of:

- formal systematic scanning
- informal scanning

that your organization undertakes.

How effective do you think the process is? What is missing from the process? Think of an example where:

- the scanning process was successful in identifying a threat
- your organization failed to detect a threat because of weaknesses in their scanning process.

What recommendations would you make to improve the scanning process within your organization?

Macroenvironmental analysis (PEST framework)

You should already be familiar with the concept of PEST (Political and legal, Economic, Social and Technological factors) – or you may use another acronym (such as PESTLE, STEP or SLEPT). Whichever acronym you prefer, the purpose is the same. To provide a useful framework for structuring thinking about the macroenvironmental factors that impact on organizations and facilitating subsequent analysis.

The purpose of this text is not to provide a detailed discussion of all the various PEST factors. These are all well documented (see Extending knowledge, below) and it is expected that you are already familiar with the framework from previous studies such as Marketing Operations. It is also important that you can describe these influences, and are able to discuss the implications of them on marketing planning. Figure 2.2 identifies some of the major factors that constitute the PEST framework.

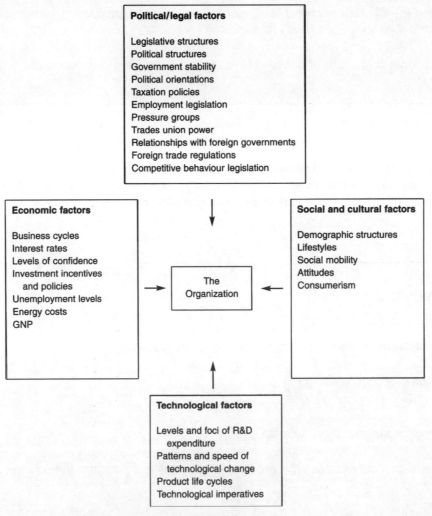

Figure 2.2
The PEST Framework (Johnson & Scholes, 1999, p.99)

Extending knowledge

To gain a good understanding of the PEST framework, and to refresh your memory, it is essential that you read: Chapter 5 of Jobber (1998).

Alternatively you can refer to any other relevant text such as Kotler (2000) or Dibb & Simkin (2000).

Drummond & Ensor (2001) provide a good summary of the major PEST factors in Chapter 2, p.15-16.

Exam hint

The analysis of macroenvironmental influences is a key theme in all the CIM Diploma modules. For example, it is a key aspect when developing integrated marketing communications and has major implications for organizations involved in international marketing. In the Analysis and Decision major case study you will be expected to undertake an extensive PEST analysis and out of this you will develop future plans. Do not think of each module in a separate box – use the knowledge you have gained from all modules to help you in all the exams.

Activity 2.3

PEST Analysis

For your own organization examine the macroenvironmental factors, using the PEST framework, that have impacted on your business over the last 5 years.

How has your organization responded to these threats/opportunities?

The Internet – a key driver of change

The case history below will provide three very different examples of companies that have seen the development of the Internet as an opportunity and have successfully capitalized on its increased use.

Case history

EMI Records

Many music companies, particularly retailers, have felt threatened by the onset of the Internet for two reasons. Firstly, there is a trend towards on-line buying, where fans no longer need to visit a store to buy CDs. Market Tracking International predicts that the global value of the on-line music market (including CDs sold over the Internet) will be $5.2 billion in 2005 (11.3% of a forecasted $46 billion music market). Secondly, the main challenge facing the music publishing business is that more fans are downloading music directly from the Internet, sometimes illegally. These trends are a significant threat to record companies, which face the loss of their very healthy profit margins on CDs. The combined force of consumers empowered by this new technology and artists keen to use the Internet to sell directly to fans has led the record companies to realize that they will have to act quickly.

EMI has joined forces with Time-Warner and AOL in an attempt to develop their Internet business. Two main strategies are to sell their music on-line using free downloads as a promotional tool. EMI has taken equity in musicmaker.com, a site that allows consumers to custom-make their own CDs from a selection of 100,000 tracks. The concept is proving popular – unusually for e-commerce sites it is making money! EMI is also digitizing its entire catalogue of music, making it possible to sell all its 'artists' music over the Internet.

Possibly one of the greatest opportunities arising from the Internet is the ability to target and develop stronger relationships with key customers through email and the use of special promotional offers.

The Internet is changing the face of the music business and many believe that the record companies will have to concentrate on the skills of creating acts and marketing them, and leave the distribution to others.

Source: Adapted from Murphy (2000).

Case history

Totalbet

Totalbet (www. totalbet. com) is the Tote's on-line betting site. It was set up as a joint venture with the sports news site PA Sporting Life, itself a joint venture between the Mirror Group and the Press Association. Totalbet went live on April 10 1999, to coincide with the Grand National.

'We realised a long time ago that the Internet was a medium that had a fairly major future and we wanted to have a major presence,' says Rob Hartnett, Public Relations Director. 'We wanted to do it in partnership with someone who had Internet capability, and the site set up by PA Sporting Life was by far the most popular in Europe.'

When it was launched, the site was able to take bets only for the Grand National – but the range has since been extended. 'In the interim we've added other events and sports – soccer, rugby league and union, motor racing, golf and cricket,' says Hartnett. Totalbet also carries editorial content from the *Sporting Life* site.

'The site has built up 5000 registrations in its first three months,' Hartnett adds. 'To put that in context, our telephone betting operation has 50,000 accounts and it's one of the biggest in Europe.' The level of on-line business per bet is higher than for the Tote's telephone betting service, which is in turn higher than it is in shops. Hartnett says this reflects the fact that Internet users still tend to be relatively affluent.

To promote the site, the Tote initially relied heavily on its link with *Sporting Life*. An on-line and print advertising campaign was launched at the end of July, targeting sports sites and newspaper sports sections. Totalbet also sponsored three horse races. The introduction of pool betting to the site is also scheduled for the autumn. The Tote has the exclusive UK licence for pool betting on horse racing.

Because this form of betting requires less human intervention than bookmaking, which involves complex risk assessment, it is expected to be well suited to the Internet.

Source: Reed (1999).

Case history

Berry Bros. & Rudd

Berry Bros & Rudd is a privately owned specialist wine retailer that can trace its origins back to 1698. In 1995, it became the first UK wine merchant to have a web site, according to John-Paul Cockain, Berry's Internet shop manager.

Initially the site, at www.bbr.co.uk, acted as a shop window, but in November 1998 it became a shop in its own right. 'With Internet shopping expected to explode, it just seemed to us that the time was right,' explains Cockain. The site is regularly reworked to improve navigation. It focuses on Berry's 300-year history to build trust in on-line shopping, and features special offers and J-P's Wine Surgery, which explains wine mysteries.

The Internet shop now accounts for 5% of Berry's London-based sales, with 60% of Internet purchases made by new customers. About 40% of sales are to customers outside the UK. 'The Internet has certainly opened us up to a much broader audience in the UK and overseas,' says Cockain. Berry also supplies international shoppers through its duty free shop at Heathrow Terminal 3, which opened in 1994.

The company used print advertising and Internet banner ads to promote its on-line operations. The bulk of its on-line advertising is focused on sites where visitors are likely to be comfortable with on-line shopping.

Source: Reed (1999).

All these cases were sourced using www.Lexis-Nexis.com

Question 2.1

PEST

Answer question 6 of the December 2000 paper on the development of the Internet and related e-commerce activity in the context of a B2B organization and compare your answer with the outline answer provided in the appendix at the back of the book.

Industry analysis

Once an organization has undertaken an analysis of the macroenvironment they can move on to analysing the microenvironment. A key component of this is the industry within which an organization is operating. It is important that marketing managers have a good understanding of the industry dynamics and the relationships that exist within it. A useful framework for undertaking this type of analysis is Porter's five forces model (Figure 2.3), which enables companies to gain greater insight into the level of competition and where the balance of power lies within a particular industry.

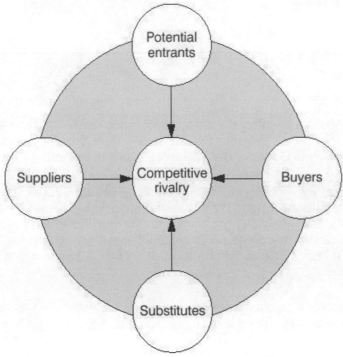

Figure 2.3
The five forces model (Adapted from Porter, 1980)

This is a very brief overview of the five forces model. For more detailed coverage of this model refer to the reading referred to in the extending knowledge bellow.

Buyers

Buyer power relates to the bargaining power of a firm's customers. If customers have relatively more power than sellers they can put pressure on companies to reduce prices. Buyer power will be greater in situations where a few buyers hold a large proportion of the market or where there are many small suppliers. This is the situation in the UK, where multiple grocers such as Tesco and Sainsburys dominate the food retail market. They put great pressure on their suppliers, such as farmers and vegetable growers, to reduce prices.

Suppliers

This is concerned with the bargaining power of suppliers. Supplier power will be stronger when there are few suppliers that sell to a range of customers in diverse markets. For example, oil production is concentrated in the hands of a few powerful companies.

Substitutes

Substitutes are concerned with the products that compete indirectly with an organization's product offering. The intensity with which substitute products compete is generally less intense that for direct competitors. However, the impact of substitutes can be significant and have major implications for a firm. For example, the increased use of email could threaten traditional mailing systems.

Potential entrants

The extent to which new players may enter the market is determined by the number of barriers to entry that may exist in an industry. These may include level of capital investment required to enter the market, economies of scale, ability to access distribution channels, brand strength and other factors such as patent protection or government policy. The Internet has had a major impact on barriers to entry and many traditional competitors have been attacked by new competitors that have used the Internet to break down the barriers to entry. For example, new retailers have become established that do not have to rely on traditional distribution channels such as those selling books, CDs and toys.

Competitive rivalry

This relates to the intensity of competition that exists within an industry. This will be determined by factors such as number and size of competitors, level of exit barriers, ability to differentiate, industry life cycle and presence of high fixed costs.

Extending knowledge

For a more detailed discussion of Porter's five forces model refer to the following texts:

Chapter 5 (p.84-86) of Aaker (1998).

and/or

Chapter 2 (p.24-26) of Drummond & Ensor (2001).

Exam hint

The five forces model can often be helpful in analysing the industry in the mini-case of the Planning and Control exam. However, it is insufficient to just draw and describe the model; you must also be able to apply it to the industry in question.

Activity 2.4

Porter's five forces model

Undertake a five forces analysis of one of your organization's strategic business units.

What conclusions can you draw regarding the balance of power?

Competitor analysis

The industry analysis provides a broad understanding of the microenvironment in which an organization is operating; however, it is necessary to undertake a more detailed analysis of competitors within that industry. In order to gain a sustainable competitive advantage it is essential that companies know their competitors and develop effective competitor information systems to monitor their activity. There is a wealth of information available on competitor analysis and therefore this text will highlight the key issues. For a more detailed discussion please refer to the Extending knowledge in the end of this section.

Kotler (2000) suggests that in order to evaluate competitors organizations need to answer the following questions:

- Who are our competitors?
- What are their objectives?
- What are their strategies (past and current)?
- What are their strengths and weaknesses (capabilities)?
- How are they likely to react?

Who are our competitors?

This may seem to be an obvious question. Many companies will have a number of competitors with which they compete directly, and which are visible and easily identifiable. For example, Ford obviously competes with companies such as Vauxhall, Nissan and Toyota. However, one can take a much broader perspective of competition and look at companies that are indirect or potential competitors. For example, it could be argued that Ford, in the widest sense, is competing with any company that produces a product/service that competes for the same disposable income as a car – a conservatory, holiday or house extension. It is impossible for companies to monitor all the different levels of competitors and therefore in the medium term they should concentrate on companies within the same strategic group. However, in the long-term companies should be monitoring the threat of new entrants or indirect competitors.

Strategic groups

According to Aaker (1998) a strategic group is a group of firms that:

- Over time pursue similar competitive strategies (e.g. similar promotional and pricing strategies).
- Have similar characteristics (e.g. size, attitudes).
- Have similar assets and competencies (e.g. strong brand).

The strategic group framework is useful for identifying the companies with which a firm is in most direct competition. It also helps an organization to understand on the basis of which competitive rivalry is taking place. There are many different criteria with which to identify strategic groups. According to Drummond & Ensor (2001) these may include:

- Size of the company.
- Assets and skills.
- Scope of the operation.
- Breadth of the product range.
- Choice of distribution channel.
- Relative product quality.
- Brand image.

Definition

Strategic group analysis

This aims to identify organizations with similar strategic characteristics following similar strategies or competing on similar bases (Johnson & Scholes, 1999, p.127).

In the financial services industry it is possible to identify a number of different strategic groups as illustrated in Figure 2.4.

- Group 1 – local building societies (e.g. Cumberland Building Society)

- Group 2 – national building societies (e.g. Nationwide)
- Group 3 – multi-national financial service institution (e.g. HSBC)

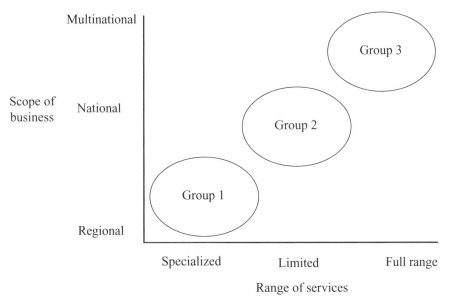

Figure 2.4
Strategic groups in the financial services industry (Meek & Meek 2000)

Activity 2.5

Strategic groups

For an industry of your choice identify:

- The attributes that would be most appropriate in identifying the various strategic groups.
- The various strategic groups that exist within the industry.
- Plot these on a matrix similar to the one presented in Figure 2.4.

Problems associated with identifying competitors

There are a number of problems that can arise when trying to identify a firm's competitors. It is often too easy to concentrate on large visible competitors whilst ignoring smaller competitors, which may be equally dangerous. There is also a possibility that attention will be given to existing competitors rather than potential new entrants. This has been the case for high-street banks in the UK. Many established traditional banks have been monitoring the direct competition within their strategic group. However, whilst they have been preoccupied by their direct competitors, the threat has in fact come from new entrants such as Virgin Financial Services. International competitors are in some cases also overlooked.

What are their objectives?

Once competitors have been identified it is necessary to identify their objectives in order to try and predict their future direction. Objectives may include market share domination, survival, short-term profits, long-term growth, etc.

What are their strategies?

In order to analyse strategies, both current and past, it is necessary to identify current markets and segments. A comparison of past and current strategies can provide useful insight into the possible direction in which the competitor is moving.

What are their strengths and weaknesses?

A strengths and weaknesses analysis will reveal the extent to which a firm is in a position to compete within the industry. It will help to identify competitors' capabilities such as their assets and resources, management ability, marketing capabilities, ability to innovate, production capabilities and financial standing. Porter's value chain (1980) can be a useful framework for analysing competitor's strengths and weaknesses. This model is discussed in unit 'Auditing tools'.

How are they likely to react?

A key element of competitor analysis is trying to predict how competitors may react when faced with competitor activity. Kotler (1999) identifies four types of competitor response:

- Laid back – unlikely to respond to any initiative.
- Selective – will only react to certain types of attack.
- Tiger – will respond to any type of attack aggressively.
- Stochastic – their response is largely unpredictable.

From this analysis it will be possible to identify those competitors to attack and which to avoid.

Competitive Intelligence System (CIS) and sources of competitive information

Gathering information to answer the questions posed above is often not easy. Some types of information will be readily available (such as annual reports, articles gleaned from the press, government statistics) and it is also possible to collect information using observational techniques (e.g. evaluating competitors advertising strategies, pricing policies and distribution management). Other types of information may be gathered using more *ad hoc* and informal methods, such as conversations with customers who also buy from your competitors, mutual suppliers, etc. The key to an effective CIS is that is flexible enough to deal with data gleaned from a variety of sources ranging from formal systematic research to ad hoc informal conversations. The lengths that some competitors will go to gather competitive intelligence sometimes push the boundaries of legality. For example, there have been instances where companies have stolen their competitors' rubbish in the hope of finding useful information. On another occasion bogus job interviews were held with competitors' employees, the purpose being to elicit information about their competitors. Companies can develop creative means of gathering competitive intelligence but they should ensure they are working within the law.

Competitive intelligence cycle

The collection of competitive intelligence is not a one off activity. It is a continuous cycle of data collection, analysis and decision-making. The firms that were once competitors may no longer be a threat and new competitors may enter the market at any time. It is essential that firms develop systems that not only collect data on existing competitors but also identify new ones.

Extending knowledge

Competitor analysis is well documented in a variety of texts. For a detailed discussion please refer to the following:

For a useful discussion of competition see chapter 2 of Drummond & Ensor, (2001) *Strategic Marketing Planning and Control*, Butterworth-Heinemann, Oxford.

Chapter 16 of Jobber (1998).

Chapter 7 of Hooley, Saunders and Piercy (1998).

and/ or

Chapter 4 of Aaker (1998).

For a practical discussion of competitive analysis refer to chapter 5 (p.203-211) of Davidson (1997).

Activity 2.6

Competitor analysis

Undertake a review of your three main competitors, either for an SBU or an individual product/service, by completing table 2.1. What conclusions can you draw about which competitors to attack and which to avoid?

Table 2.1: Competitive Analysis			
	Competitor 1	Competitor 2	Competitor 3
What are their objectives?			
What are their strategies (past and current)?			
What are their strengths?			
What are their weaknesses?			
How may they react?			

Case history

Sources of Competitor Information

One of the most valuable services the Internet can offer is a short cut to information about millions of companies – whether potential collaborators, suppliers or competitors.

To check the identity, reliability or credit-worthiness of another organization, try Dun and Bradstreet's site (www.uk.dnb.com). Its Globalseek service provides one-off information on companies. Detailed data for USA companies costs between $20 and $90

For more detailed UK information, turn to UK Data (www.ukdata.com), which provides reports on every company registered with Companies House in the UK. Costs range from £6 for a simple company overview to £24 for a comprehensive report.

For a more analytical edge, Business Credit Management UK, (www.creditman.co.uk) provides International Chamber of Commerce information on 5 million businesses, live and defunct. A full report, at £42, includes the ICC/Juniper risk score.

If you wish to monitor the activities of particular organizations, Company Sleuth (www.companysleuth.com) is a free service that tracks the performance and business activities of selected companies, producing a daily e-mail report.

For sheer volume of information, Interactive Investor (www.iii.co.uk) provides reams of free information on UK shares and other investments; Reuters (www. reuters.com) provides near-live market indices from around the world and Investext (www.investext.com) has more than 1.8 million reports from across the world, at an average price of $20.

For tailored competitor analysis – in both on-line and off-line markets – you may wish to try outsourcing their research. Smarterwork (www.smarterwork.com) links its users with an expanding pool of more than 3,000 accredited 'experts' who will bid for, among other things, market research contracts. Smarterwork acts as a mediator, ensuring prompt payment and quality control by testing researchers before allowing them on its books. This is a powerful opportunity to cut costs and save time. The site gathers researchers from throughout the world. Offers from outside the European Union or North America consistently undercut those from inside – a truly global marketplace.

Question 2.2

Competitor analysis

Answer question 3 of the December 2000 Planning and Control exam on a competitor analysis of a cosmetics firm and compare your answer with the outline answer provided in the appendix at the back of the book.

Market analysis

Once an analysis of the macroenvironment, the industry and competitors has been undertaken it is appropriate to start analysing the market itself in greater detail. According to Drummond & Ensor (2001) market analysis would normally include the following:

- Actual and potential market size (total market sales and growth potential).
- Trends (analysing general trends that may highlight important market developments).
- Customers (this will address questions such as 'who buys?'' How do they buy? ' 'Where and when do they buy?') This issue will be dealt with in the next section.
- Customer segments (identifying current, and possible, market segments and establishing the benefits they seek).
- Distribution channels (analysing changes in distribution channels).

Extending knowledge

For further information on market analysis see the following sources:

Chapter 4 of Aaker (1998).

and/or

Chapter 2 (p.21-22) of Drummond & Ensor (2001).

Customer Analysis

This section is concerned with analysing customers and trying to understand them. This information will help organizations in developing their segmentation, targeting and positioning strategies, (this will be discussed in detail in the unit 'Developing a specific competitive position'). Understanding customers is probably one of the most challenging activities that a firm will engage in. Many companies commit large sums of money every year in an attempt to predict the behaviour of their often elusive customers. Companies are increasingly recognizing that their customers are not a homogenous mass with similar needs and wants and similar profit potential. Thus the need for relevant and timely information is a key aspect of the auditing process. Customer analysis is well documented in many texts. Therefore, the purpose here is to highlight the key topics with which you should be familiar and direct you to further reading to gain greater insight into these core concepts. You should already be familiar with many of these concepts from previous studies, such as Marketing Operations and the Marketing Customer Interface.

Exam hint

Planning and Control exam questions may not always relate to the consumer market. There are many occasions when students are examined on B2B markets and therefore it is essential that you are familiar with both consumer and organizational buyers and the influences upon them.

Consumer Markets

There are a number of key questions that must be answered when analysing consumer buyers:

- What factors influence their behaviour?
- Does behaviour vary according to the type of product/service purchased?
- What process of decision-making do they go through?
- Who is involved in the decision-making process?

A useful framework in helping to understand the relationship between these key questions is the black box model, illustrated in Figure 2.5. The black box model suggests that we can observe the inputs (i.e. the external environmental influences and the controllable marketing stimuli) in the form of the marketing mix. We can also observe the outputs in terms of whether buyers purchase our product or not, or their levels of brand loyalty. What we cannot observe is what is going on in the mind of the customer. The aim of customer analysis is to try and understand what is going on inside this black box (i.e. try to answer the above questions).

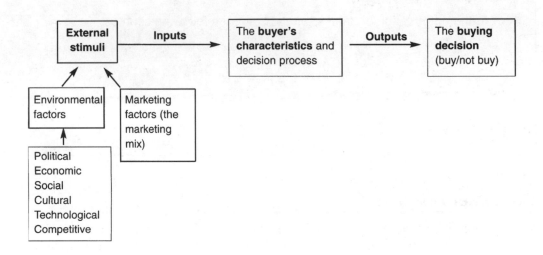

Figure 2.5
A black box model of the buying process

What influences consumer buying behaviour?

Most authors agree that there are four main influences on consumers, beginning with general factors moving and to increasingly specific factors:

1. Cultural factors such as:
   - culture
   - sub-cultures (e.g. religious groups, ethnic groups.
   - social class.
2. Social factors, such as:
   - reference groups
   - family
   - roles and statuses.
3. Personal influences, such as:
   - age and life cycle stage
   - occupation
   - economic circumstances
   - lifestyle
   - personality and self-concept.

4. Psychological aspects, such as:
   - o motivation
   - o perception
   - o learning
   - o beliefs and values.

Extending knowledge

For a detailed discussion of these factors refer to Jobber (1998), Chapter 3, p. 68-77 .

Activity 2.7

Influences on behaviour

For the following two products outline how an understanding of cultural, social, personal and psychological influences can aid our understanding of consumer buying behaviour. Which influences do you think are the most important? What are the implications for a marketing manager of these products?

- Beer or Lager.
- Financial services.

Does behaviour vary according to the type of product/service purchased?

The same individual may behave differently depending on the type of purchase they are making. It is important for marketers to understand the various types of buying behaviour. Two important criteria that can be used to identify types of buying behaviour:

- the level of involvement that the customer has with the product
- the extent to which the customer perceives differences between the various product offerings. .

Using these two criteria it is possible to develop a matrix that highlights four different types of buying behaviour as shown in Figure 2.6

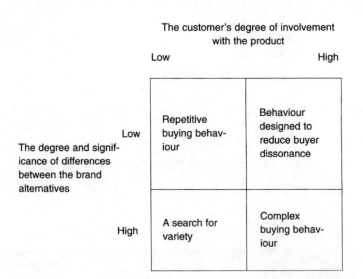

The customer's degree of involvement
with the product

	Low	High
Low	Repetitive buying behaviour	Behaviour designed to reduce buyer dissonance
High	A search for variety	Complex buying behaviour

The degree and significance of differences between the brand alternatives

Figure 2.6
The four types of buying behaviour (Adapted from Assael, 1987, p.87)

Activity 2.8

Types of Buying Behaviour

Identify at least one example of products/ services that would fit into each quadrant of the matrix illustrated in Figure 2.6. What are the implications for marketing managers?

What process of decision-making do they go through?

The buyer is going to be influenced by the factors that have already been outlined and the type of purchase situation. However, the process through which the buyer progresses when purchasing is also going to be an important consideration. Marketers need to have a good understanding of this process in order to tailor their marketing offering. Buyers typically go through the following stages, which are illustrated in Figure 2.7.

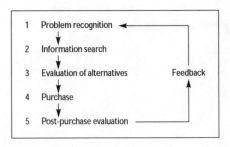

1 Problem recognition
2 Information search
3 Evaluation of alternatives   Feedback
4 Purchase
5 Post-purchase evaluation

Figure 2.7
The five stages of the buying process (Adapted from Assael, 1987, p.87)

This model has been criticized for being too simplistic and for failing to acknowledge that many buyers do not move through these stages sequentially. However, it is useful in highlighting the key stages through which a buyer progresses.

Who is involved in the decision-making process?

On many occasions purchase decisions are made by a group rather than by an individual. For example, when a new car is being purchased it is rare that the decision will be made by one individual. Those individuals involved in the purchase decision have been referred to as the decision-making unit (DMU). The DMU consists of:

- The *initiator* – the person who suggests the purchase.
- The *user* – the consumer of the product.
- The *influencer* – anybody that may affect the decision.
- The *decider* – the person ultimately responsible for making the decision.
- The *purchaser* – the person who actually buys the product.

These roles may all be performed by one person, or more than one person may perform each role. However, it is important that marketers understand the various roles involved and are in a position to identify to whom they should be targeting their marketing activity. This is illustrated in the following case study.

Extended knowledge

For a detailed discussion of the types of buyer behaviour, the decision-making process and the decision-making unit refer to Jobber (1998), Chapter 3.

Case history

Consumer Shopping Habits

Consumer buying behaviour is changing due to the increased usage of technology. Traditionally, consumers had little choice but to shop in the high street. However, consumers can now buy what they need from the Internet, catalogues or interactive TV. Although home shopping accounts for only 5% of retail sales these still amounts to £10 billion lost revenue by the high street (Knight Frank Retail Review 1999). Price WaterhouseCoopers estimate that this will grow from 1% of retail sales today to 6% by 2003. The high street is no longer a necessity but an option and retailers are now having to respond to the increased competition from the Internet. Shopping on the Internet is undeniably convenient and in many cases cheaper than the high street, but it is a very limited experience compared with the three-dimensional branded environment of the store. This is the competitive advantage that high-street retailers have over Internet retailers and many are beginning to capitalize on this unique selling point (USAP).

One of the most prominent expressions of this trend in the UK so far is Niketown in Oxford Circus. Visitors can join running clubs, attend sports clinics, meet athletes and play with any number of interactive displays. It's as much an entertainment centre as a shop and is one of 14 Nike has built around the world.

The Waterstone's store in London's Piccadilly Circus has six floors, all themed around the books on display. The children's floor, for example, features a juice bar and a play area, while the art, architecture and design top floor has a trendy cocktail bar. The basement is a café, with newspapers, magazines and Sky TV.

Boots has launched healthcare and beauty services. For example, it is offering dental services and homeopathy treatments. It has also opened a walk-in medical centre at a Birmingham store, offering basic nurse-led services.

In London, Ford has been working with Imagination to open its first site, called Capital Ford, which is allegedly the largest dealership in Europe. Outside, it features a specially landscaped off-road driving area for testing 4×4 models, while inside the environment is similar to a motor show. There is a cafe, Internet stations, interactive CD-ROM terminals, a merchandising display and staff trained in communicating the wider aspects of Ford's brand.

Girl Heaven is the ultimate little girls' store. Situated in the Bluewater complex, it is targeted at 2-to 12-year-old girls who may want to have their picture taken in a princess costume, braid their hair or experiment with make-up.

REI's, Seattle-based flagship outdoor equipment store features a rain-room to test out waterproof gear, a 65 ft climbing wall for rock climbers and an outdoor rough-terrain track for testing mountain bikes and hiking boots.

Source: Adapted from Curtis (1999) www.Lexis-Nexis.com

Question 2.3

Consumer Buying Behaviour

Answer the following question from the June 1996 paper and compare your answer with the outline answer in the paper.

> Your company is thinking of entering a number of foreign markets with a range of fashion products that is have previously sold in its home markets. What factors would you take into account in analysing patterns of customer buying behaviour in the new markets?

Organizational Buying Behaviour

Organizational buying behaviour can be more complex than consumer buying behaviour because not only do organizational purchasers still have their own individual characteristics, but they are also influenced by organizational factors. In addition, there are generally more people involved in the purchase decision.

Definition

Organizational buying behaviour

The decision-making process by which formal organizations establish the need for purchased products and services, and identify, evaluate and choose among alternative brands and suppliers (Webster & Wind, 1972).

Influences on organizational Buyers

There are a number of influences on organizational buyers:

- Environmental.
- Organizational.
- Interpersonal.
- Individual.

These are illustrated in Figure 2.8. It has been traditionally thought that organizational buyers are wholly rational in their purchase behaviour. However, it is now becoming apparent that this is far from true and that organizational buyers are still human beings at work, susceptible to the same influences as consumer buyers.

Figure 2.8
Influences on the organizational buyer

The decision-making unit (DMU)

The DMU exists in an organizational context in the same way as it exists in consumer markets, but to a greater extent. In many instances there are large DMUs and more formal processes for purchasing products. There is often the presence of a 'gatekeeper' who filters information. A key task of industrial marketers is to identify the members of the DMU and to target the most influential members or those that make the final decision.

Types of purchases

As in consumer markets the buying situation or type of purchase will influence the decision-making process.

Jobber (1998) identifies three types of purchase situations:

- *Straight Rebuy* – routine orders such as stationery reordering.
- *Modified Rebuy* – a situation in which the buyer wants to modify product specifications, prices, delivery etc.
- *New Task* – appointing a new advertising agency.

Each of these types of purchase holds different challenges for marketers. For example, for an established supplier of a straight rebuy product their main task would be to provide a good level of service so that customers are satisfied and do not seek new suppliers. Non-established suppliers would concentrate their efforts on offering something new and trying to get small orders that with time would grow into larger orders.

The decision-making process

Organizational buyers move through a number of stages from initial problem identification to purchase, in a similar manner to consumer markets. However, it has been suggested that there are a further three steps in the organizational decision-making process. Figure 2.9 illustrates the decision-making process with reference to the differences that exist for each of the three types of purchase behaviour.

	Buy classes		
Buy phases	Straight rebuy	Modified rebuy	New task
1 The recognition of the problem	N	Possibly	Y
2 The determination of the general need	N	Possibly	Y
3 The specific description of the required product	Y	Y	Y
4 The search for potential suppliers	N	Possibly	Y
5 The detailed evaluation of suppliers	N	Possibly	Y
6 The selection of a supplier	N	Possibly	Y
7 The establishment of an order routine	N	Possibly	Y
8 Performance review and feedback	Y	Y	Y

Figure 2.9
The buy grid matrix (Adapted from Robinson, Faris & Wind, 1967)

Extending knowledge

For a detailed discussion of organizational buying behaviour refer to Chapter 4 of Jobber (1998).

Many of these models that have been discussed in relation to buying behaviour suggest that customers are rational creatures that look to maximize the utility of their purchase. This is a feature of "economic man" a term developed by Marshall, an economist. However, as we all know in reality customers can be fickle and unpredictable. This does not, however, diminish the efforts of marketing managers to try and understand their customers. Understanding customers and trying to predict their changing tastes and preferences is the essence of marketing.

Summary

- The external environment consists of the macroenvironment (PEST) and the microenvironment (industry, market, competitors and customers).

- The macroenvironment is continually changing and marketers need to monitor these changes via environmental scanning in order to identify threats and opportunities that may arise.
- Organizations must develop effective environmental monitoring systems that collect relevant information, translate this information into a usable format and disseminate it to the right people at the right time to aid decision-making.
- Porter's five forces model provides a useful framework for analysing industry structure and for identifying where the balance of power is located.
- Companies need to know who they are competing against in order to gain a sustainable competitive advantage. They should be able to answer the following questions. 'Who are our competitors?' 'What are their objectives?' 'What are their strategies?' 'What are their strengths and weaknesses?' 'How are they likely to react?'
- Organizations must develop effective systems for gathering and managing competitor information.
- It is essential that firms have a good understanding of the market in which they are operating. A market analysis would include information such as actual and potential market size, market trends, customer buying behaviour and distribution channels.
- A great deal of time and effort is spent trying to understand customer behaviour and attempting to predict their behaviour. Customers can be classified into consumer buyers and organizational buyers.
- Consumer behaviour is influenced by a wide variety of factors – cultural, social, personal and psychological factors. The type of purchase will also influence behaviour, as will the buying process.
- Purchases are often not made independently, and in many cases will be made by a decision-making unit including the initiator, the user, the influencer, the decider and the purchaser.
- Organizational buyers are influenced by environmental, organizational, interpersonal and individual factors. The type of purchase whether it is a straight rebuy, a modified rebuy or a new task purchase will also influence buying behaviour, as will the decision-making process.

Further study

Extending knowledge

Bibliography and links

Aaker D (1998), *Strategic Market Management*, 5th Ed, John Wiley & Sons.

Aguilar F J (1967), *Scanning the Business Environment*, Macmillan

Assael H (1987), *Consumer Behaviour and Marketing Action*. Wadsworth Publishing.

Curtis J (1999), *What is The Future of UK Shopping?*, *Marketing*, 4 November.

Davison H & O'Reilly T (1997), *More Offensive Marketing*, Penguin.

Dibb S, Simkin L, Pride W & Ferrel OC (2000), *Marketing: Concepts and Strategies*, 4th Ed., Houghton Mifflin.

Drummond G & Ensor J (2001), *Strategic Marketing Planning and Control*, Butterworth-Heinemann.

Fahey L & Narayanan VK (1986), *Macroenvironmental Analysis for Strategic Management*, West Publishing.

Hooley GJ, Saunders JA & Piercy NF (1998), *Marketing Strategy and Competitive Positioning*, 2nd Ed, Prentice Hall.

Jobber D (1998), *Principles and Practice of Marketing*, 2nd Ed, McGraw-Hill.

Johnson G & Scholes J (1999), *Exploring Corporate Strategy,* 5th Ed, Prentice-Hall

Meek R & Meek H (2001), *Marketing Management*, Financial World Publishing.

Kotler P (1999),*Marketing Management, The Millenium Edition*, Prentice-Hall.

Murphy C (2000), *Brit pop wakes up to net revolution – The web is the new rock and roll – and music companies are trying to figure out how best to protect themselves in an age of direct downloads*, Marketing, 16 March.

Mutel G (2000), *Do Upmarket stores 'own' organic? – Organic food is becoming a big part of supermarkets' strategies*, Marketing, 14 September.

Porter ME (1980), *Competitive Strategy*, Free Press.

Porter ME (1985), *Competitive Advantage: Creating and Sustaining Superior Performance*, Free Press.

Reed M (1999), *Real-world outfits make most of net – A wide range of businesses are taking steps to benefit from the explosion of e-commerce*, Marketing, 26 August.

Robinson PJ, Faris CW and Wind Y (1967), *Industrial Buying and Creative Marketing*, Allyn & Bacon.

Webster FE & Wind T (1972), *A General Model of Organizational Buying Behaviour*, Journal of Marketing, 26 April, p.12-17.

Objectives

By the end of this unit you will be able to:

- Conduct and evaluate a detailed marketing audit, both internally and externally
- Identify the elements that can be used to create competitive advantage
- Understand and be able to critically appraise a wide variety of marketing techniques, and concepts including:
    - Resource-based approach to marketing (organizational assets, competencies and capabilities):
        o Technical resources
        o Financial standing
        o Managerial skills
        o Organization
        o Information systems
    - Understand and be able to critically appraise an asset-based approach to marketing:
        o Customer-based assets
        o Distribution-based assets
        o Alliance-based assets
        o Internal assets
    - Understand and be able to undertake a marketing activities audit:
        o Marketing strategy audit
        o Marketing structures audit
        o Marketing systems audit
        o Productivity audit
        o Marketing functions audit
    - Understand and be able to undertake an innovation audit.

Study guide

- This unit will take you about 2 hours to work through
- We suggest that you take a further 3 hours to do the various activities and questions in the unit.

Introduction

The second unit concentrated on analysing the external environment faced by organizations. This unit will focus on the internal analysis of an organization's resources. This stage of the auditing process creates the information necessary for an organization to identify the key assets and competencies upon which a strategic position can be built. In particular the unit explores the nature of organizational assets, competencies and capabilities. It then goes on to cover the fundamental elements of a marketing activities audit, including an innovation audit.

Organizational assets

Organizational assets are both tangible and intangible (Hooley et al., 1998) and include:

- **Financial assets** – Working capital, access/availability of investment finance, credit worthiness.
- **Physical assets** – ownership or control of facilities and property. In the retail sector ownership of an outlet in a prime location could be a significant asset.
- **Operational assets** – production plant, machinery and process technologies.
- **People assets** – the quantity of human resources available to the organization and the quality of this resource in terms of their background and abilities.
- **Legally enforceable assets** – ownership of copyrights and patents, franchise and licensing agreements.
- **Systems** – management-information systems and databases and the general infrastructure for supporting decision-making activities.
- **Marketing assets** – marketing assets fall into four main categories:

1. **Customer-based assets** – assets that customers perceive to be important such as:
   - **Image and reputation** – of the company and the recognition of its corporate identity
   - **Brand franchises** – effective brands have high levels of customer loyalty, create competitive positions that are more easy to defend and achieve higher margins
   - **Unique products and services** – a number of features such as price, quality, design or level of innovation can be used to create distinctive products and services
   - **Country of origin** – consumers associate particular attributes to different nations, these then become associated with a company or brand that has its origin in that particular country. For instance, Audi benefits from the perception of Germany as the source of quality engineering products.
2. **Distribution based assets** – a number of potential assets are associated with the critical activity of distributing products and services, such as:
   - **level of control over distribution channels** – control over the main channels of distribution in a market is a key marketing asset as it confers a major competitive advantage to an organization.
   - **the geographical coverage and quality of the distribution network** – the quality of a distribution network is not just a function of geographic spread or how intensive that coverage is on the ground but also other key factors such as ability to guarantee supply, lead times, or ability to react quickly.
3. **Internally based assets** – other assets that lie outside the marketing functional area but can be exploited to give advantages to marketing activities. It is important to remember that the aim of the internal audit is to identify the underlying asset rather than just the activity. It is the asset itself that may have the potential to be used innovatively to create additional advantages. A range of internal assets have the potential to provide advantages to marketing activities:
   - **cost structure** – an organization may be in the position to realize lower costs than its competitors through fuller use of capacity or by the creative use of new technology. This in turn could give marketing the option to set lower prices for products and services than the competition. Although the asset itself is the manufacturing cost base, it can be exploited to enable an advantage to be gained in the marketing activity of pricing.
   - **information systems** – marketing research activities (such as collecting and analysing customer, competitor and market information) can be supported by information systems. These systems can be configured to create sophisticated databases, which are essentially a key marketing asset that an organization can exploit.
4. **Assets based on external relationships** – agreements with third parties, both formal or informal, can permit an organization to gain access to a number of different assets:
   - **access to markets** – agreements with local distributors can allow an organization to cover markets that it would be unable to address within the constraints of it's existing resource base.
   - **access to technological developments or processes** – licensing or joint ventures allow an organization to operate at the leading edge of technological developments or production processes.
   - **exclusive agreements** – third parties can be used to exclude competitors. An example would be where a building society agrees to offer only a particular insurance company's policies to its mortgage customers.

Case history

HBOS

In May 2001 the Halifax Building Society and the Bank of Scotland announced a £28 million merger. The combined organization, called HBOS, would become the fifth biggest bank in the UK. The merger proposal was based on an analysis of the current assets of the companies.

The Halifax's strengths are in consumer markets, where it is the UK's largest mortgage lender and the market leader in the savings market. The company has 800 branches in England and Wales but only 60 in Scotland. In contrast, the Bank of Scotland has 300 branches in Scotland and a mere 28 branches in England and Wales. The Bank of Scotland's strengths lie in the corporate and business banking sector.

The companies have little physical overlap and have complementary strengths. The aim will be to enhance revenue by allowing both brands access to the other's partners distribution channels of the other partner. HBOS also believes that the new larger organization will allow it to introduce new product developments more quickly.

Combining assets through a merger can make strategic sense. The unanswered question is whether the new organization has the competencies to ensure that the full potential of the merger is realized.

Exam hint

In the exam questions based on a mini case, you will be expected not only to be able to identify the organizational assets but also to show how they can be used to advantage in the future strategy of the company.

Organizational competencies

Definition

Organizational competencies

'The abilities and skills available to the company to marshal the effective exploitation of the company's assets' (Drummond & Ensor, 2001).

Organizational competencies are necessary for an organization to effectively exploit its assets. It is the combination of assets and these skills that deliver an organization's strategic capabilities in a market. Activities, such as producing a range of distinctive products, arise out of the underlying assets and competencies of an organization. Skills are located at a strategic, functional and operational level. Within these levels they may also be competencies that are to be found throughout an organization, within specific teams or within specific individuals (Hooley et al., 1998).

- **Competencies at a strategic level** – refer to a range of management skills that drive the strategic direction of an organization including the ability to: communicate, motivate, create strategic vision, implement strategy, assess changing circumstances, innovate and learn.
- **Competencies at a functional level** – are the skills available to an organization to manage its various functional activities such as finance, operations and marketing. In the area of marketing the function should be assessed on skills relating to its ability to handle customer relationships, channel management, product management and product innovation.

There are also some organizational competencies that lie outside the marketing function that can be used to create advantages in marketing activities such as:

- **Innovatory culture** – the ability to be able to create and sustain a culture that supports innovation is an important competence. This enhances activities such as new product development, customer service (through empowering front-line staff to develop creative solutions to customers' problems), and promotional campaigns through a willingness to implement creative ideas
- **Production skills** – these may allow an organization to produce products or services more flexibly, at higher quality or to shorter lead times, all of which can be used to gain an advantage by the marketing function.

- **Competencies at an operational level** are the skills involved in the day-to-day operations, across the functional areas, of the organization. In the marketing function, for example, these would include skills of co-ordinating and implementing sales force activities, promotional and public relations activities, special offers and discounts, updating of packaging and labelling.
- **Competencies present corporation wide** are the skills that are relevant to the entire organization, and which impinge on its ability to execute tasks at strategic, functional and operational level. An example would be the ability to foster creativity and innovation throughout the activities of the whole organization.
- **Competencies within teams**. Individuals in organizations generally work together in teams, both on a formal and informal basis. Alongside the specific skill base each individual offers, a group requires the skills necessary to work together effectively as a team. Successful project management relies on these team competencies.
- **Competencies within individuals** are the abilities and skills that individuals have to execute the tasks they face in their area of responsibility, whether at strategic, functional or operational level.

Not all competencies lie within an organization: they can be gained through external association:

- **Competencies based on external relationships** organizations may subcontract entire areas of activity to third parties, such as, promotional campaigns to advertising agencies. Alternatively, the company may choose to bring new skills into the organization temporarily by – for instance, contracting a management consultancy practice to co-ordinate specific one-off projects. Where this takes place, a key skill to review in an internal audit is the ability to co-ordinate and control these external relationships.

Once the assets and competencies of an organization have been detected some assets are more likely to be critical than others. The connection between these assets and competencies can be charted to uncover the key relationships.

Activity 3.1

Analyse your organization, or an organization of your choice, to establish its assets and competencies. Compare these with those of other organizations in your company's strategic group. Does your organization have any unique capabilities?

Question

Read the mini-case study 'easyJet' in the December 1999 exam paper and carry out the following task.

As a consultant you have been asked, as an initial step, to identify the core capabilities of easyJet that can be used to grow the family of companies that Haji-Ioannou envisages.

Give yourself 10 minutes to read the mini-case study and no more than 25 minutes to write your answer. Compare your answer with the specimen answer in the paper.

The auditing process

Initially any audit will need to carry out a corporate internal audit in order to establish those assets and competencies from other functional areas that either currently, or potentially could assist the marketing function and support strategic marketing developments. Hooley et al (1998) suggest that these wider non-marketing assets and competencies will fall into the following categories: financial resources, managerial skills, technical resources, organizational structures and information systems.

The internal marketing audit

Once this corporate overview has taken place the specific marketing activities of the organization should be evaluated. This is undertaken by an internal marketing audit, which is specifically aimed at reviewing the marketing activities of the enterprise. It is split into five distinct areas (Kotler et al, 1996):

- **Marketing strategy audit**, which analyses the organization's current corporate and marketing objectives. The objectives need to be reviewed to establish if they are relevant, realistic and explicit as the current marketing strategy will be evaluated in terms of its fit with these objectives. This element of the audit should also allow the organization to identify whether adequate resources have been allocated for the successful implementation of the strategy.
- **Marketing structures audit** examines the structure of the marketing function and its relationship with other areas of the business. In particular the profile that the marketing function has, within the business, is reviewed. Communication is a key element of this part of the audit, both within the marketing function and between marketing and other functions, as it is an indicator of how effective the function is at co-ordinating its activities.
- **Marketing systems audit** examines the planning systems, control measures and new product development processes in an organization, as well as reviewing the information systems that support these activities.
- **Productivity audit** inspects the organization's activities using financial criteria such as profitability and cost-effectiveness applied to assess the relative productivity of products, market sectors, distribution channels and geographic markets.
- **Marketing functions audit** explores in detail all aspects of the marketing mix: the products and services the organization produces, pricing policy, distribution arrangements, the organization of the sales team, advertising policy, public relations and other promotional activities.

Innovation

Many organizations are operating in markets where they are increasingly confronting global competition, which tends to lead to rapidly changing market conditions. This is compounded by shorter product life cycles and a technological revolution of increasing competitiveness, which is shaping the way in which organizations manage their business practices and processes. If they wish to survive in this external environment organizations need to foster creativity and innovation. Thus, any audit of an organization's internal activities should include a review of its performance in the area of innovation.

The innovation audit

This element of the auditing process reviews how effectively an organization is able to deliver the level of innovation necessary to create new products, new services, and new ways of undertaking activities. Success in these activities is heavily dependent on a company successfully harnessing the creative ideas of individuals at all levels and within all functions of the organization. The innovation audit examines current performance and establishes whether the underlying assets and competencies necessary to foster innovation are present. The innovation audit reviews four key aspects of the organization:

- The organization's current performance in delivering innovation.
- The organization's policies and practices that are currently used to support innovation.
- The organizational climate with regard to innovation.
- The balance of the cognitive styles of the senior management team.

Current performance

A range of performance measures can be utilized to establish an organization's current level of achievement in the area of creativity and innovation.

Davidson (1997) suggests that two measures are used. Firstly the total rate of new product launches in the last three years needs to be established. Then the percentage success rate of these developments must be analysed to clarify the actual performance in the market (see Figure 3.1).

Innovation criteria	3 years ago	This year
Number of significant innovations in past 5 years	14	7
Number successful	4	4
% Success rate	29%	57%
% Total sales in product/ services launched in past 5 years	18%	30%
% Incremental sales	11%	13.5%
Average annual sales per new product/service (£m)	5	8
Incremental payback per new product/service (years)	3	4

Figure 3.1
Example of product and service innovation performance measures. (Adapted from Davidson, 1997)

These product and service innovation performance measures show the following:

- New product and service developments are lower in the last five years, but the rate of successful market launches has risen from 29% of developments to 57%.
- Sales per new development have risen from £5 million to £8 million.
- Although 30% of sales, in the last 12 months, are from products launched in the last five years (up from 18% three years ago) only 13.5% of these sales are new (incremental) sales. The remaining 16.5% are sales that have cannibalized current products. This is an indication of poor planning.
- The payback period for new developments is lengthening.

One action the organization could take is to have more effective segmentation and targeting processes, so that new product sales are developmental rather than cannibalizing existing sales. This type of analysis allows an organization to explore its current performance using hard output measures.

Another important hard measure is an organization's customer satisfaction ratings. These should be established not only for the performance of the core product but also across all the areas of customer service.

An innovation/value product portfolio analysis

Kim & Mauborgne's (1998) research suggests that products that offered only incremental improvements were likely to generate lower sales and substantially less profitability than truly pioneering innovations. They grouped innovations into three categories:

1. **Settlers** – businesses or products that offer the normal ('me-too') market value.
2. **Migrators** – businesses or products that offer value improvements over competitors.
3. **Pioneers** – businesses or products that represent value innovations and create new markets. An example is the Sony Walkman. They may also recreate/redefine an existing market, for example Dyson in the vacuum cleaner market.

The clear implication of this study is that organizations that are driven by future profitability need to have a spread of business across the portfolio. Companies that find that most of their businesses or products are in the settler area are paying insufficient attention to the innovation process. For the audit organizations should undertake a portfolio analysis based on the innovation/value matrix (see Figure 3.2).

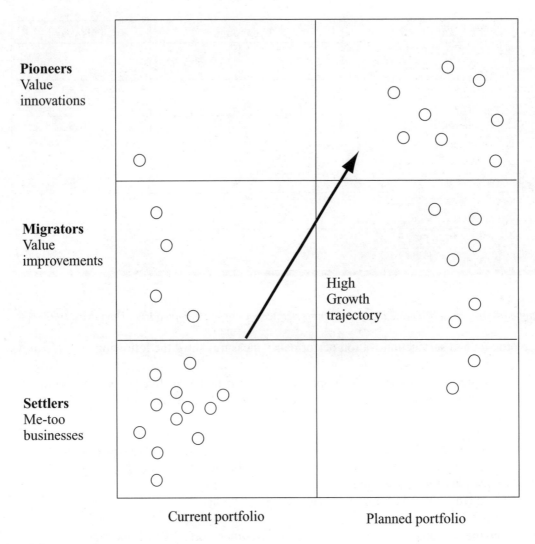

Pioneers
Value
innovations

Migrators
Value
improvements

High
Growth
trajectory

Settlers
Me-too
businesses

Current portfolio

Planned portfolio

Figure 3.2
The innovation/value matrix (Kim & Mauborgne, 1998)

Review of the organization's policies and practices that are currently used to support innovation

This stage of the audit consists of identifying the current policies that are in place in an organization to support innovation. It will also include a review of the structures or procedures that have been developed to foster creativity and innovation.

The organizational climate

In order to produce creative ideas and foster innovation, a supportive organizational climate which facilitates innovative activity is needed. Two approaches can be taken in reviewing an organization's climate. The first approach is to undertake a standard attitude survey the second approach is to use metaphors as a way of discovering staff attitudes.

An attitude survey of key areas of the organizational climate that affect creativity

The aim of this element of the audit is to uncover the staff's perceptions of the current organizational climate. These should centre on eight influential factors that are critical supports to innovation and four areas that act as barriers (Burnside, 1990).

Factors that support creativity and innovation include:

- **Teamwork** – The level of teamwork undertaken within a company and familiarity of individuals to forming new project teams are important factors in fostering successful teamwork. Other factors include the amount of trust between team members, the level of willingness to help each other and the commitment to the current projects.
- **Resources** – The level of access individuals and teams have to appropriate resources in terms of facilities, staff, finance and information.
- **Challenge** – The level of challenge involved in the work undertaken in terms of the nature of the task and the level of importance associated with it. Individuals and teams are invigorated by projects that set about solving intriguing problems (solving the problem alone provides the individuals involved with an implicit reward).
- **Freedom** – The level of freedom devolved to individuals and teams is critical. The more control and freedom individuals have over their work and ideas the more likely they are to be innovative in the ways in which they undertake a project or task.
- **Supervisory encouragement** – Innovation is facilitated by managerial support that provides a clear set of clear goals, good communication channels and is focused on building staff morale.
- **Creativity infrastructure** – Innovation can be nurtured in a company by formal organizational structures consciously put in place by senior management to support the development of creative ideas.
- **Recognition** – As well as the implicit rewards of successfully undertaking challenging projects, individuals are encouraged by more formal recognition of their ideas and actions. This includes, but as only one aspect, the use of formal financial rewards.
- **Unity and co-operation** – A shared vision within an organization that values creativity clearly facilitates innovation. Also a culture that breeds a collaborative and co-operative atmosphere is beneficial.

Several elements of an organization's climate may act as constraints on innovation. These including:

- **Insufficient time** -Time pressure erodes the ability to consider alternative approaches to projects.
- **Status quo** – Signified by an unwillingness of managers and other staff to change the 'traditional' ways of doing things.
- **Political problems** – Lack of co-operation between different areas of the organization and battles over areas of responsibility.
- **Evaluation pressure** – Evaluation or feedback systems that are focused on criticism and external evaluation are unlikely to facilitate creativity and innovation. This is a common characteristic of public-sector organizations, which have to demonstrate the probity of their actions to the public. This probity is demonstrated by the external scrutiny of their activities by independent external bodies. One effect may be to stifle the development of creative and innovative services.

Case history

Nokia

Since 1998 Nokia has increased its share of the mobile phone handset market from 20.6% to 30.6%. This has been gained at the expense of other companies such as Ericsson, whose share of the market has dropped from 16.4% to 10% over the same period.

Nokia's success has been down to the company identifying early on, that consumers would treat mobile phone handsets as a fashion accessory. Rather than concentrating on creating products with sophisticated services, Nokia developed a range of inexpensive phones that came in a wide array of colours and designs. The result has been a dramatic increase in sales. By being market-oriented and correctly identifying a significant trend in buyer behaviour Nokia managed to develop a range of products to address this market segment. Nokia's ability to 'rethink the product' created an innovation that has been very successful in the market. Note, however, that the product development itself was not the most technologically sophisticated – yet it was truly innovative.

Nokia is now demonstrating an innovative approach in the network infrastructure market. The company recently announced a deal with Orange, worth £930 million, to provide infrastructure in France, Germany and the UK. The innovation was the financial deal whereby Nokia offered Orange 'vendor financing', under the agreement Nokia offered Orange a loan to help buy the new equipment.

Industry observers see Nokia's management as being highly pragmatic and action oriented. Competitors, by contrast, tend to get locked in internal discussions and are therefore slower to deliver new products and services. Nokia's success emphasizes the importance to an organization of having a market orientation and a culture that embraces and encourages innovation.

Exam hint

Get into the habit of reading the business section of any broadsheet newspaper and of watching the business programmes on television. Try to identify stories that are practical examples of issues raised in the workbook. These will be useful examples to include in your answers to exam questions. They will demonstrate to the examiner that you are able to use theory to analyse situations faced by contemporary businesses.

Metaphors

Metaphorical description (Morgan, 1993) is a proven creativity tool. The strength of this approach is its ability to overcome the limitations of literal language to describe far more complex relationships and connections. It is therefore an entirely appropriate tool to use in order to ascertain staff perceptions of a company's organizational climate.

The metaphorical description approach asks individuals to describe their organization in terms of a metaphor. For example: ' This organization is like a "lead weight", it holds you back and drags you down' or 'This organization is like a "rowing team" we all pull together'. These metaphors are then analysed. Generally they tend to be positive or negative observations of seven key organizational features:

- strategic orientation
- organizational structure
- organizational life cycle
- management skills
- people orientation
- power orientation
- operations practices.

The use of metaphor allows a rounded perspective to emerge of the organizational climate that supports innovation.

Summary

This unit has outlined the elements of a detailed internal marketing audit. It had also demonstrated that an internal analysis is undertaken in order to identify an organization's assets and competencies. Combined, these resources make up an organization's capabilities. It is these organizational capabilities, based on an identification of assets and competencies, that are used to create competitive advantage.

Further study and examination preparation

Extending knowledge

Bibliography

Burnside R (1990), *Improving corporate climates for creativity*, in *Innovation and Creativity at Work*, Ed West M A, & Farr J, L Wiley.

Davidson M (1997), *Even More Offensive Marketing*, Chapter 2, Penguin Books.

Higgins JM (1996), *Innovate or Evaporate: Creative Techniques for Strategists*. Long Range Planning, 29: 3, pp.370-380.

Hooley GH, Saunders JA and Piercy NF (1998), *Marketing Strategy & Competitive Positioning*, 2nd Ed, Prentice-Hall.

Hurst DK, Rush JC and White RE (1989), *Top management teams and organizational renewal*, Strategic Management Journal, 10; pp.87-105.

Johnson G & Scholes K (1999), *Exploring Corporate Strategy*, 5th Ed, Prentice-Hall.

Kay J (1993), *Foundations of Corporate Success*, Oxford University Press.

Kim CW & Mauborgne R (1998), *Pioneers strike it rich*. Financial Times, August 11.

Kotler K, Armstrong G, Saunders J & Wong V (1996), *Principles of Marketing: the European Edition*, Prentice-Hall.

Martensen A & Dahlgaard JJ (1999), *Strategy and Planning for Innovation Management – Supported by Creative and Learning organizations*, International Journal of Quality and Reliability Management, 16:9, pp.878-891.

Montanari JR & Bracker JS (1986), *Strategic Management Journal*, 7: 3. pp.251-265.

Morgan G (1993), *Imaginization, The Art of Creative Management*, Sage Publications.

Objectives

By the end of this unit you will:

- Be able to describe, apply and critically evaluate a range of auditing tools:
    1. Product life cycle
    2. The diffusion of innovation process
    3. Experience curves and the role of market share
    4. Profit impact of marketing strategies (PIMS)
    5. Portfolio analysis
    6. Value chain
    7. Gap analysis
- Know the key components of, and be able to undertake, a marketing audit and SWOT analysis

Study guide

- This unit will take you about 4 hours to work through
- We suggest that you take a further 4 hours to do the various activities and questions in this unit.

Introduction

The last two units have focused on the current situation in terms of external and internal analysis. There are many tools that can be used to help interpret the current situation. These are often referred to as auditing tools. These models can not only be used for auditing the current situation but can also play an important role in helping to develop future strategy (i.e. can be used for identifying both 'where are we now?' and also 'where do we want to be?' questions). This unit will outline the various models and frameworks that can be used for both strategic analysis and strategy development. For example, portfolio analysis tools such as the General Electric matrix can be used to identify the current location of strategic business units or products but can be equally valid in determining future strategies.

You will have already been introduced to many of these models in previous CIM modules such as Marketing Operations where you will have encountered the product life cycle. It is expected that at Diploma level students will not only be able to describe each of the models but that you will also be able to apply them and provide a critical evaluation of their uses and limitations.

Exam hint

On each of the recent Planning and Control exam papers there has been at least one question on techniques for analysis and strategy development. They have appeared in both Section A (compulsory question) and Section B (choice). For example, on the December 2000 paper there was a question on portfolio analysis and in the June 2000 paper there was a question on the value chain.

Value chain

The value chain (Porter 1980) can be a very valuable auditing tool as well as proving useful for identifying strategies to gain competitive advantage. This model shown in Figure 4.1 was originally developed for accounting purposes to identify the profitability of the various stages of the manufacturing process. More recently it has been acknowledged that the model can be applied to measures of competitive advantage rather than just profit. Porter (1985) suggests that competitive advantage is determined to a large extent by the way in which companies manage each element and the interactions between them. The value chain provides companies with a means of identifying ways of creating more customer value and analysing an organization's capabilities. The model was traditionally applied to manufacturing companies but more recently it has been recognized that it can be applied equally well to service organizations.

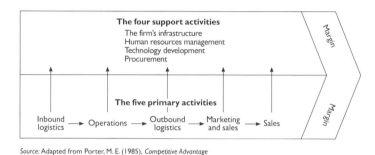

Source: Adapted from Porter, M. E. (1985), *Competitive Advantage*

Figure 4.1
The Value Chain (Porter, 1985)

The model highlights nine interrelated value-creating activities that can help to create value. These are divided into primary and support activities.

Primary activities

- **Inbound logistics** – activities concerned with receiving, storing and the internal distribution of raw materials.
- **Operations** – the means by which the raw materials are converted into the final product.
- **Outbound Logistics** – activities that relate to the process of delivering the product to the customer such as storage, warehousing and transportation.
- **Marketing and Sales** – involves making sure the customers are aware of the product.
- **Service** – includes activities such as customer service, after-sales service, installation and training.

Support Activities

- **Firm Infrastructure** – this relates to the organizational structure, management style, culture and systems.
- **Human Resource Management** – recruitment, training and rewarding of staff.
- **Technology Development** – includes research and development, IT and process improvements.
- **Procurement** – purchasing of various inputs.

By focusing on these various functions companies can improve performance and effectiveness and identify areas in which they can add customer value. It not only provides a structured framework for examining costs and performance within organizations but also provides a sound basis for interfirm comparisons. The value chain can be extended to include suppliers, distributors and customers, to analyse the relationships between companies and to identify ways of adding value in the supply chain such as Just-in-time delivery (JIT). It can also be a valuable tool for analysing competitors, for example for identifying cost advantages.

Extended knowledge

For further reading on the value chain see either Hooley et al. (1998), pp.159-162.

Case history

The media value chain

During the 1980s and 1990s electronic media companies were highly successful. The owners of licences such as the ITV companies and Capital Radio were exceptionally profitable. These companies dominated the key portion of the 'value chain' described by Porter (1998). In most electronic media markets this chain is simple. Each link is a separate stage in the process that takes the raw talent of an actor, comedian or football player and turns it into great media that the consumer will listen to or watch.

At each stage value is added, but separate links in the chain are rewarded very differently for the contribution they make. The key question in assessing the value of media businesses and deciding which companies to invest in is to understand which of these links in the chain will hold the greatest value in the long-term.

In the 1980s there were just four links in the chain:

1 The **talent**, be it a writer's, performer's or someone who creates powerful formats. It is the raw material of great media.
2 **Production**, the ability to take creative talent and turn it into a programme or a website that consumers really want.
3 **Content packaging and marketing**. Channel 4 typifies this. The channel does not produce any programmes, but creates channel brands.
4 **Distribution** – the ability to get the media to the consumer through control of spectrum, telephone wires or cables. This final link has for many years been the most profitable of all. The spectrum was so limited that the companies that controlled it had tremendous power over the entire chain, and took the largest proportion of the value created.

But two things have changed all that:

1 The spectrum isn't as limited as it once was. There are now more than 200 TV channels broadcasting in the UK and more than 250 analogue radio stations, there is the Internet and soon the new broadband and third-generation mobile media will be offering greater access to the consumer. When the analogue TV signal is switched off there will be another slice of spectrum to sell. There have never been so many routes to carry media content to the consumer, and it will become easier in the future.

2 A new link has also appeared in the value chain that has further devalued companies that simply have access to broadcast spectrum. This is the consumer gateway. Sky and ONDigital gain their power through their TV set-top boxes, which allow them to control access to the consumer. And there are also new and powerful operators being created by the Internet, such as AOL.
   At the other end, the stock market already puts a high value on companies such as AOL and ONDigital, which control the consumer gateway.

The real value seems to lie in vertically integrated businesses that have 'must-see' content and control the gateway. This lies at the heart of BSkyB's strategy and is the rationale for the merger between AOL and Time Warner.

Applying this logic to the mobile phone industry makes the companies that paid £22.48 billion for third-generation spectrum in Britain – the weakest link in the media value chain – rather nervous. To make an acceptable return on capital employed, they will need to generate substantial profits from the content, packaging and consumer gateway links in the value chain.

This will require some big changes. These companies must convert their existing billing relationships into gateway relationships where they are at the heart of everything the customer does. They also have to offer their customers 'must-see' content that is exclusive to their network. The final step would be to vertically integrate the whole operation, as BSkyB has in television. This would create significant synergies.

To achieve this will require a huge cultural shift. Companies that have core skills in network and subscriber management must understand and adopt the very different skills of integrated content providers. It is a tough proposition.

Source: Ewington, (2000); www.Lexis-Nexis.com

Exam hint

In the exam you will be expected not only to be able to outline and discuss the value chain but also to critically evaluate the model and even apply it to a particular scenario. In December 1999 students were asked to apply the value chain to EasyJet as a means of identifying competitive advantage.

Limitations of the value chain

Despite being a valuable auditing tool the model does have limitations. It is very inwardly oriented, rather than being focused on the external environment (in particular the market and customers). It is also worth remembering that in most industries a single organization rarely undertakes all the value-creating activities and therefore any analysis should recognize the wider value system.

Question 4.1

Value chain

Answer Question 2 for the exam paper for June 2000. Compare your answer with the outline answer provided in the appendix at the back of the book.

Product life cycle

The product life cycle (PLC) – See Figure 4.2 – appears in almost every textbook on marketing and yet it is often described as the least understood marketing tool. This is because, although most marketers can describe the various stages of the PLC, few seem to take any real account of the concept when planning future strategies. The PLC recognizes that products, like humans, have a finite life and move through a variety of distinct stages from introduction to growth, maturity, decline and eventually death. Therefore, marketers need to modify their strategies and tactics to ensure that the maximum profit is generated from each stage. The PLC concept has many limitations (which will be discussed below); however, it does highlight a range of important considerations:

- Products have a finite life and will eventually die.
- During their existence they will move through a variety of stages that will all require different strategies in order to try and extend the life and generate the maximum profit.
- It also highlights that the profit potential from each stage will vary considerably.
-

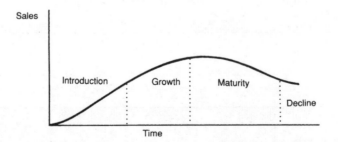

Figure 4.2
The classic S-shaped PLC curve

The product life cycle can be applied at a number of levels:

- **Total industries** – such as the motor industry.
- **Product classes** – such as cars, vans and lorries.

- **Product forms** – such as people movers, estate cars and sports cars.
- **Brands** – such as Renault Espace, VW Beetle and Ford Escort.

Rink & Swan (1979) believed that in order for managers to fully understand the context in which the brand is developing it is essential they understand the distinction between the various categories of the PLC. The length of each stage will vary considerably depending on which category we are considering. For example industry and product classes tend to have the longest PLC's. However, it is often difficult to judge the nature of the PLC for individual brands. For example, the Persil brand (washing product) has endured longer than each of the product classes – washing powder, liquid detergents and now tablets. Product forms tend to conform to the classic PLC curve to a greater extent than the other categories.

Table 4.1 summarizes the various marketing mix decisions for each stage of the PLC. It must be remembered that this table simplifies the decisions and provides guidance only. Each product must be viewed independently. For example, the table suggests that a low price strategy should be adopted in the introductory stage. However, this may not always be the case. For example, organizations may choose to adopt a skimming strategy by setting a high initial price to cream off profits in the short-term. This is often used by new, innovatory, products for which customers are prepared to pay a high price. The strategic use of the PLC will be focused on in this text. However, the decline stage will be discussed in some detail because this is a major strategic decision facing companies in deciding whether to rejuvenate or withdraw products.

Table 4.1

Marketing mix strategies	Introduction	Growth	Maturity	Decline
Product	Basic product, limited range	Develop product extensions and service levels	Modify and differentiate Develop next generation	Phase out weak brands Consider leaving market
Price	Low price strategy	Penetration strategy	Price to meet or beat competitors	Reduce
Distribution	Selective Build dealer relations	Intensive. Limited trade discounts	Intensive. Heavy trade discounts	Selective. Phase out weak outlets
Advertising	Heavy spending to build awareness and encourage trial among early adopters and distributors	Moderate to build awareness and interest in the mass market. Greater word of mouth	Emphasize brand differentiation and special offers	Reduce to a level that maintains hard core loyalty. Emphasize low prices to reduce stock
Sales promotion	Extensive to encourage trial	Reduce to a moderate level	Increase to encourage brand switching	Reduce or stop completely
Planning time frame	Short to medium	Long range	Medium range	Short

Activity 4.1

Product life cycle in practice

In the exam it is essential that you illustrate your answers with current examples. Collect articles from current marketing press such as *Marketing Week*, *Marketing*, *Campaign* and national newspapers that illustrate the product life cycle in practice. In particular, identify products or services that have reached maturity/decline and identify the strategies being used to either rejuvenate or delete these products/services.

Value of the PLC

The PLC can be a valuable tool for a number of reasons. Jobber (1998) p. 225 identifies a number of the insights that the PLC provides:

- **Product termination** – The PLC emphasizes that nothing lasts forever. There is a danger that marketers will fail to recognize this and become complacent, not developing new products to replace established ones.
- **Growth projections** – The PLC warns against the dangers of assuming that growth will continue indefinitely. This is particularly critical when companies are facing major investment decisions based on existing products.
- **Marketing objectives and strategies change during the PLC** – This emphasizes the need to review marketing objectives and strategies as the product/service moves through the various stages. For example, promotional objectives may change from raising awareness (initial stages) to reminding customers (latter stages of the cycle).
- **Product planning** – The PLC emphasizes the need to have a balanced portfolio of products, i.e. to have new products in the pipeline to replace those in maturity or decline. Companies should be using the cash generated by mature products to fund new product development. It is essential that this is managed effectively to avoid cash-flow problems when established products enter decline and there are no new products to fill the gap. This links in with the Boston Consulting Group Matrix, which will be discussed later in the unit.
- **Dangers of overpowering** – Companies that launch an innovatory new product ahead of competitors have the opportunity to charge a high price. However, unless they have patent protection competitors may enter the market and undercut them.

In addition, the PLC can be used as a control tool in that comparisons can be made with life cycles of similar products.

Limitations of the PLC

Despite some of the insights the PLC provides it has many limitations. Jobber (1998), p.228, provides a good overview of these:

- **Fads and classics** – Many products do not follow the traditional S-shaped PLC. For example, there are those products (described as fads) that show a rapid growth but an equally rapid decline such as Buzz Light Year toys, cabbage patch dolls and various 'executive toys'. In contrast, products (known as classics) seem to defy the PLC concept and live forever – some examples include Bisto and Coca Cola. Swan and Rink (1982) identified 17 different life cycle curves, which questions the validity of the traditional PLC S-shaped curve.
- **Marketing effects** – The PLC is the *result* of marketing activity, not the cause, and therefore marketers have to be careful they do not fall into the self-fulfilling prophecy where they expect a product to decline, withdraw marketing support and the product declines.
- **Unpredictability** – There is little indication of the timescale of the PLC. The duration of each stage varies considerably with product and may range from weeks to years. Therefore the model is of limited use as a forecasting tool.
- **Misleading objectives and strategy** – The model has been criticized for being too prescriptive in terms of the objectives and strategies that are appropriate for each stage. There is little scope for creativity.

There is also an additional problem in that it is often very difficult to identify where a product is located on the PLC (therefore management decisions may be based on incorrect assumptions). The model can also encourage marketers to be product focused rather than market focused. It is often very difficult to predict the shape and duration of the PLC due to external factors such as political, social, economic and technological and competitive activities.

Extended knowledge

For further discussion on the product life cycle read Jobber (1998), pp. 224-229.

Managing products in the decline stage

It is worth while considering the latter stages of the PLC because these often prove to be the most challenging for marketers. Do we try to rejuvenate our product or do we accept it has reached the end of its useful life and withdraw it?

Case history

Heinz Salad Cream

Heinz is hoping to make Salad Cream the UK's number one table sauce, ahead of its own Tomato Ketchup and Hellmann's Mayonnaise, following the brand's £10 million relaunch. Annual sales of Salad Cream stand at £25 million – but Heinz's director of European Sauces Stefan Barden says the brand will be axed if the figure doesn't double by 2005. Barden says: 'Salad Cream is in the last-chance saloon. We will review it on a yearly basis and if it doesn't make any money, it will go.' Salad Cream was saved following a public outcry when Heinz revealed it was considering killing it off last year. The brand is being targeted at 'twentysomething' consumers through an integrated marketing campaign consisting of an interactive Website, sponsored comedy tour and new TV, press and radio ads. Salad Cream bottles have also been redesigned and the price increased from 59p to 99p for a 285g bottle. The TV ads, which broke on April 3, have been created by Leo Burnett, with media through Starcom Motive. They carry the strapline 'Any food tastes supreme with Heinz Salad Cream. One of the TV ads, called Pizza, shows a young man using Heinz Salad Cream to revive a day-old slice of pizza found stuck to his bedclothes. If the campaign is a success, Barden says that Heinz will target the European market and even consider launching Salad Cream in the USA.

Source: Marketing Week (2000) 30 March, p.8. www.Lexis-Nexis.com

There are a number of options available to companies facing products in the decline stage of the PLC. Wilson & Gilligan (1997) identify four alternatives:

- **Non-deletion** – This option involves attempting to rejuvenate the product to extend the life cycle. This strategy has been successfully employed by companies such as the VW Beetle, Tango and Fairy Liquid.
- **Eliminate overnight** – Some organizations may decide to divest immediately and withdraw the product from the market. This strategy is most relevant where the organization does not intend to commit resources to developing the product or service. Where products at the decline stage damage corporate image, or other products and

services marketed by the organization, then the decision can be reformulated to ask: 'Can the business afford not to eliminate the product immediately?'. This can be a risky strategy because it can have repercussions for the company in terms of negative publicity and may have a knock-on effect on other products they offer.

- **Increase price or reduce promotion** – This strategy relies on products fading away naturally because marketing support is withdrawn. This option is often pursued by financial service providers that may have old savings products that have been superseded by more modern accounts. Rather than closing down all these accounts they stop promoting them and hope they will naturally fade away.
- **Stay to attract competitors' customers** – This may be an attractive option when many players have withdrawn from the market and there is still demand for a particular product. This strategy has been successfully employed by Electronic Data Services (EDS) who have invested in large-scale automated cheque clearance facilities to gain economies of scale in this overall declining market. Many financial service organizations have started to contract out this function, which was traditionally undertaken in house, to EDS.

An alternative strategy may be to look for new markets to extend the life of existing products – new segments or new geographical markets. For example, tobacco manufacturers have extended the life of tobacco products by marketing the product in countries that are less well regulated than Europe or the USA (such as African countries).

There are a number of factors, both financial and non-financial, that companies must consider when deciding how to deal with declining products. These include:

- Budget implications of each option.
- Estimated future profitability of each strategy.
- Future market potential.
- Customer/distribution expectations.
- Any opportunity to launch in other markets?
- Is a replacement product available?
- What effect will deletion have on customer perceptions?
- Any impact on provision of spare parts?
- Will there be any impact on other products within the portfolio?
- Does the product contribute to the sale of other products?

Question 4.2

Product life cycle – Decline Phase

Answer the following question of the June 1996 examination paper and compare your answer with the outline provided in Appendix 5.

You have recently taken responsibility for a product which your company has marketed for several years, but which now appears to be entering the decline stage of the PLC. Identify the strategic alternatives that are open to you and criteria that should be used in deciding between these alternatives.

Concluding Thoughts

The PLC is a useful model in prompting markers to consider the possible fate of their products and provides some useful insights into the various stages a product may pass through and strategies that may prove useful. However, in reality it is often too simplistic and generalized to be used in isolation, and it cannot replace management expertise and judgement. It may prove to be more useful as a control technique rather than as a forecasting technique. The PLC is not the marketer's panacea but it can be useful if used in combination with other models and frameworks and alongside good management judgement.

Exam hint

Exam questions on the PLC have been popular among students and yet many answers are disappointing. In the exam it is not sufficient to just draw the PLC and describe the various stages. It is important that you answer the question set rather than regurgitating everything you know about the PLC. In many cases questions have focused on a specific stage of the PLC and students have been asked to discuss the implications for marketing strategy. The Senior Examiner is looking for a critical evaluation of the model and its uses and limitations, at a strategic rather than a tactical level.

Exam Questions

Product life cycle

'Far from providing any useful insights the concept of the product life cycle is likely to mislead Marketing Managers.' Discuss this statement and illustrate with examples from you own experience.

See exam paper for December 1998

What problems would you be likely to experience in attempting to forecast the nature and shape of the product life cycle for an innovatory product aimed at a rapidly changing consumer goods market? How, if at all, might these problems possibly be overcome?

See exam paper for June 1994

What useful guidelines does the PLC provide for the development of a marketing mix programme for a service?

See exam paper for June 1995

What criteria should be taken into account when deciding whether to rejuvenate a product or service that is in the mature phase of its life cycle? Assuming that rejuvenation was felt to be worthwhile, what strategies might achieve rejuvenation?

See exam paper for December 1995

As a response to escalating costs and risks of NPD, many managers appear to be paying greater attention to the rejuvenation of products in the late maturity/early decline stages of the PLC. Making reference to products or services which appear to have reached this position on the PLC, discuss how rejuvenation might possibly be achieved.

See exam paper for June 1993

Diffusion of innovation

The PLC provides an indicator of the various stages through which a product passes but provides little indicator of the time scale. The rate at which new products will be adopted varies considerably but Rogers (1983) developed a model which is shown in Figure 4.3. Rogers' model illustrates the pattern of adoption that is often evident following the launch of a new product. This model is not explicitly stated in the Planning and Control syllabus but it usefully links in with new product development and the PLC and has therefore been included in this section.

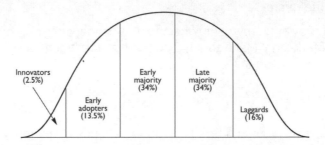

Figure 4.3
Diffusion of innovation (Rogers 1983)

Rogers' model identifies the various types of individuals and the rate at which they will be likely to purchase new products. This model is useful in helping to identify potential target markets for new products and for tailoring the marketing mix to meet the needs of each group of customers. For example, a different pricing strategy may be necessary when targeting the early majority rather than innovators. The innovators may be prepared to pay a high price for an innovative new product and yet this price may have to be reduced to appeal to other target groups. It can be a useful tool for segmenting the market. However, the difficulty lies in a marketer's ability to identify these segments and to reach them effectively, (e.g. those individuals that are innovators in the consumer electronics market may not be innovators in the golf equipment market). This poses a challenge for marketers when they are developing their marketing campaigns. The characteristics of each category of adopters are outlined below.

- **Innovators** – These customers embrace new ideas and new products readily and are often prepared to pay high initial prices to be the first in the market. They are often regarded as opinion leaders and are seen as key targets for new products. Innovators are people who currently purchase 'smart homes', where, for example, household appliances communicate with control devices by phone or via the Internet.
- **Early adopters** – This group is also willing to adopt new ideas, but not at the same speed as the innovators. They are more likely to seek information before purchasing than the innovators.

- **Early majority** – Accounts for approximately one-third of customers. In general they are more conservative than the innovators and early adopters and more likely to be risk averse. For example, people who would consider making a purchase on the Internet.
- **Late majority** – Another third of customers, including people that are often cautious about new products. Mobile phones are probably appealing to this group currently.
- **Laggards** – This group tends to be very traditional and averse to change. They may be very price sensitive and wait for prices to reduce. In fact they may change only when their current product becomes obsolete. For example, people may be forced to buy a CD player when they can no longer buy vinyl records or a record player.

The rate at which new products are adopted can also vary considerably. A number of factors will influence the speed at which the products are adopted:

- **Newness** – The extent to which the new product challenges or supports existing behaviour. For example, mobile phones where adopted rapidly because they fitted in with existing behaviour, whereas television shopping challenges traditional shopping habits and the take-up has been slower.
- **Trialability** – how easy it is for customers to try the new product. For example, a person can easily visit a showroom and try out a CD player. In contrast the take up of ISAs (Individual Savings Accounts) has been slower because it is impossible to trial the product before purchase.
- **Relative cost** – For low-priced items such as confectionery the rate of take-up may be faster than for more expensive items such as consumer electronic products.
- **Additional costs** – To what extent does the customer incur costs when purchasing? For example, for contact lenses there include ['cleaning-fluid' costs and 'time and trouble costs' associated with maintenance of contact lenses versus spectacles.
- **Complexity** – How easy is it to communicate the product and its benefits? The new stakeholder pensions due to be launched in the UK this year are quite complex and the Government

---

Activity 4.2

Diffusion of innovation

Identify one new product/service that has been adopted rapidly by customers and one that has been very slowly adopted or not at all. Compare and contrast these two products and give reasons why one has been accepted rapidly whilst the other has not.

Portfolio analysis

Much of the time in marketing we consider the management of products or strategic business units as separate entities. However, in reality many companies have multiple products servicing multiple segments and markets. Some of these products will require much investment; others will generate income. Companies need to devise a means of allocating their limited resources among products or strategic business units so as to achieve the best performance for the company as a whole. Decisions have to be made regarding which products or brands should be invested in, which to hold and which to remove support from. The process of managing groups of brands/ products or strategic business units is called portfolio planning. In the same way that financial investors try to maintain a balanced portfolio of investments with different levels of risk marketing managers strive to achieve a balanced portfolio of products.

Portfolio analysis starts with historic data but can be used to project forwards to the future and possible future strategies. Portfolio analysis tools, like the PLC, are very flexible and can be applied to products, brands and strategic business units. The overall aim of a company should be to maintain a balanced portfolio and develop a sustainable competitive advantage.

There are a number of different portfolio planning tools. These are well documented in most marketing texts but we will focus on three of the most well known models – the Boston Consulting Group Growth-Share Matrix and two multi-factor models (the General Electric Market Attractiveness-Competitive Position model and the Shell Directional Policy Matrix). Other multi-factor models, such as the Arthur D Little Strategic Conditions Matrix and the Abell and Hammons 3×3 Investment Opportunity Chart differ slightly from the GE matrix but the underlying principles are similar and will therefore not be discussed separately in this unit.

Boston Consulting Group Growth Share Matrix (BCG)

What is the BCG?

The Boston Consulting Group, a leading management consultancy, developed a 2×2 matrix that allows the portfolio of products/SBU to be positioned on the matrix according to:

- market growth rate
- relative market share (i.e. relative to the leading competitor).

The underlying principle of the BCG is the generation and management of cash within a business. According to Drummond & Ensor (2001), p. 96 'Relative market share is seen as a predictor of the product's capacity to generate cash' and 'market growth is seen as a predictor of the product's need for cash'. This would suggest that products with high market share will achieve high sales, but will need relatively less investment than new brands and should have lower costs due to scale economies. Products in fast-growing markets require higher levels of investment than those in slower growing markets. Products in low-growth markets with a high market share will be generating cash, which can be used to help fund other products that require investment; cash flow is not the same as profitability.

Figure 4.4 outlines the BCG. Market growth rate indicates the growth rate of the market in which each product/SBU operates and is used as a proxy for market attractiveness. The scale on the axis will depend on the market and the general economic conditions. Relative market share refers to the market share of each product/SBU relative to the leading competitor. Market share acts as a proxy for competitive strength. The scale is a logarithmic one and the division between high and low market share is 1. For example, if our product had a market share of 50% and the next leading competitor had 25% this would be indicated as 2 on the horizontal axis. If our market share was 15% and the leading competitor is 30% our score would be 0.5. The products/SBUs are represented on the matrix by circles and fall into one of the four quadrants, as illustrated in the figure.

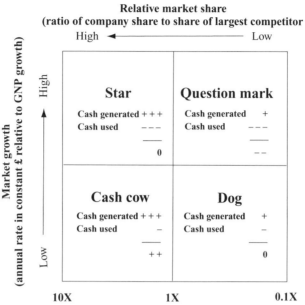

Figure 4.4
The Boston Consultancy Group's growth share matrix (BCG)

Table 4.2	
Stars • Build strategies by increasing sales or market share • Invest to maintain leadership status	**Question Marks** • Build selectively • Identify and focus on niche markets • Harvest and divest others
Cash Cows • Hold strategies to maintain sales or market share • Defend position • Use cash generated to sustain stars, invest in NPD and support a select number of question marks	**Dogs** • Harvest or • Divest or • Identify profitable niche markets and focus on these.

Once products have been plotted on the matrix it is possible to identify the potential strategies for each type (Table 4.2 outlines the options for each type of product.) It is also possible to identify the number of cash cows, stars, question marks and dogs present in the portfolio. If the portfolio is unbalanced action should be taken to improve it.

What are the limitations of the BCG?

The BCG is a very simple tool that can be highly effective in helping managers to understand their portfolio. However a number of criticisms have been directed at it. For instance, Jobber (1998) identifies a number of limitations of the model:

- Pre-occupation with focusing on market share and market growth rates. There may be other factors that are of equal importance, such as profitability.
- Too simplistic – treats market share as a proxy for competitive strength and marketing growth rate as proxy for market attractiveness.
- Unhealthy preoccupation with market share gain.
- Ignores interdependencies between products.
- Many low-growth markets are still attractive.
- Many successful low-share companies.
- How does one define market? Does Mercedes have a low share of the car market or a high share of the luxury car market?.
- Ignores external factors such as competitive activity.
- Lacks precision in identifying products to build/harvest or drop.
- Based on cash flow – perhaps profitability may be a more accurate criterion?

General Electric Market Attractiveness Competitive Position Model (GE)

What is the GE model?

The GE matrix was developed by McKinsey and Company in conjunction with General Electric in the USA, in response to some of the weaknesses of the BCG matrix. This model built on the success of the BCG but acknowledged that market growth rate alone was an insufficient measure of market attractiveness and market share in measuring competitive strength. A multi-factor matrix was developed that enabled managers to build in the measures that were relevant to their industry.

Market attractiveness criteria could include measures such as:

- Market factors (size, growth rates, segment size, price sensitivity).
- Competition (types and strength).
- PEST factors.
- Profit potential.

Competitive strength criteria could include measures such as:

- Market share (total market, segments).
- Bargaining power of suppliers and customers.
- Reputation.
- Patents.
- Relationships/strategic alliances.
- Distribution capabilities.
- Ability to develop a competitive advantage or cost advantages.

Once the criteria have been selected each factor should be given a weighting that recognizes their relative importance. Table 4.3 gives an example of the weighting (totals 10).

Table 4.3: Weighting the Criteria	
Market attractiveness	
Market growth rate	2
Market size	2.5
Strength of competition	1
Social factors	0.5
Profit opportunity	4
Total	**10**
Competitive strength	
Market share	2.5
Patents	1
Distribution capabilities	2
Relationships	2
Cost advantages	2.5
Total	**10**

Each market attractiveness factor and competitive strength is scored out of 10 (1 = very unattractive/weak and 10 = very attractive/strong) for each product/ SBU. Each score is multiplied by the weighting to produce an overall score for market attractiveness and competitive strength for each product/SBU. These can then be plotted on the GE matrix.

Once the products have been plotted on the matrix it is possible to identify potential strategies for each portion of the matrix. This is illustrated in Figure 4.5.

The GE matrix provides managers with greater flexibility than the BCG and enables them to select the criteria that are most relevant to their particular situation.

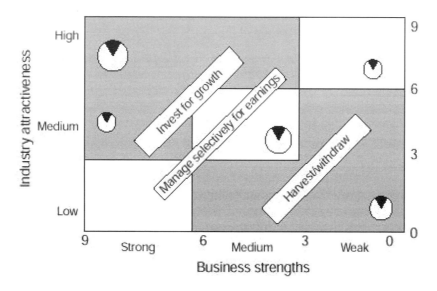

Figure 4.5
The General Electric Multi-factor Matrix

Limitations of the GE matrix

The GE matrix allows a much richer analysis than the BCG; however, it does receive some criticism. It can be a difficult model to use due to the amount of information required and the need for managers to agree the criteria and weighting. There is also an additional problem in that, due to the flexibility of the model, there is opportunity for bias to enter the analysis. It has been suggested that to avoid this the analysis should be conducted at a managerial level higher than the one being analysed.

Activity 4.3

The GE matrix

Using your own company or an organization of your choice select three products or strategic business units on which to base a GE matrix. Complete the table.

- Identify four relevant measures of market attractiveness and four measures of competitive strength.
- For each market attractiveness measure weight their importance out of 10. Repeat for competitive strength.
- For each product/ strategic business unit give a score out of 10 for each of the measures (1 meaning very weak and 10 being very strong).
- Calculate the rating for each factor by multiplying the score by the weighting and produce a total (out of 100) for each product/ strategic business unit.

Plot the products/SBUs on the GE matrix.

Table 4.4 Market Attractiveness	Product/ SBU 1			Product/ SBU 2			Product/ SBU 3		
	Weighting	Score	Rating	Weighting	Score	Rating	Weighting	Score	Rating
1									
2									
3									
4									
Total	10			10			10		

Table 4.5 Competitive Strength	Product/ SBU 1			Product/ SBU 2			Product/ SBU 3		
	Weighting	Score	Rating	Weighting	Score	Rating	Weighting	Score	Rating
1									
2									
3									
4									
Total	10			10			10		

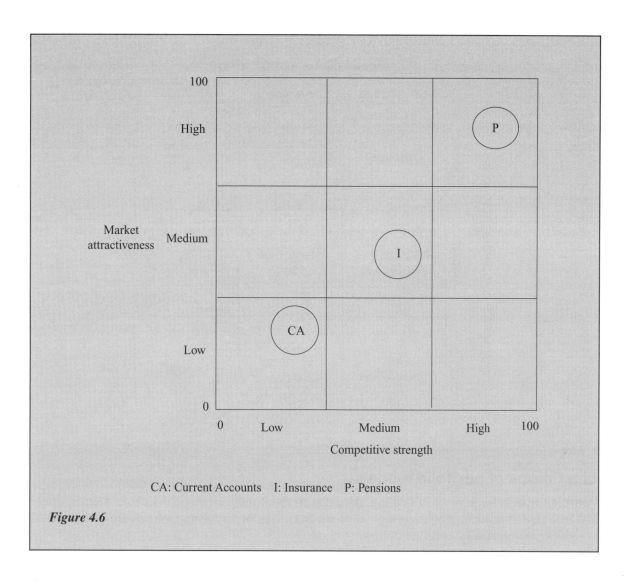

CA: Current Accounts   I: Insurance   P: Pensions

Figure 4.6

Shell Directional Policy Matrix

The Shell Directional Policy Matrix adopts an approach similar to that of the GE matrix, the main difference being the axes. The axes on the Shell Directional Policy matrix are Prospects for Sector Profitability and Enterprises' Competitive Capabilities (see Figure 4.7).

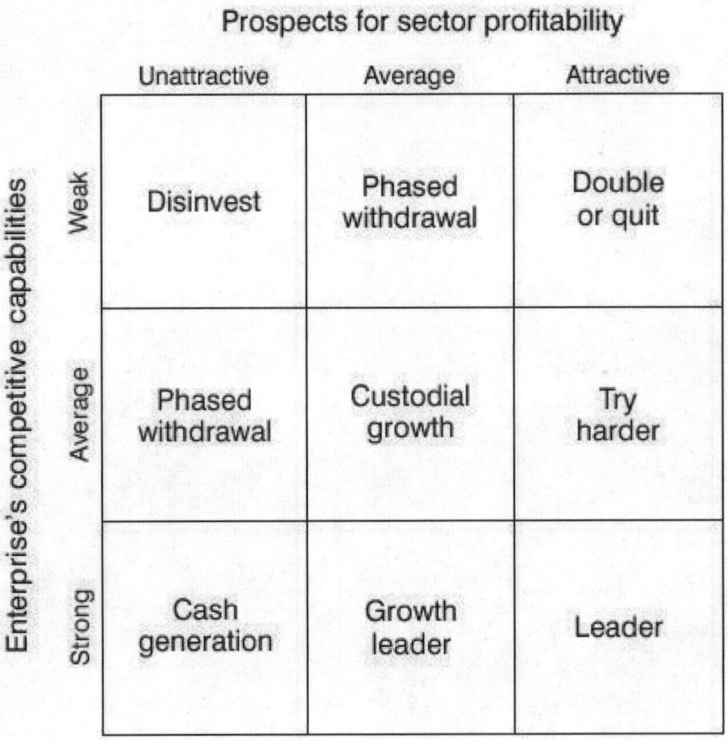

Prospects for sector profitability

	Unattractive	Average	Attractive
Weak	Disinvest	Phased withdrawal	Double or quit
Average	Phased withdrawal	Custodial growth	Try harder
Strong	Cash generation	Growth leader	Leader

(Enterprise's competitive capabilities)

Figure 4.7

Limitations of portfolio models

Portfolio models have value in helping managers to think more strategically about their business and resource allocation. However, they have not been free of criticism. Douglas Brownlie (1983) criticizes portfolio analysis for the following reasons:

- It is over-simplified.
- Often offers a misleading representation of strategy options.
- Makes use of inappropriate and overly generous measures.
- Rests on an assumption that market leadership invariably offers benefits.
- Ignores the real benefits of market inching.
- Ignores a series of important and strategic factors in the competitive environment.

Concluding thoughts

Despite the limitations of the portfolio models they have made a significant contribution to portfolio planning. Jobber (1998) identifies a number of ways in which portfolio analysis tools are of value to the strategic planner.

- **Different products and different roles** – The models highlight that all products should not be treated equally and may have different roles, such as cash generation or profitability.
- **Different reward systems and types of managers** – Because different products should have different profitability objectives it is fair to say that managers may require different skills and reward systems. For example, new products that are being built may require marketing-led managers, whereas managers of harvested products may have to be more cost-orientated.

Like any model portfolio planning provides guidelines for strategic thinking but the tools should not be seen as a replacement for management judgement.

Experience curves and importance of market share

The experience curve

Many marketing strategies are based on the premise that market leadership is a desirable goal. It is important that we understand the rationale behind this premise. The experience curve suggests that as a firm accumulates experience of carrying out an activity or function there is evidence of decreasing costs, the result of this being that unit costs reduce as a company becomes more experienced (see Figure 4.8). The implication of this is that the first company to enter a market and attain a large market share will have cost advantages over those entering the market later.

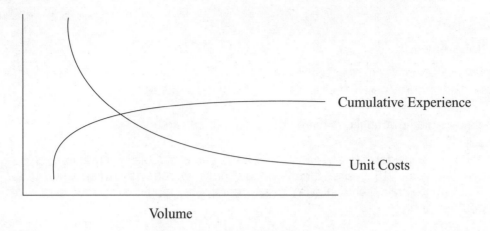

Figure 4.8
Experience curves

According to Aaker (1998) the experience curve may be based on:

- **Economies of scale** – Scale economies can be derived from more efficient methods of production at higher volumes.
- **Learning** – People learn to undertake tasks faster and more efficiently simply by repetition.
- **Technological improvements in production/operations** – The use of new machinery/IT systems, etc. to improve production or operations can reduce costs dramatically, particularly in capital-intensive industries.
- **Product redesign** – Simplification of products can sharply reduce costs.

Aaker (1998) also acknowledges that there are several considerations when using the experience curve:

- Multiple products can complicate the concept – there may be several experience curves to analyse.
- The experience curve does not apply in every situation.
- Technological developments may make the experience curve obsolete.
- Lowest costs do not have to equate to lowest prices.

It is essential that managers focus on the customer, not the process. Sometimes preoccupation with economies of scale and the experience curve can detract from the customer and changing needs. Companies can fall into the trap of focusing on how to improve current processes and ignore the fact that the process is becoming obsolete.

Extended knowledge

For further discussion of the experience curve read p.187 – 189 of Aaker (1998).

Importance of market share

Companies with higher market share gains have more experience than their competitors. This experience results in lower costs; lower costs mean that at a given market price the market leader in terms of market share will have the highest profits, and therefore will have more to spend on R&D, which in turn enables them to maintain their high market share. This partly explains why many companies strive to be market share leaders but there are other reasons as to why achieving market share as desirable:

- Economies of scale – explained above.
- Increased bargaining power – with suppliers, etc.
- Security – for various stakeholders.
- Status – there is often a sense of status associated with being number 1 in the market.
- Measure of managerial performance – market share gain is often used as such a measure.
- Supported by PIMS research (see below).

However, there are a number of factors companies must take into account when deciding to pursue a share-gaining strategy – such as competitive reactions, cost of gaining market share, how long the strategy can be maintained, level of maturity in the market, effect on other areas of the company's activity and level of customer loyalty.

Profit impact of marketing strategy (PIMS)

PIMS research found a strong relationship between market share and return on investment. This research set out to identify the key factors influencing profitability by examining the performance of approximately 3,000 strategic business units. The results of this study showed that market share was a key factor in profitability and in general terms there was a linear relationship between profits and relative market share, as shown in Figure 4.9. For example, the study found that organizations with a market share of 40% or more will achieve a return on investment of 30%, three times that of companies with a market share of under 10%. organizations have been encouraged by this research to pursue market share gains, as this should lead to an increase in profitability.

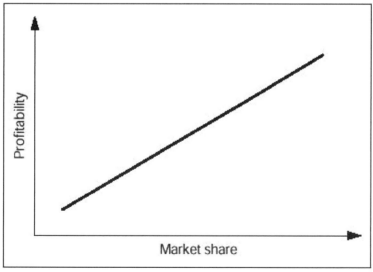

Figure 4.9
PIMS research – profit related to market share

Criticisms of PIMS

High market share will not automatically improve profitability and several criticisms have been directed at the PIMS research:

- Definition of the market – Porter (1980) wrote: 'there is no single relationship between profitability and market share, unless one conveniently defines the market.' and it has been suggested that research findings are more as a result of flexible definition than reality. For example, does easyJet have a large market share of the budget airline industry or small share of the total airline industry?

- Evidence of many successful low share businesses.
- Evidence of 'V-shaped ' curve rather than linear relationship between market share and profitability see Figure 4.10. For example, in the June 1999 Analysis and Decision case study of Biocatalysts (an industrial enzyme manufacturer), there was evidence that small niche players and large dominant competitors were profitable but it was those medium-sized companies that were 'stuck in the middle' which did not see a good return on investment.

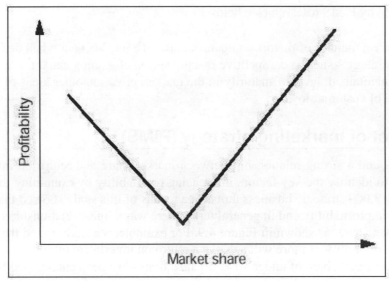

Figure 4.10
V-Shaped profit/market share relationship

Extended knowledge

For further discussion of the PIMS research see Wilson & Gilligan (1997) p.104 – 107 and 342 – 347.

Concluding thoughts

The PIMS research provides useful insights into the factors contributing to profitability. However, it must be used (as should all models) with some caution. A high market share does not always equate to high profits; these will also depend on a number of other factors such as the level of maturity of the market, level of customer loyalty, likely competitive reactions, PEST factors and the effect on other areas of the organization's activities. For example, market share gain may be at the expense of damaging a premium image.

Question 4.4

PIMS

Answer the following question taken from the June 1999 paper. Compare your answer with the CIM specimen answers.

Gap analysis

Gap analysis is a fairly simple diagrammatical method of presenting 'where are we now?' and 'where do we want to be?' as illustrated in Figure 4.11.

The strategic analysis will identify the current situation and then forecasts can be made of how the company will perform in the future. It is then possible to identify the gap between the two and develop strategies to try to close this gap. Units 'Creating strategic advantage' and 'developing a specific competitive position' will discuss the ways in which companies can achieve their objectives and close this gap.

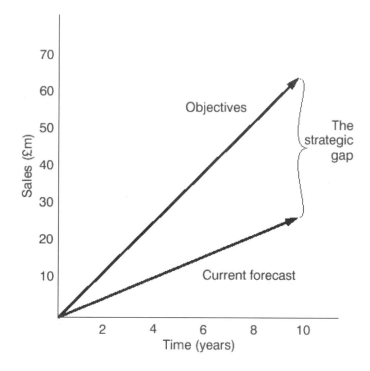

Figure 4.11
Gap analysis

Marketing audit

The marketing audit is a comprehensive framework for undertaking an analysis of the current situation.

Definition

Marketing audit

'An audit is a systematic, critical and unbiased review and appraisal of the environment and of the company's operations. A marketing audit is part of the larger management audit and is concerned with the marketing environment and marketing operations.' McDonald (1999)

The marketing audit helps to identify:

- The organization's environment and the nature of the environmental threats and opportunities.
- Its marketing systems (strengths and weaknesses).
- Its marketing activities.

According to Kotler (1997) there are six elements to a marketing audit:

1. The marketing environment – both the macro and microenvironments.
2. The marketing strategy – appropriateness and success.
3. The marketing organization – structure and staffing.
4. The marketing systems – such as the planning process and the MKIS.
5. Marketing productivity – cost effectiveness and profitability.
6. The marketing functions – detailed evaluation of the marketing mix.

A key aspect of the marketing audit is that it should be independent. This is often difficult to achieve if it is conducted by internal staff with a vested interest in the results. Therefore, many companies elect to periodically employ external agencies such as marketing consultants to undertake the audit to ensure that the analysis is independent.

Extended knowledge

For a detailed discussion of the marketing audit please refer to either Wilson & Gilligan (1997), Chapter 2, or Kotler (1997) pp. 777 – 781.

SWOT Analysis

SWOT (strengths, weaknesses, opportunities and threats) is a well known tool often used during the auditing process. This framework is a useful way of summarizing all the information gathered from the auditing process and should be used to identify the critical factors. Often too many SWOTs contain extensive lists of factors rather than focusing on the key aspects. It can be helpful to produce a weighted SWOT that identifies the critical factors and relates the internal strengths and weaknesses to the external threats and opportunities. The main purpose of the SWOT is to focus attention on the critical issues when developing strategies.

Extended knowledge

Refer to Wilson & Gilligan (1997) Chapter 2 for a comprehensive discussion of SWOT analysis.

Summary

- There are a number of models/tools that can be used for auditing the current situation and for developing future strategy – value chain, PLC, diffusion of innovation model, experience curves, PIMS, portfolio analysis and gap analysis.
- The value chain is a tool that helps marketers identify ways of creating more customer value and analysing company capabilities. The model identifies nine interrelated value-creating activities, divided into primary and secondary activities.
- The PLC is often described as the most familiar but least understood marketing tool. The model suggests that products and services have a finite life and will move through a series of different stages. Each stage will require different strategies in order to try to extend the product's life and generate maximum profit. The model is criticized for being over-simplistic.
- The rate at which consumers adopt products will vary depending on a number of factors such as level of newness, complexity of the product and trialability. The diffusion of innovation model helps to identify the various groups of customers in relation to the speed at which they will adopt a new product.
- Most companies do not just offer one product or service: many have multiple products serving multiple segments and they are faced with decisions relating to how to manage their portfolio (i.e. which products/SBUs to invest in and which to divest). Portfolio analysis tools can help marketers to manage their portfolios by categorizing their products/SBUs.
- The Boston Consulting Group (BCG) matrix is a simplistic model that categories products/SBUs according to market growth rate and relative market share. It is a useful starting point for many marketers but it has been criticized for being over-simplistic and for misleading managers because of its reliance on only two factors.
- To overcome some of the limitations of the BCG model multi-factor portfolio analysis techniques were developed such as the General Electric model, Shell Directional Policy matrix and the Arthur D. Little matrix. These models use a whole range of factors in addition to market growth rate and relative market share. They have also been criticized for being highly subjective.
- Many companies often regard market leadership as a desirable goal and market leadership is based on the experience curve. The experience curve suggests that as a firm accumulates experience of carrying out an activity its costs fall.
- The Profit Impact of Marketing Strategy (PIMS) research identified a strong relationship between market share and return on investment. This research has encouraged firms to pursue market share objectives.
- Gap analysis is a diagrammatical method of presenting 'where we are now and where do we want to be in the future?'
- The marketing audit is a framework for undertaking an analysis of the current situation, both internal and external. SWOT analysis is a tool for drawing together the information from the audit that highlights key strengths, weaknesses, opportunities and threats.

Further study

Extending knowledge

Bibliography

Aaker D (1998), *Strategic Market Management*, 5th Ed, John Wiley & Sons.

Brownlie DT (1983), *Analytical frameworks for strategic market planning* cited in Baker MJ (ed) (1983), *Marketing Theory and Practice*, Macmillan.

Drummond G & Ensor J (1999), *Strategic Marketing Planning and Control*, Butterworth-Heinemann.

Ewington (2000), *Financial Times*, 21 November, p.15.

Hooley G, Saunders J & Piercy N, (1998) *Marketing Strategy and Competitive Positioning*, Prentice Hall.

Jobber D (1998), *Principles and Practice of Marketing*, 2nd Ed, McGraw Hill.

Kotler P (1997), *Marketing Management Analysis, Planning, Implementation and Control*, 9th Ed, Prentice-Hall.

McDonald M (1999), *Marketing Plans How To Prepare Them, How to Use Them*, 4th Ed, Butterworth-Heinemann.

Porter M (1980), *Competitive Strategy: Techniques for analysing Industries and Competitors*, Free Press.

Porter (1985), *Competitive Advantage: Creating and Sustaining Superior Performance*, Free Press.

Rogers EM (1983), *Diffusion of Innovations*, Free Press.

Rink DR & Swan JE (1979), *Product life cycle Research: A Literature Review*, Journal of Business Research, 78 (Sept), pp.219-42.

Swan JE & Rink DR (1982), *Variations on the Product life cycle*, Business Horizons, 25: 1 January – February, pp.72-6.

Wilson RMS & Gilligan CT (1997) *Strategic Marketing Management: Planning, Implementation and Control,* Butterworth-Heinemann.

Unit 5
Financial analysis and techniques
for developing a view of the future

Objectives

By the end of this unit you will:

- Be able to discuss a variety or techniques for forecasting the future, including:
    - o Trend extrapolation
    - o Modelling
    - o Individual forecasting
    - o Intuitive forecasting
    - o Consensus forecasting
    - o Scenario planning
    - o War gaming
    - o Synthesis reports
- Understand the strategic use of information
- Understand and be able to discuss market sensing and its role in marketing planning.
- Be familiar with a variety of tools for financial analysis, including:
    - o Balance sheets
    - o Profit and loss accounts
    - o Ratio analysis
    - o Productivity analysis
    - o Segmental analysis
- Be able to demonstrate an understanding of the financial implications of marketing planning

Study guide

- This unit will take you about 3 hours to work through
- We suggest that you take a further 4 hours to do the various activities and questions in this unit.

Introduction

The last unit provided an overview of the various tools that can be used in the auditing process and to help develop future strategies. The first part of this unit will continue this discussion with reference to the role of financial analysis. Understanding the current situation is a vital part of developing a marketing strategy. However, in order to develop a strategy that is looking towards the future, it is essential that organizations utilize techniques for developing a view of the future. This unit will outline the various tools available to do so. The future is uncertain; however, it is essential that companies develop techniques to identify new trends, in the hope that they can capitalize on any opportunities.

Financial auditing tools

These tools can support answers to major marketing planning questions:

1. 'Where are we now?', as the financial component of a marketing audit.
2. 'Where do we want to be?', when used in the context of objective setting, from which planners must generate appropriate strategies.
3. 'How do we know we have arrived?', used in the context of marketing control.

It is assumed that students have an understanding of profit and loss accounts, balance sheets and ratio analysis. You can revise these topics by reading the appropriate sections in the Advanced Certificate module 'Management Information for Marketing Decisions'. This unit will provide a brief overview of financial analysis and highlight the key issues in relation to the Planning and Control syllabus.

Profit and loss accounts

The profit and loss account measures the operational performance of a company over a period of time. It does this by summarizing revenues and costs over a period of time, which allows profits, or losses, to be determined. The Advanced Certificate module MIMD would have introduced you to profit and loss accounts. Activity 5.1 will also check your understanding of this concept.

Balance sheets

A balance sheet provides a snapshot of the financial position of an organization in terms of its assets, liabilities and capital at a particular moment in time. This is in contrast to a profit and loss account, which measures profits over a period, usually an accounting year. You should be familiar with the format and contents of a balance sheet from studying the CIM Advanced Certificate module MIMD. To check your understanding undertake activity 5.1.

Ratio analysis

In corporate and strategic planning the focus tends to be on topline financial values. These are derived from the profit and loss account and from the balance sheet. The main categories of ratios, with some examples of each, are summarized in Table 5.1

Table 5.1: Classification of topline financial variables more commonly used in strategic planning

Type of ratio	Example topline ratios
Fundamental strength of the business	1. Profitability ratios • Gross profit margin = (GP / Sales) ×100 • Net profit margin = (NP / Sales) ×100 2. Capital structure ratios, also termed 'gearing' ratios • debt ratio = total debt/total assets where: total debt = current liabilities + long-term liabilities Total assets = Fixed assets + current assets
Operational efficiency of the business	3. Liquidity • current ratio = current assets/current liabilities • liquid ratio = (current assets − stock) / current liabilities 4. Asset utilization • stock turnover ratio = cost of goods sold/stock at cost on balance sheet • debtor turnover = sales turnover/debtors • credit turnover ratios = cost of goods sold/trade creditors from the balance sheet
Investment performance ratios	5. Investment performance ratios • Price to earnings ratio (i.e. P/E ratio) = Market price per share[1] / earnings per share[2]

[1] From stock market

[2] Declared annually or twice per year by the company

Marketing planners consider ratios in monitoring their own organization, and in contrasting its financial strength with that of other organizations. Profitability ratios are most commonly used for this purpose. They also provide an insight into how efficiently and effectively an organization is managed and indicate the amount of resources a competitor may be accumulating for future competitive action. Investment performance ratios are used by financial stakeholders, especially potential financial stakeholders. In some organizations, the influence of these key stakeholders can even be translated into share price and P/E ratio targets for chief executive officers. Low and/or falling share prices are a clear sign of competitive weakness: they are a sign of poor past performance, a consensus market view (which includes many informed and important stakeholders and analysts) which anticipates weak future performance and, even more crucially, makes the organization vulnerable to takeover. While one organization may not wish to buy a particularly weak business with a low share price, a competitor may gain strategic advantage from an acquisition. Investment performance ratios may be viewed as summarizing the conclusions that may be drawn from profitability, capital structure, liquidity and asset utilization ratios.

Table 5.2: Profit and loss 'Pantronics Limited'				
	£	£		
Sales		1,160,000	A	
Opening stock (1 January 20xx)	90,000			
Purchases	762,000			
B	852,000			
Less closing stock (31 December 20xx) C	100,000			
Cost of sales		752,000	D	D = B – C
Gross profit		408,000	E	E = A – D
Less overheads:				
Directors' remuneration	90,000			
Debenture interest	7,200			
Other overheads	270,000			
		367,200	F	F = Sum of overheads
Net profit for year before taxation		40,800	G	G = E – F
Less corporation tax		14,280		
Profit for year after taxation		26,520	H	
Less interim dividends paid:				
ordinary shares	12,000			
preference shares	2,000			
final dividends paid				
ordinary shares	22,000			
preference shares	2,000			
		38,000	I	I = sum of all dividends
Retained profit for year		-11,480	J	J = H – I
Add balance of retained profits at beginning of year		82,000	K	Profits retained *
Balance of retained profits at end of year		70,520	L	L = J + K

* i.e. from last year

Table 5.3: Balance Sheet – Pantronics Limited		DEP'N			
	COST	TO DATE	NET		
	£	£			
Fixed assets					
Intangible					
Goodwill	90000	36000	54,000		
Tangible					
Freehold land and buildings	324000	36000	288,000		
Machinery	414000	162000	252,000		
Fixtures and fittings	180000	45000	135,000		
	1008000	279000	729,000	A	Total fixed assets
Current assets					
Stock		85,000			
Debtors		64,600			
Bank		37,400			
Cash		3,400			
		190,400		B	Total current assets
Less current liabilities					
Creditors	51,000				
Proposed dividends	20,400				
Corporation tax	25,500				
		96,900		C	Total current liabilities
Working capital			93,500	D	D = B – C
			822,500	E	E = A + D
Less long-term liabilities					
10% Debentures			60,000	F	G = total assets less total liabilities
Net assets			762,500	G	G = (A + B) – (C+F)
Financed by					
Issue share capital					
40,000 10% preference shares of £1 each, fully paid			40,000		
630,000 ordinary shares of £1 each, fully paid			630,000		
			670,000	H	
Capital reserve					
Share premium account			21,980	I	
Revenue reserve					
Profit and loss account			70,520	J	
Shareholder funds			762,500	K	K = H + I+ J

Also assume: Market share price = 165p

Productivity analysis

Productivity analysis considers the relationship between inputs and outputs and is sometimes referred to as input-output analysis. Table 5.4 provides the general formula for this, along with two examples to illustrate the principle.

Table 5.4: Productivity analysis		
General formula	Marketing outputs/ Marketing inputs	The general principle is that any output may be expressed as a ratio of any input. The particular variable selected depends on the reason for calculating the productivity ratio.
Example 1	Change in sales turnover/ Change in communications expenditure	The assumption behind this ratio is that a communications campaign has been undertaken and that this is the sole, or main reason behind an increase in sales turnover. Additional information must be gathered at the time of collecting ratio data, in order to confirm that another factor has not been the cause of the change. For example, poor distribution by a competitor, or a competitor withdrawing from the market.
Example 2	Increase in consumer awareness/Change in advertising expenditure	This provides a useful measure by which to judge, at least in part, the performance of the company. This example is to illustrate that the ratio need not always be purely of financial measures. It may be of a physical and financial measure (see real indices), (below).

Real indices

One note of caution in using productivity ratios must be taken when using a mixture of a financial measure and a physical measure to calculate a single ratio, for example sales turnover (£)/number of salespeople. The danger arises from inflation of financial values such that any increase in the ratio could arise purely from a general rise in prices (i.e. inflation) rather than be caused by the influence of marketing activity. The solution to this problem is to remove the influence of inflation from any data expressed in monetary terms (in principle by dividing by an appropriate inflation index). The ratio that results is termed a 'real index' or measure.

Comparative analysis

In applying productivity ratios, organizations may monitor how the indices have changed over time, by comparing:

1. How individual ratios for the organization (i.e. internal ratios) have changed over time.
2. Ratios for competitor organizations to assess how their productivity, as well as relative productivity, has changed. Assessments based on these types of ratios must in particular consider how data is compiled to ensure that correct inferences are made from using comparative data.

Segmental analysis

Segmental analysis forces the marketer to consider the market that is the focus of analysis. This, to some people, seems an excessively simple task, but is often ill considered. It is at the core of much marketing analysis. Hours of marketing planning can be wasted if the market has not been defined correctly. Segmental analysis may consider three main areas: product areas, geographical areas and consumer segments.

For example, consider the market for pasta.

Product areas

1. Do you include fresh, tinned, atmosphere packaged and dry pasta?
2. Should pasta products be included which include some other processed product (e.g. cannelloni or tortellini?)
3. Should pasta be included in ready meals with a pasta component?

Geographical areas

1. If the European pasta market is being considered, is this defined as some or all member countries of the European Union? Should countries that are about to join the Union be considered? Should Switzerland and Norway be included, even though they are not members of the EU?

Consumer segments

1. There are many possible approaches to considering the segmentation of this market, for example, income, lifestyle, household composition and measures that combine all or some of these segmentation criteria.

Defining the market, which is the foundation for much marketing analysis, is not always a simple process. Marketing strategists must be informed in this decision by a clear view of the markets they are in, which they wish to enter and who is defined as a 'competitor'.

Segments and organizational size

The analysis may generate very different results as the subject for analysis changes. The analysts may need to change the subject of analysis in order to understand its effect. Which definition is considered will depend on the marketing decision the analysis supports. For example, where a SME from Australia wishes to launch on the UK market, most of the analysis will be on the UK market. However, a multinational enterprise will be interested in as wide a definition of 'the market' as possible, probably starting with the EU, but undertaking particularly detailed studies in markets considered to be significant currently or with the potential to grow.

Combining the segments

Which products and sub-products to include, will depend on the view taken on the elasticity of demand and on the relative substitutability of different products. Analysts will start by considering the most substitutable products as most relevant for inclusion in their analysis. Time and resources available as well as, for example, marketing research information on consumer perception of substitutes, will determine how wide the analytical net is spread. From a product market perspective low-cost tinned pasta, shaped into circles, in tomato sauce purchased for ease of eating by children (i.e. family life cycle stage with dependent children) will have few highly substitutable competitors. Obviously from a consumer segment perspective pasta rings is only one solution to the 'quick, simple childrens' meal, for which there are many substitutes.

In contrast, from a product market perspective, high-income singles or 'empty nesters' with active lifestyles are likely to include 'quality and speed of preparation with minimal effort' as important product attributes. As long as a solution is presented to this problem, then quite a wide range of pasta offerings (in combination with other meal elements presented in the food outlet) is likely to be acceptable. From a consumer segment perspective, a multitude of non-pasta potential competitors exists.

Techniques for developing a future orientation

Organizations operate in dynamic environments. In order to develop marketing plans that reflect these changes it is necessary to utilize techniques that can help forecast the future. Organizations that can effectively forecast future trends and developments will be well positioned to capitalize on the opportunities arising out of these changes. A variety of techniques can be used to develop a vision of the future

A crucial initial decision, before selecting a particular analytical tool, is the perspective that will be taken of 'the market'. This perspective will be influenced by the size of firm conducting the analysis. These issues were discussed in segmental analysis, and Table 5.5 summarizes the three main perspectives.

Table 5.5: Main elements forecast		
	Electronics industry example	Airline industry example
Industry	Mobile telecommunications	Inter continental air traffic
Market sector	Consumer mobile phones	Transatlantic (Europe – USA) business travel
Product	Text messaging mobile phones	Supersonic business travel

A variety of techniques are available to support analysis. Which technique is most appropriate will depend on the data that is available, the complexity and type of problem and the timescales involved.

Students naturally like to know which models to use in particular contexts. It is difficult to provide a simple guide as many models may be used in a variety of contexts. In addition, some of the syllabus 'techniques' are approaches rather than detailed, specific methods (e.g. 'individual forecasts', 'intuitive forecasts', 'scenario planning'). Perhaps the most simple classification approach is to consider techniques in relation to (a) forecasting horizon and (b) breadth of forecast. In the three-level 'breadth' classification of Table 5.3, 'product' is narrowest and 'industry' broadest. 'Trend' extrapolation, a type of statistical technique, is best suited to narrow, short time horizons as the technique can take account of only a limited amount of 'narrowly defined' information. 'Individual forecasts', 'intuitive forecasts' and modelling may be used for all types of forecasting, from individual product sales forecasts for the next three month period to the outlook for the industry over the next 20 years. Techniques best suited to broad, long-range forecasts include consensus forecasting and scenario planning. The time-consuming nature of such forecasts, and their resource requirements, mean that they are mainly suited to decisions where the cost implication of success, and of failure, is relatively great. They are helpful where data is difficult to obtain, where numerical information is insufficient, or where long-run datasets do not allow the use of statistically based techniques.

Trend extrapolation

This technique uses information on the past to predict the future. The assumption is that the relationships between variables that held in the past will continue to hold in the future. If sales revenue growth averaged 3% in each of the last four years, trend extrapolation will predict that this will be the case in the future. In practice data, is more variable than this and extrapolation is likely to be based on a statistical 'best fit' line. The principle is, however, the same.

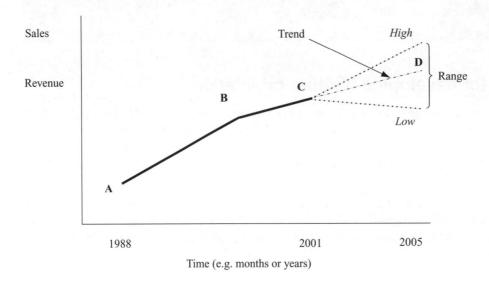

Figure 5.1
Trend forecast

Trend forecasting is conceptually quite simple but more difficult in practice. Even when a decision has been made to use the past as the basis for predicting the future, two main questions arise:

1. How far into the past should you go to calculate the trend?
2. How should you summarize the past in a way that can then be extrapolated into the future? See the Advanced Certificate module MIMD, where, for example data smoothing is discussed.

In Figure 5.1 the trend line C-D has been based on sales revenue data for the period B-C (i.e. the recent part is considered the most relevant basis on which to predict the future). If it were considered that the period B-C is somehow unusual then the whole period A-C would be used to develop a trend prediction. The decision must be taken based on specialist market knowledge.

When considering trends, forecasters must be clear about the underlying market forces that are influencing demand for individual products and services. These can be separated, or decomposed, into separate elements:

- **Seasonal variation** during any single year. Many industries are influenced by this: frozen foods in the summer, consumer goods at Christmas, chocolate sales increase at gift-giving festivals (especially Christmas and Easter), etc. This has a knock-on effect in the associated business-to-business markets.
- **Cyclical variation** due to changes in economic activity associated with business cycles. These can extend over periods from a few to over 15 years.
- **Random variation** due to unpredictable events. Demand fell rapidly in the UK tourist sector in 2001 due to adverse publicity following the foot and mouth outbreak and the negative imagery presented to potential customers throughout the world. Perrier suffered a large deduction in demand due to temporary benzene contamination of their product in the early 1990s. Individual companies have suffered from random reductions in demand for their products and services as special-interest groups have targeted their environmental or employment policies – e.g. oil companies and the environment and footwear and clothing retailers sourcing from suppliers who use 'child labour'. Figure 5.2 illustrates these variations graphically.

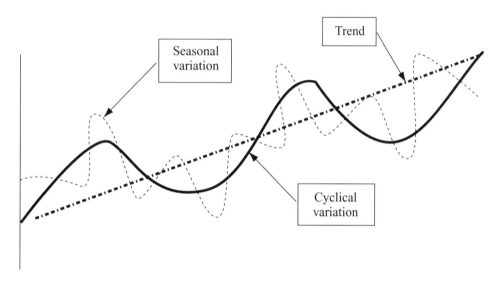

Figure 5.2
Decomposition of data

Modelling

Models are simplifications of the 'real world'. Much marketing theory may be described as models. For example, that successful marketing implementation will be achieved if each of the 7 'Ps' is managed effectively. However, the context in which 'models' are discussed here focuses on their application to forecasting. There are various approaches to classifying models. Here we consider models in terms of whether or not they describe the 'black box'. Figure 5.3 illustrates the 'black box' model.

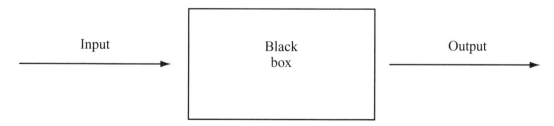

Figure 5.3
A conceptual representation of the 'black box' model

The general approach to modelling is that, after analysis, it will be possible to predict outputs if a given level of inputs are known. Black box, or input-output, models attempt to establish a relationship between inputs and outputs (assuming all other factors remain constant). For example:

- £20,000 advertising expenditure will result in an increase in sales of £50,000.
- A 20% price reduction over four weeks will result in 10% increase in sales revenue over the following year.

Such models do not try to explain what takes place within the black box. Simple regression models exemplify black box modelling. In contrast, simulation-type models attempt to explain what takes place within the box. Examples are models of consumer behaviour which attempt to explain each stage, in detail, of the decision-making process.

One application of simulation modelling has been implemented by food retailers. For example, a supermarket layout may be represented in a computer model, with customers arriving and leaving the store and moving around the store represented by queues or by individual dots (pixels on a computer screen). The management team wishes to know how to optimize:

- store layout (and their ability to influence customer flow around the store and to encourage unplanned purchasing behaviour)
- product shelf space allocation
- allocation of staff between shelf stacking and checkout duties
- location for merchandising activity.

In working with this model, assumptions may be made about the numbers of customers arriving at the store each hour, time spent in the store, checkout processing time, purchases made in each type of shelf location (e.g. bottom, middle, top), etc. and these can be experimented with in a store simulation model. Such modelling techniques enable managers to experiment with the influence of different parameters on the system and to understand the system more clearly.

Case history

An example of a retail store simulation

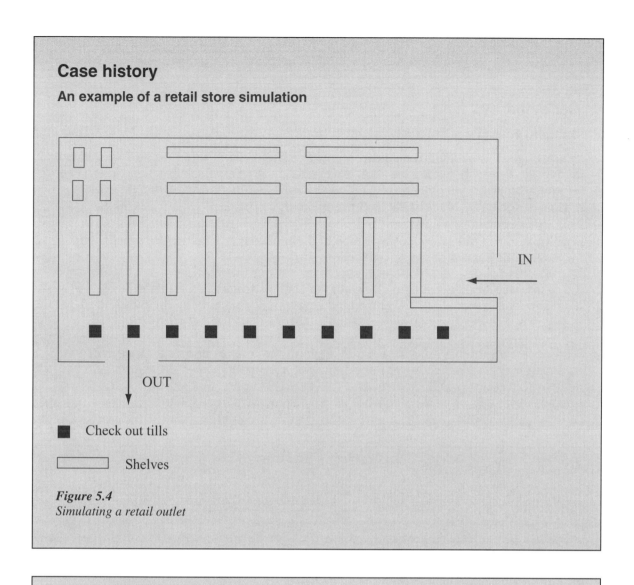

Check out tills

Shelves

Figure 5.4
Simulating a retail outlet

Assumptions:

1. 120 shoppers arrive each hour.
2. Each shopper spends on average £60.
3. The average time in store is 15 minutes.
4. Time to process a shopper at the checkout averages five minutes.

In this simulation, the shopper moves around the store and arrives at the checkout. Queues develop at the checkouts and the supermarket manager must decide on the relative balance between shelfstacking staff and checkout staff; too many shelf stackers and customer satisfaction declines rapidly at the checkout and the potential to lose repeat business rises; too many people on the checkout and the shelves start to run out of products. There are many other issues; for example, how to get the customer to stay in the store longer, to browse the shelves (i.e. move away from the narrow confines of the shopping list) and so spend more money. The simulation can be expanded to include the impact of changing store layout, inclusion of more merchandising activity and altering the marketing mix and outside the store. In addition to affecting movement around the store, the spread of arrival times over the day and the numbers arriving are likely also to be affected. By changing one single assumption of the simulation, the impact on queue development (an associated revenue flow) can be examined and assessed.

Individual forecasting

This is where an organization regards an individual's view of the future as especially significant. The organization does not want this particular individual's view to be diluted by coming to a consensus with other less expert individuals. Individual experts may be used for a wide range of forecasts, from the demand for individual products and services, to future scenarios of industry sectors or of economies. Arthur C. Clarke, for example, has been used by many organizations, including the National American Space Administration (NASA) to provide a view of the future of space technology and travel. Such future views allow planners to create more realistic business and marketing plans, in the case of NASA for lobbying government for funds. There is a line of debate which suggests that accounting for future views actually causes the future to happen. This is especially probable where experts are exceptional and have a track record of being right. For example, if significant experts, acting for each major automobile manufacturer, believe a breakthrough in fuel cell technology is imminent, then each company will fund this not to be left behind. This therefore increases the probability of the breakthrough happening.

It is difficult to deconstruct the processes that occur when experts provide a forecast. Often no specific technique is used: the forecast is based on a life's accretion of knowledge and experience. Such forecasts have been termed **intuitive**, but that has in the past stood for 'predictions' that have been little more than guesses. Expert 'intuition' is increasingly being modelled by computer scientists using complex models and principles such as neural networks, which try to replicate the functioning of a human brain. This is still some way off from practical marketing planning application.

Consensus forecasting

Rather than relying on the expertise of a particular individual, it is more common to use groups of people, especially where the forecast has a substantial influence on the success of the business. There are two approaches to group forecasting:

1. Where group members interact in person with each other (for example, jury forecasts).
2. Where group members are in separate locations and interaction is purely through reporting group findings, usually in the form of written summary results (for example, Delphi forecasts).

The aim of consensus (group) forecasting is to develop a forecast by reaching some form of consensus agreement. The general principle of Jury forecasting was introduced to the Advanced Certificate in the module Marketing Information for Management Decisions, and particular reference is made in that module to Delphi forecasting.

Jury forecasting

Jury forecasting involves bringing together a group of individuals, either internal staff or external experts, to discuss their views on the future and to ultimately come to a consensus decision. The accuracy of the forecast will depend to a large extent on the quality of the individuals within the group. There can be problems with jury forecasting, mainly due to the group dynamics. For example, long-established managers may dominate the group and junior members with valid suggestions may feel intimidated. There is also a tendency for 'groupthink' where the views of dissenting individuals are ignored. According to Drummond and Ensor (2001) there are four key factors that affect the level of 'groupthink':

- High cohesiveness.
- Strong leadership.
- Lack of objective search and evaluation.
- Insulation of group.

Groupthink can result in a number of problems for jury forecasting according to Drummond and Ensor (2001):

- Illusions of invulnerability.
- Collective rationalization.
- Belief in the inherent morality of the group.
- Pressure on dissenters.
- The illusion of unanimity.
- Self-appointed mind guards.

Jury forecasting can be a valuable forecasting technique as long as companies recognize the problems associated with groupthink.

Extended knowledge

For further amplification of groupthink refer to:

Drummond and Ensor, (2001), Strategic Marketing Planning and Control, Butterworth-Heinemann. Chapter 6, pp. 109-11.

Delphi forecasting

Delphi forecasting can help to overcome some of the problems associated with jury forecasting. Instead of the group meeting together the views of experts are sought independently. In most cases the 'experts' will remain anonymous and will have no communication with each other. The whole process is co-ordinated by somebody not involved in the forecast. The Delphi method has several stages:

1. Forecasts are invited from a variety of experts.
2. The co-ordinator reviews these forecasts and may remove any spurious forecasts.
3. The experts are then sent the various forecasts and asked to comment or amend their own forecast in light of the other forecasts.
4. The co-ordinator reviews these forecasts and the process continues until a consensus opinion is arrived at.

This method overcomes some of the problems of groupthink. However, it does have its own problems. For example, it is a very time-consuming process and the time delays may result in the participants becoming demotivated. *The FT Mastering Marketing* (1998) series included an interesting article on forecasting. This article suggested that the following principles should be followed when using Delphi forecasting techniques:

- Structure the forecasting problem so that it makes good use of the experts' knowledge (this may call for breaking the problem into a series of smaller problems).
- Write out the problem and check that it is comprehensible.
- Prepare alternative written statements of the problem.
- Use at least five experts but no more than 20.
- Ensure that experts do not receive incentives that could compromise objectivity.
- Ask each expert to make an independent forecast.
- Choose experts who differ from one another.
- Choose experts with some expertise in the problem area (although high expertise is not necessary).
- Allow the experts to revise their forecasts in light of information from other experts.

Source: *Financial Times Mastering Marketing Series* (1998).

Scenario planning

Scenario planning is planning for different futures. An implicit assumption of this technique is that the forecaster understands how the present has been determined, i.e. the external environmental factors which contribute to the present, and the external environmental factors that will be important in the future. Forecasters will construct different scenarios based on assumptions about changes in one of two variables, or influential factors:

1. Assumptions about how a key variable will change.
2. Assumptions about likely combinations of a range of relatively important variables.

For example, critical in any scenario of the future of the airline industry are assumptions behind (1) the growth in demand for air travel, the particular routes that will grow fastest (short, medium and long haul), (2) the size (i.e. carrying capacity) and (3) speed of next-generation passenger aircraft. Scenario planning for a 20-year time horizon for the airline industry is likely to be based on several assumptions for each of these three key variables. According to Drummond & Ensor (2001) there are four main stages in the development of simple scenarios:

1. **Identify critical variables** – This involves establishing the factors that will act as drivers of change in the future. Once identified they should then be evaluated in terms of their importance to the organization and the extent to which they can be predicted.
2. **Develop possible string of events** – Using the important drivers of change it is then possible to develop a number of different scenarios
3. **Refine the scenarios** – Once a whole range of scenarios has been developed it is then necessary to evaluate the alternatives.
4. **Identify the issues arising** – The robust strategies produced from this process should then be reviewed, the objective being to assess whether any critical issues have been identified that may impact on the business.

Scenario planning is concerned with encouraging managers to think 'outside the box' and to identify possible future events that may have major implications for the organization. Drummond & Ensor (2001) p.72 suggest three benefits of using scenario planning:

- It helps managers to understand the critical issues that lie at the heart of the organization.
- It encourages managers to consider the future and the possibility of discontinuities in the external environment.
- It places strategic issues on the management agenda.

Extended knowledge

For a detailed discussion of scenario planning refer to:

Mercer D (1998) *Marketing Strategy: The Challenge of the External Environment*, The Open University, Sage Publications. Chapters 6 – 8.

Question 5.1

Scenario planning

Answer question 7 on scenario planning from the June 2000 Planning and Control exam and compare your answer with the outline provided in the appendix at the back of the book.

War gaming

This is a term that is taken from military planning, where actions and counter-actions of opponents are simulated, using either physical models in large dioramas or, more commonly, using computer models. In marketing, war gaming may be enacted by individuals or teams, with the strategies and tactics of opponents represented. Where this is undertaken, simulation tends to be favoured as a technique. The advantage of this approach is that it allows multiple options to be investigated. Planners may then allocate probabilities to the occurrence of each simulated option, in order to generate most probable/least probable scenarios. Benefits accrue simply from the process of simulated planning and when this is undertaken by teams, the process additionally encourages team building. The strength of the conclusions resulting from the simulation is dependent on the accuracy of the data on which the simulation is based, and on the algorithms used to resolve strategy and tactics decisions.

Synthesis reports

This approach has its origins in clippings libraries where all newspaper articles on a given topic, for example fast food or a particular company, would be filed into a selected, common 'clippings' folder. This approach is now undertaken electronically and is available as a themed electronic 'clippings' service that several publishers currently provide free on a trial basis. Subscription services also provide summaries (i.e. abstracts) of specified topics for worldwide publications. This also includes abstracts, in English, from non-English-language publications. In addition to these services, marketers have access to a growing number of electronic synthesis tools. For example, 'intelligent agents' are software programmes which can 'learn' the type of material the user requires and may then search the World Wide Web automatically for similar material. This moves beyond the constraints of 'key word' searches.

Case history

Forecasting and planning in practice

How Boeing forecasts aircraft demand

Boeing's planning horizons are long-term. The NPD process can take 20 years from idea generation to commercialization. Boeing must attempt to forecast the future demand for air travel to ensure they are manufacturing the right types of aircraft. There are a number of critical issues to consider when building long-range forecasts:

'inventory' issues, i.e. annual replacements of aircraft.
The markets which drive demand for aircraft. A long-range forecast is developed annually at Boeing to forecast demand for world air travel and cargo growth. This includes forecasts for each main size category of airplane. It consists of the following:
- o Air travel market forecasts (by econometric model) based on
   1. changes in the cost of air travel
   2. changes in the income of the travelling population
- o Airplane retirement assumptions.
- o Forecasts for commercial jet planes:
   1. airplane deliveries in dollars
   2. airplane deliveries in units
   3. categorization by range and size.

These forecasts are then used within the Boeing business planning process to develop:

Financial and production plans.
Competitor analyses.
Workforce and inventory requirements.
Resource allocations.
New-product evaluations.

These forecasts, combined with forecasts involving risk and opportunities, drive internal planning. Boeing does not include any consideration of unpredictable and random events such as energy crises or wars in their forecasts. The forecast is then broken down into three sections:

1. The world market demand involving growth in air travel and cargo with assumptions about the replacement of retired airplanes.

2. The airplane supply requirement
3. The manufacturer's position in the industry.

Source: Adapted from Cravens (2000)

Extended knowledge

Visit the website www.marketing.wharton.upenn.edu/forecast to find out more about the principles behind successful forecasting, based on a substantial amount of research activity. This site has links to other relevant sites.

Market sensing

Market sensing focuses on the need for managers to understand the market in which they are operating. Piercy (2000) provides the following comments that help to explain the concept of market sensing:

> how those of us inside the company understand and react to the marketplace and the way it is changing (p.388).

> our focus is on market understanding not marketing research techniques and marketing information systems (p.426).

> the real challenge is not making market research more sophisticated, it is trying to ensure that the things that managers' know' and 'understand' are the right things (p.396).

Information is a key requirement of the decision-making process. However, the type and amount of information available will vary considerably depending on the level at which it is being used in an organization. It is possible to produce copious amounts of market information but this is unlikely to be particularly helpful at a strategic level. Strategic decisions are concerned with the future and much market information is based on the past. It is dangerous to assume that what happened in the past will be of relevance to the future, particularly for firms operating in a dynamic environment. Figure 5.5 illustrates the relationship between the availability and predictability of information in relation to the level of decision-making. At an operational level there is likely to be much available information that is largely predictable. This may take the form of market research, internal records and marketing intelligence. However, at a strategic level it is likely there will be a shortage of reliable information.

Low

Predictability of information

Availability of information

Strategic level

Management level

High ► Operational level ◄ High

Decision-making pyramid

Figure 5.5
Decision-making pyramid (Adapted from Piercy, 2000)

A key difference between marketing research and market sensing is that market sensing focuses on a manager's understanding of the market place. Marketing research frequently provides information on 'what is', i.e. the current attitudes of consumers, current product preferences and levels of demand. Market sensing is about interpreting these relationships to understand how they impact on the market place and consequently on marketing planning.

Question 5.2

Market sensing versus marketing research

Answer the following question from the December 1999 exam paper and compare your answer with the CIM specimen answer.

Your Marketing Director has asked you to write a briefing paper, outlining and evaluating the techniques available to help the organization form a view of the future. In particular, she has asked you to explain the difference between the concept of market sensing and market research.

Extended knowledge

For further information on techniques for developing a view of the future refer to:

Drummond & Ensor (2001) *Strategic Marketing Planning and Control*, Butterworth-Heinemann. Chapter 6.

Mercer (1998) *Marketing Strategy: The Challenge of the External Environment*, The Open University, Sage Publications. Chapters 2 and 5 – 8.

Marketing information systems (MkIS) and use of strategic intelligence

Marketing information is a key requirement for any successful marketing plan and therefore the development of effective management and marketing information systems is an important task for marketers. The Planning and Control syllabus does not explicitly include MkIS. However, it is expected that you will be familiar with this subject from studying at Certificate and Advanced Certificate levels, in particular within the Management Information for Marketing Decisions module. Therefore this workbook will highlight the areas that you should be familiar with and refer you to further reading, rather than covering the topic in detail.

Senior Marketing Managers should not become too heavily involved in the details of the MKIS and marketing research but should be concentrating on how to utilize the information in helping to understand the market and develop successful marketing programmes.

Marketing information systems (MkIS)

You should already be fully conversant with the concept of MkIS from previous CIM modules. This section will provide a brief overview of the key issues and refer you to further reading. It is essential that organizations develop integrated systems for managing their, often huge, amounts of data. It is a waste of time collecting data if it is then inaccessible and unavailable to decision makers at the right time and in the right format. Effective and flexible MkIS can provide organizations with a competitive advantage if developed appropriately. Figure 5.6 illustrates a typical MkIS.

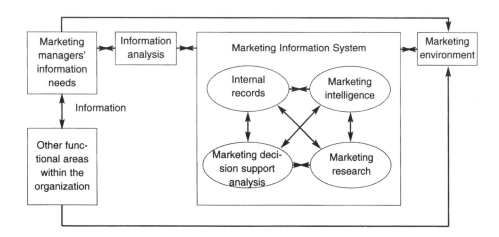

Figure 5.6
The marketing information system (Adapted from Piercy, 2000)

It is clear that a MKIS has four main components:

1. **Internal records** – there is a wealth of information available within the organization and it is essential that it is organized in such as way to facilitate its usage. This may include sales data, customer orders, prices, stock levels, customer complaints, etc.

2. **Marketing research** – this is concerned with the systematic collection of information that is specific to a particular problem. For example, a piece of marketing research may be commissioned to investigate attitudes to a new advertising campaign.
3. **Marketing intelligence** – this may include any information that is collected on an *ad hoc* basis, such as competitor intelligence gleaned from the press, customer trends, registered patents etc.
4. **Marketing decision support systems** – the processes that convert the data into usable information. For example, statistical tools or modelling techniques.

Extended knowledge

For further discussion of marketing information systems and marketing research refer to:

Jobber (1998) *Principles and Practice of Marketing*, 2nd Ed, McGraw Hill. Chapter 6.

Question 5.3

Market information

Answer the following question from the December 1998 exam paper and compare your answer with the CIM specimen answer.

Your Taiwan-based organization has been approached by a major UK clothing retailer with a view to franchising their operation in your home market. Write a report outlining the information that is needed in order to make a management decision on this proposal. Show how you would acquire this data.

Summary

- The Planning and Control syllabus assumes an understanding of the profit and loss account and of the balance sheet. However of greater interest in the Planning and Control module is the use of these accounts in the analysis of businesses. This tends to be undertaken using ratio analysis.
- There are five main types of ratios: profitability ratios, capital structure ratios, liquidity ratios, asset utilization ratios and investment performance ratios.
- Productivity analysis concerns the relationship between outputs and inputs. These are expressed as a ratio to measure the efficiency of the relationship, for example the increase in sales revenue over the increase in advertising expenditure.
- Segmental analysis forces the marketer to consider the market that is the focus of the analysis and how to segment the market. Consideration of how to segment the market will depend on market attributes, product attributes company size and objectives.
- A variety of techniques are available to predict the future and to allow the organization to develop a future orientation. The event/situation (including issues concerning breadth and detail) which are to be forecast, and the forecast time horizon, influence the selection of forecasting technique.

- Market sensing is much more than marketing research and marketing research techniques. Its focus is on understanding the market and its future direction, rather than developing an ever-greater understanding of the market in the past. Past analysis has traditionally been the focus of attention, in an attempt to predict the future, based on a detailed understanding of the past. However, the future may be so different that the past may contribute little to future understanding; on the contrary it may hinder it.
- Senior marketing managers should be concerned with how to use the information generated from the MkIS rather than with the details of the system.

Further study

Extending knowledge

Bibliography and links

Craven S D, (2000), *Current Market Outlook Boeing Commercial Airplane Group,* February 1992, p.11, cited in Craven S D, *Strategic Marketing* (1999) 6th Ed, McGraw-Hill.

Cox D, Fardon M (1997), *Management of Finance. A Guide to Business Finance for the Non-Specialist,* Osborne Books ISBN 1 872962 238

Drummond G & Ensor J (1999), *Strategic Marketing Planning and Control,* Butterworth-Heinemann.

Drummond G & Ensor J (2001), *Strategic Marketing Planning and Control,* Butterworth-Heinemann.

Financial Times Mastering Marketing Series (1998) Part 1, 21 September

Jobber D (1988) *Principles and Practice of Marketing,* 2nd Ed, McGraw-Hill.

Mercer D (1998), *Marketing Strategy: The Challenge of the External Environment,* The Open University, Sage Publications.

Piercy N (2000), *Market-Led Strategic Change,* 2nd Ed, Butterworth-Heinemann.

www.hps-inc.com.

www.marketing.wharton.upenn.edu/forecast

Objectives

By the end of this unit you will:

- Be able to define the terms 'strategic intent'/ vision' and 'mission statement'
- Know the components of 'good' mission statements
- Be able to identify the factors that influence the selection of visions and mission statements, and the setting of goals and objectives
- Be able to discuss the development of appropriate objectives
- Be able to describe and critically evaluate the balanced score card

Study guide

- This unit will take you about 3 hours to work through.
- We suggest that you take a further 3 hours to do the various activities and questions in this unit.

Introduction

The next three units are all concerned with strategy formulation and selection. This unit will discuss the strategic intent of an organization and the factors that influence their overall strategic direction. The Unit 'Creating strategic advantage' will then concentrate on how companies can develop a strategic advantage with reference to the generic models that companies can use. 'Developing a specific competitive position' is concerned with how companies can translate this generic advantage into a specific competitive advantage with particular reference to the role of segmentation, targeting and positioning. Before an organization can make decisions about their strategy and how they are going to compete in terms of their competitive advantage it is necessary to first establish the general areas in which they wish to operate. Organizations need to have a clear vision of where they want to go in the future in order to decide how they are going to get there.

Strategic intent/vision and mission

Strategic intent refers to the aspirations of an organization rather than just its current activity. Writers often use the terms 'strategic intent' and 'vision' interchangeably because they are essentially referring to the same concept. According to Aaker (1998), p.158, strategic intent provides:

> A long-term drive for advantage that can be essential to success. It provides a model that helps break the mould, moving a firm away from simply doing the same things a bit better and working a bit harder than the year before. It has the capability to elevate and extend an organization, helping it reach levels it would not otherwise attain.

It is apparent that many organizations that have an appropriate and well-constructed vision are focused on the future and ways of continually attaining sustainable competitive advantages. A vision can help guide strategy, identify and maintain core competencies and provide inspiration and motivation to its managers and its employees by providing them with a sense of purpose.

Hamel & Pralahad (1989) suggested that strategic intent combines:

- 'a dream that energizes the company' (i.e. acts as a motivator)
- implied 'stretch', (looks for new opportunities rather than relying on existing business)
- sense of direction
- sense of discovery
- coherence to plans.

Definition

Strategic intent/vision

The desired future state or aspiration of the organization (Johnson & Scholes, 1999, p243)

Case history

Microsoft's vision

' Microsoft's vision is to empower people through great software – any time, any place and on any devices. As the worldwide leader in software for personal and business computing, Microsoft strives to produce innovative products and services that meet our customer's evolving needs. At the same time, we understand that long-term success is about more that just making good products.'

There are two key aspects to Microsoft's past and future success: its vision of technology and the values by which we live, every day, as a company. The values you see below are a set of principles which have evolved since our founding, and which capture the spirit, philosophy and day-to-day business practices of our company. They are not new values, but rather a reinforcement of long-held company principles that underscore our relationships with customers, partners and employees.

Customers: Helping customers achieve their goals is the key to Microsoft's long-term success. We must listen to what they tell us, respond rapidly by delivering new and constantly improving products, and build relationships based on trust, respect and mutual understanding. We will always back up our products with unparalleled service and support.

Innovation: In an industry that moves at lightning speed, innovation is critical to our competitiveness. Microsoft's long-term approach to research & development, combined with our constant efforts to anticipate customer needs, improve quality and reduce costs will enable us to deliver the best products and technologies.

Partners: Helping our partners succeed and grow their businesses with the best plafforms, tools and support is central to our mission.

Integrity: Our managers and employees must always act with the utmost integrity, and be guided by what is ethical and right for our customers. We compete vigorously and fairly.

People: Our goal is for everyone at Microsoft to develop a challenging career with opportunities for growth, competitive rewards and a balance between work and home life. In a fast-paced, competitive environment, this is a shared responsibility between Microsoft and its employees.

Mission statements

A mission statement (in contrast to a vision) is more concerned with providing daily guidance rather than a vision of the future. According to Piercy (2000), p.180-181, mission statements that are to contribute anything must:

- Reflect an organization's core competencies and how it intends to apply and sustain them.
- Be closely tied to the critical success factors in the marketplace.
- Tell employees, managers, suppliers and partners what contribution is required from them to deliver the promise of value to the customer.

Definition

Mission statement

A generalized statement of the overriding purpose of the organization (Johnson & Scholes, 1999, p.241)

Case history

Mission statement

The following provides you with examples of mission statements.

Cranfield University

Cranfield's particular mission is to transform world-class science, technology and management expertise into viable, practical, environmentally desirable solutions that enhance economic development. Cranfield will transfer its solutions through its students, and its research, development and consultancy.
Source: www.cranfield.ac.uk

Mission statements are influenced by a number of factors such as the history of the organization, resource availability, the external environment, the core competencies of the organization and the current preferences of the current chief executive and senior management. The extent to which the mission statement serves its purpose is influenced not only by the quality and relevance of the mission but also by how it is communicated to staff and other stakeholders. A successful mission statement is one that is wholly embraced and 'believed' by staff. Just having a mission statement is insufficient; the staff must also 'buy into' the idea. One organization that failed to understand this, did not involve staff in the process of developing the mission, and then out of the blue all employees were sent a letter and a laminated card informing staff of the organization's new vision and mission. How successful and motivating do you think this mission will be?

Drummond & Ensor (2001) suggest that successful mission statements should demonstrate the following characteristics:

- Credibility – it must be realistic and believable.
- Uniqueness – not bland and generic.
- Specific capabilities – embrace core capabilities.
- Aspirational – needs to motivate individuals.

Activity 6.1

Evaluating mission statements

Piercy (2000) in his text *Market-Led Strategic Change* (p.193) proposes a method for testing mission statements. Refer to this list of criteria and then complete the following:

- Select two different organizations and seek out their mission statements (include your own organization if possible).

The relationship between the vision and mission within the strategic marketing planning framework is illustrated in Figure 6.1.

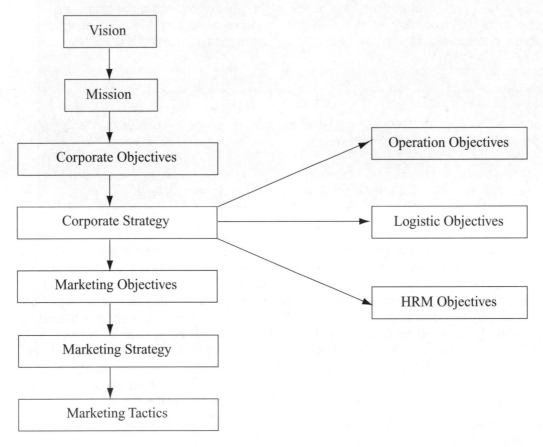

Figure 6.1
Corporate and marketing hierarchy

Many mission statements were widely adopted by organizations in the 1980s and 1990s but were criticized for being bland and lacking uniqueness, and therefore for not fulfilling the role they were set out for. Many organizations have been accused of paying 'lip service' to mission statements, because they believe that it is necessary to have a 'mission', but did not invest time or energy in producing a relevant and motivating statement. However, advocates of mission statements believe that if written well they can have a powerful influence over strategy and act as a great motivator for staff. Some organizations combine their vision and mission statements whilst others recognize a difference between the two and therefore develop separate statements.

Influences on organizational strategic direction

The vision, mission and overall strategic direction of an organization will be influenced by a number of factors. Johnson & Scholes (1999) suggest that there are four major types of influence (illustrated in Figure 6.2):

- **Corporate governance** – to whom should the organization be accountable?
- **Stakeholders** – employees, customers, shareholders, suppliers, wider social community, etc.
- **Business Ethics** – social responsibility.
- **Cultural context** – at a broad national level and within organizational culture.

The strategic direction of an organization is subject to such influences and it can often be difficult to accommodate all of these, often conflicting, influences. For example, shareholders may make demands on the organization to improve their return on the investment. However, this may be contrary to the organization's commitment to improving their social responsibility, for example by reducing the amount of pollution it creates.

Figure 6.2
Influences on an organization's mission and objectives (Adapted from Johnson & Scholes, 1999)

Goals and objectives

The vision and mission provide guidance on the overall direction of an organization. Objectives, whether corporate or marketing, are the expected outcomes of the strategy. Goals are often regarded as less specific than objectives and more difficult to measure. However, it is normally accepted that objectives should be SMART:

- **S**pecific.
- **M**easurable – expressed in quantifiable terms.
- **A**cceptable – to stakeholders.
- **R**ealistic – attainable.
- **T**ime bound – achievable within a certain time frame.

Some writers argue that it is not possible to quantify all types of objectives. For example, it can be difficult to quantify objectives such as innovation leadership.

Definition

Goals and objectives

Goal – general statement of aim or purpose. *Objective* – Quantification (if possible) or more precise statement of the goal (Johnson & Scholes, 1999, p.14)

There are many different types of objectives with which an organization should be concerned. Drucker (1954) identified the following:

1. Market Standing – e.g. market share objectives
2. Innovation – e.g. number of new products launched
3. Productivity – e.g. inputs compared with outputs such as increase sales whilst maintaining the same number of sales staff
4. Physical and financial resources – relating to the use of resources
5. Profitability – e.g. return on investment
6. Manager performance and development – performance criteria
7. Employee performance and attitude – loyalty
8. Public responsibility – e.g. reduce dependency on fossil fuels

It is likely that many organizations will place greater weighting on some areas than others. For example, the Co-operative bank places great emphasis on their responsibility to the public in the form of their ethical banking policy. There may be the danger that some organizations are preoccupied with productivity objectives and trying to improve efficiency of existing activities without actually questioning whether they are doing the right things.

Levels of Objectives

Objectives exist at a number of levels within an organization (such as corporate and marketing levels). At whatever level, their purpose is the same: to set out what is to be achieved. There is often confusion as to what constitutes a corporate objective and how this differs from a marketing objective. Corporate objectives are influenced by the vision and mission, relate to the companies overall direction and are often expressed in financial terms such as return on investment and profitability. From this the corporate strategy will be developed that will hope to meet these objectives. These objectives then need to be translated into functional objectives such as marketing, human resources and operations. For example, marketing objectives will be concerned with markets, products and customers. Appropriate marketing objectives may include market share or sales volume. These objectives will then be cascaded down and be translated into operational plans. In the case of marketing these will relate to the elements of the marketing mix – for example promotional, distribution and pricing objectives. This can be further broken down – for example promotional objectives could be separated into advertising, public relations and sales promotion objectives. The relationship between these various levels of objectives is illustrated in Figure 6.3.

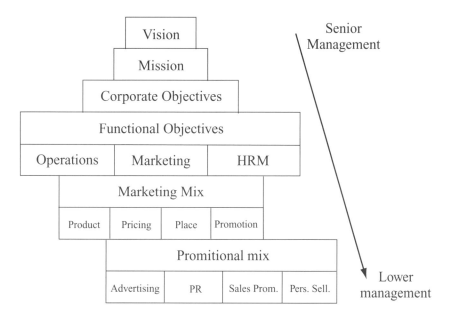

Figure 6.3
Levels of objectives

Activity 6.2

Writing objectives

Drummond & Ensor 2001 p. 86 provide a good example of the different types of objectives that may exist in a hotel. Refer to Figure 6.3 and produce a similar table for either your own organization or an organization of your choice.

Strategic direction – trade-offs

It is inevitable that organizations will have to make trade-offs between different types of objectives when developing their strategic direction. For example, they may wish to pursue environmental objectives but this could be at the expense of profitability. Weinberg (1969) suggests that the following trade-offs may have to be made:

- Short-term versus long-term.
- Profit margin versus competitive position.
- Marketing penetration versus market development.
- Related versus non-related growth.
- Profit versus non-profit objectives (social, ethical, environmental etc.).
- Growth versus stability.
- Risk avoidance versus risk taking.

Many organizations struggle to achieve a balance between these various types of trade-offs. The balanced scorecard framework can be used to help organizations take a balanced approach to their objectives.

Question 6.1

Strategic objectives and trade-offs

Answer the following question from the December 1999 exam paper and then compare your answer with the CIM specimen answer.

The strategic direction of an organization is subject to a number of influences. Discuss the trade-offs that managers should consider when formulating an organization's strategic objectives.

Balanced scorecard

Objectives cannot be set in isolation from the various organizational stakeholders (see below for a discussion of stakeholders). The balanced scorecard approach was developed by Kaplan & Norton (1992) as a means of acknowledging the various perspectives of different stakeholder groups, whilst at the same time linking objectives with performance measures. In the planning and control cycle a key part of the process is monitoring and control. Kaplan and Norton suggest that a set of consistent objectives must be established, but that at the same time these should be linked to performance measures. The balanced scorecard approach, illustrated in Figure 6.4, suggests that an organization should view itself from four different perspectives:

- **Customer perspective** – how customers view a company is of obvious importance. They will be concerned with issues such as quality and customer service.
- **Financial perspective** – this is often the area with which many organizations become preoccupied. This represents the view of the shareholders and relates to the financial performance of the company.
- **Internal perspective** – this identifies the internal processes that lead to external customer satisfaction. For example, employees' attitudes and performance.
- **Innovation and learning** – relates to an organization's ability to continually innovate and learn.

•

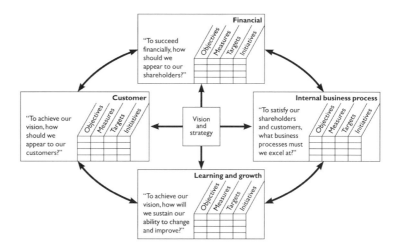

Figure 6.4
The balanced scorecard framework (Kaplan & Norton, 1996)

Definition

Balanced scorecard

Balanced scorecards combine both qualitative and quantitative measures, acknowledge the expectations of different stakeholders and relate an assessment of performance to choice of strategy. Johnson & Scholes, 1999, p.468.

This model helps organizations to develop a balanced range of objectives and also relate them to relevant performance measures. Examples of these are illustrated in Figure 6.5.

	Strategic objectives	Strategic measures
Financial	F.1 Return on capital F.2 Cash flow F.3 Profitability F.4 Profitability growth F.5 Reliability of performance	⇨ ROCE ⇨ Cash flow ⇨ Net margin ⇨ Volume growth rate vs. industry ⇨ Profit forecast reliability ⇨ Sales backlog
Customer	C.1 Value for money C.2 Competitive price C.3 Customer satisfaction	⇨ Customer ranking survey ⇨ Pricing index ⇨ Customer satisfaction index ⇨ Mystery shopping index
Internal	I.1 Marketing ■ Product and service development ■ Shape customer requirement I.2 Manufacturing ■ Lower manufacturing cost ■ Improve project management I.3 Logistics ■ Reduce delivery costs ■ Inventory management I.4 Quality	⇨ Pioneer percentage of product portfolio ⇨ Hours with customer on new work ⇨ Total expenses per unit vs. competition ⇨ Safety incident index ⇨ Delivered cost per unit ⇨ Inventory level compared to plan and output rate ⇨ Rework
Innovation and learning	I.L.1 Innovate products and services I.L.2 Time to market I.L.3 Empowered workforce I.L.4 Access to strategic information I.L.5 Continuous improvement	⇨ Percentage revenue from pioneer products ⇨ Cycle time vs. industry norm ⇨ Staff attitude survey ⇨ Strategic information availability ⇨ Number of employee suggestions

Figure 6.5
The balanced scorecard (Source: Kaplan and Norton 1992, 1993)

As illustrated in Figure 6.6 there are causal relationships between the four different perspectives. The knowledge, skills and systems that employees need and the culture that is engendered (innovation and learning) go towards building the right strategic capabilities such as marketing and logistics (internal processes) and in turn this delivers value to the market (customer), which will eventually lead to greater shareholder value (financial).

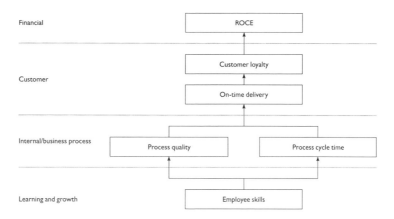

Figure 6.6
Causal Relationships Within the Balanced Scorecard (Source: Kaplan and Norton 1992, 1993)

Kaplan & Norton (2000) have developed the balanced scorecard further by suggesting that the framework can be used to help map out organizations' strategies using the cause and effect chain that connects desired outcomes with the drivers of those results.

Case history

Bass Brewers

Many companies are beginning to recognize the value of the balanced scorecard. Bass is one company that is integrating the principles of this approach into their strategy development and evaluation process. According to USA consultant Dr David Norton, one of the early proponents of the balanced scorecard approach, measuring not just financial outcomes but also areas like customer and employee satisfaction is having a big impact on companies:

'What the balanced scorecard forces management to do is look holistically at the organization and to look at the strategy in its totality.

'Instead of asking the marketing person to come in and talk about the marketing plan, and then the manufacturing person to talk about the quality plan, you address the strategy as a team.

'The scorecard creates a management tool that allows this team view of strategy to be translated into a structure you can use to manage. As simple as that may seem, it has created some pretty dramatic changes in organizations.'

Over the past few years, Bass Brewers has been developing a more targeted approach to its customers, who are becoming more sophisticated and are demanding more customized service. Central to dealing with these groups of customers on an individual basis is an information system that the company has been working on since 1993, and which it wants to build on and make sophisticated enough to take it through to the millennium and beyond. This system will also enable the company to maintain a far better grasp on measurement overall, from customer value through to the key performance indicators at board level.

Customer satisfaction is one of the key performance indicators included in the balanced scorecard at board level. That scorecard has a mix of financial and non-financial figures. Net profit, net profit as a percentage of turnover, capital expenditure, return on capital, cashflow, margin per unit, sales volume and value are all monitored. New brands as a percentage of total volume is included because in such a mature industry, while improving performance and productivity is essential, innovation is equally required to invigorate the market. And, as well as customer satisfaction, there are other customer measures, like returns and complaints. The information gathered for the board is then cascaded down through the business.

Extending knowledge

For a more detailed discussion refer to:

Drummond & Ensor, (2000), pp. 139-140

The balanced scorecard was introduced in the Marketing Customer Interface module at Advanced Certificate.

If you would like more information on Kaplan and Norton's approach to mapping out strategy then read:

Kaplan & Norton (2000), pp. 167-176

Question 6.2

Balanced scorecard

Answer question 4 on the June 2000 planning and control exam paper about the balanced scorecard and compare your answer with the outline answer provided in the appendix at the back of the book.

Stakeholders

A key consideration when developing strategic direction relates to an organization's various stakeholder groups. Stakeholders refer to all the different groups of individuals that are influenced by the activities of an organization. Stakeholders have different expectations and can exert varying levels of influence over the organization. It is important that organizations have a good understanding of the varying needs of their various stakeholder groups. There are three main groups of stakeholders:

- Internal stakeholders (employees, management).
- Connected stakeholders (suppliers, distributors, shareholders, customers).
- External stakeholders (community, government, pressure groups).

Figure 6.7 illustrates an outline stakeholder map.

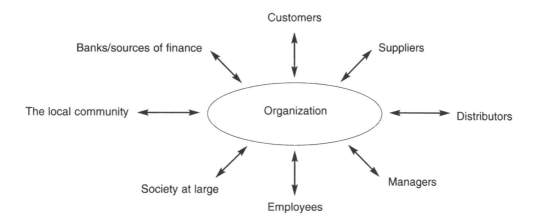

Figure 6.7
A *stakeholder map* (Kaplan and Norton 1992, 1993)

Summary

- Strategic intent relates to the aspirations of an organization and is sometimes referred to as the organization's vision. An appropriate and well constructed vision can help guide strategy, identify and maintain core competencies and can act as a motivator for staff by providing them with a sense of purpose.
- Mission statements are more concerned with providing daily guidance rather than a vision of the future. They should reflect an organization's core competencies, relate to the critical success factors in the market and also inform employees and other stakeholders what contribution is required from them to deliver value to the customer.
- There are a number of influences on strategic direction – corporate governance, stakeholders, business ethics and cultural context. It can be difficult to accommodate these, often conflicting, influences.
- Objectives are a statement of what an organization wants to achieve and, wherever possible, they should be SMART. Objectives exist at a number of levels within an organization. Whatever the level of the objective the purpose is the same, to set out what is to be achieved.
- Organizations will have to make trade-offs between different types of objectives when developing their strategic direction. For example, short-term versus long-term, profit versus non-profit goals, growth versus stability.
- The balanced scorecard, developed by Kaplan & Norton, is a framework that acknowledges the various perspectives of the various stakeholder groups, whilst at the same time linking objective setting with performance measures. The four different perspectives are the customer perspective, the financial perspective, the internal perspective and innovation and learning.
- Stakeholders are a key consideration when developing strategic direction. Stakeholders consist of all those individuals that are influenced by the activities of an organization and include internal stakeholders (employees and management), connected stakeholders (suppliers, distributors, shareholders and customers) and external stakeholders (community, government and pressure groups).

Further study

Extending knowledge

Bibliography

Aaker D (1998), *Strategic Market Management*, 5th Ed, John Wiley & Sons.

Drucker P (1954), *The Practice of Management* Harper & Row, pp.65-83.

Drummond G & Ensor J (2000), *Strategic Marketing Planning and Control*, Butterworth-Heinemann pp.79 – 84.

Hamel G & Pralahad C K (1989), *Harvard Business Review*, 67:3, pp.63 – 76.

Johnson G & Scholes K (1999), *Exploring Corporate Strategy* 5th Ed, Prentice-Hall, pp.13-16 and 241 – 244.

Kaplan R S & Norton D P (1992), *The Balanced Scorecard: Measures that drive performance*, Harvard Business Review, 70:1, pp.71-79.

Kaplan R S & Norton D P (1993), *Putting the Balanced Scorecard to Work*, Harvard Business Review, 71:5, pp.134-147.

Kaplan R S & Norton D P (2000), *Having Trouble with your Strategy? Then Map It*, Harvard Business Review, Sept-Oct, pp.167-176.

Piercy N (2000), *Market-Led Strategic Change*, 2nd Ed, Butterworth-Heinemann.

Weinberg R (1969), *Developing Marketing Strategies for Short-term Profits and Long-term Growth*, paper presented at *Advanced Management Research Inc. Seminar*, New York.

www.cranfield.ac.uk

www.bp.com

www.microsoft.com/mscorp

Objectives

By the end of this unit you will:

- Understand the term strategic advantage
- Be able to describe, discuss and apply the following approaches to developing strategic advantage:
    - Porter's generic strategies
    - Sustainable advantage (Davidson's approach)
    - Competitive positions and strategy
    - Ansoff's matrix
- Be able to discuss and apply offensive and defensive strategies
- Understand the various types of alliances and networks, be able to discuss the motivations for, and the factors that should be considered when, establishing such relationships
- Be able to discuss the alternative strategies for declining and hostile markets.
- Understand the concept of and the reasons for, strategic wearout.

Study guide

- This unit will take you about 4 hours to work through.
- We suggest that you take a further 4 hours to do the various activities and questions in this unit.

Introduction

Once an organization has undertaken its business analysis as outlined in units two and three and developed a view of the future (see Unit 'Financial Analysis and techniques for developing a view of the future') they need to translate their findings into a winning strategy. The previous unit discussed strategic intent and how this influences the overall strategic direction of an organization. This unit is concerned with analysing the various ways in which organizations can create strategic advantage in an attempt to develop a winning strategy. A number of approaches will be outlined that organizations can use to help them develop strategic advantage. Alliances and partnerships are increasingly being seen as means of gaining strategic advantage. The growth in, and issues relating to, these relationships will be explored. Successful strategies will not endure indefinitely and this unit will conclude with a discussion of the dangers of, and reasons for, 'strategic wear-out'.

Strategic advantage

One of the greatest challenges for any organization is developing a coherent and appropriate strategy that builds on their internal resources and capabilities, capitalizes on external opportunities and will provide a distinct competitive advantage. Competitive advantage is the process of identifying a unique and enduring basis from which to compete, some authors refer to it as strategic advantage. Aaker (1998) provides a useful framework for considering sustainable competitive advantage (SCA) (see Figure 7.1). According to Aaker there are numerous ways in which organizations can compete – through their distribution strategies, their pricing strategies, global strategies and their positioning strategies. However, Aaker believes that how you compete is only part of the equation. The basis of competition, the markets in which you compete and to whom you compete against are all key elements of SCA.

Basis of competition

Aaker (1998) suggests that organizations must also consider the basis of competition (i.e. in terms of available assets and competencies). Without the support of assets and competencies it will be unlikely that the SCA can be sustained. Aaker gives the example that anyone can distribute cereal or detergent through supermarkets but few actually have the assets and competencies needed to do it effectively.

Where you compete

This relates to the market in which you decide to compete. An organization may have an excellent distribution strategy and the assets and competencies to deliver this strategy but may fail because the market does not value them. Aaker provides the example of Pringles crisps, which had great assets – long shelf life and a crushproof container. However, it failed in the market because customers did not value these characteristics, being primarily concerned with taste, which this product failed to deliver. It was not until the taste was improved that the product succeeded.

Whom you compete against

For an asset or competency to lead to a SCA it may need the right set of competitors. For example, many financial services were traditionally regarded as poor at customer service. Companies such as Virgin saw this as an opportunity to enter this market due to their ability to deliver high levels of customer service.

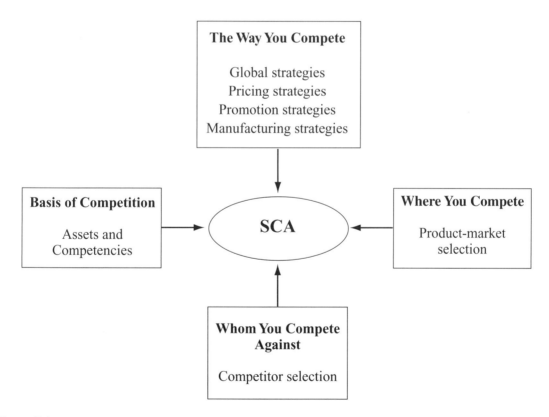

Figure 7.1
The sustainable competitive advantage (Adapted from Aaker, (1998), p.142)

Approaches to developing strategic advantage

The next section will outline a number of approaches to developing strategic advantage. They are not mutually exclusive and many organizations use a combination of approaches to develop their own distinctive competitive advantage.

Porter's generic strategies

Porter (1980), a major contributor to the discussion of competitive strategy, suggests that there are three generic types of strategy that can provide organizations with a competitive advantage:

- Cost leadership
- Differentiation
- Focus

Figure 7.2 illustrates the alternative sources of competitive advantage and highlights the options open to companies in terms of defining their source of advantage and their competitive scope (i.e. targeting a broad or narrow range of customers).

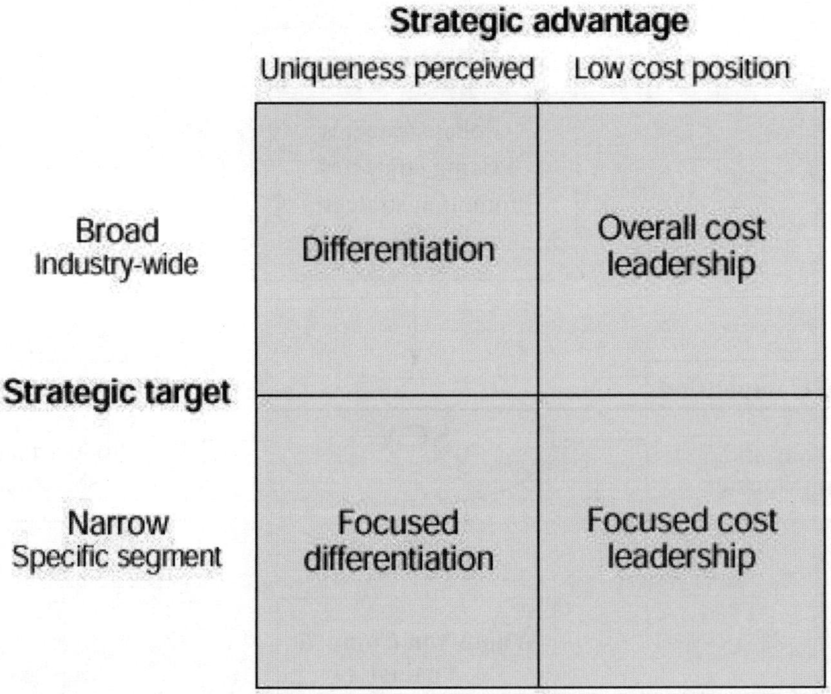

Strategic advantage

	Uniqueness perceived	Low cost position
Broad Industry-wide	Differentiation	Overall cost leadership
Narrow Specific segment	Focused differentiation	Focused cost leadership

Strategic target

Figure 7.2
Competitive advantage (Adapted from Porter, 1980)

Cost leadership

One possible source of competitive advantage lies in the ability of a firm to be the lowest cost producer in the industry. Firms pursuing a cost leadership strategy would typically concentrate on continually striving to reduce their cost base and improving efficiencies. This could be achieved through activities such as achieving economies of scale, cutting costs, global sourcing and using technology to develop more efficient means of production. Low-cost producers do not necessarily need to offer the lowest price. Instead, they could use the additional revenue to invest back into research and development so that new ways can be identified to reduce costs. Cost leadership relies on large-scale production and the presence of the experience curve. Retailers specializing in a narrow product range that seek out-of-town locations, (such as PC World) are able to achieve economies of scale and therefore pursue a cost leader strategy.

Cost leadership can be a difficult strategy to sustain in the long-term due to the threat of competitors that may have even lower cost structures. For example, the UK based discount retailer Kwik Save was threatened by the entry of German-based Netto and Aldi into the low cost retail market.

Differentiation

Companies pursuing a differentiation strategy strive to offer products or services that are regarded as superior to those offered by competitors. The uniqueness of the product enables companies to charge a premium price. For this strategy to be successful customers must perceive that the higher price is justified in terms of the additional features and benefits they accrue. For example, Gap sell children's clothing at a significantly higher price than other high-street retailers. Many parents are prepared to pay this price premium because of the imagery and brand values associated with Gap clothing. A differentiation strategy is sustainable as long as customers perceive a firm's offering to be of greater value than those of its competitors. For example, Marks & Spencer's differentiation strategy based on quality failed because the competitors were matching their quality standard and selling similar products at a lower price. The company is currently striving to find a meaningful way of differentiating themselves from its competition.

Focus

Cost leadership and differentiation strategies both target a broad market. In contrast, a focus strategy concentrates on a narrow segment of the market that is particularly attractive. A focus strategy, sometimes referred to as a niche strategy, is based on the assumption that these niche markets can be served more effectively and/or efficiently than by companies that are competing more broadly. Companies pursuing a focus strategy can adopt either a cost focus or a differentiation focus strategy.

Cost focus

Companies pursuing a cost focus strategy are concentrating on a niche market but are also concentrating on reducing costs. It can be argued that easyJet has adopted a cost focus strategy. It has concentrated on a narrow segment of the population and has driven costs down by direct bookings and removing all the peripheral services associated with air travel, such as on-board meals. It could be argued that easyJet is now moving from a narrow focus to more broad market appeal.

Differentiation focus

This is concerned with producing superior products for narrow market segments. Such as, Rolex watches and Ferrari.

Case history

Small is beautiful – Palmair

Palmair Express, based at Bournemouth airport, has just one aircraft and its 73-year-old Chairman waves off every flight. The airline was founded in 1957 by Peter Bath, the current Chairman, employs 22 cabin crew and operates 14 flights a week, mainly to European destinations. The Chairman is keen that the airline should maintain the personal service for which it has become famous, and to help ensure the personal touch he greets every passenger on their departure. In March 2001 Palmair was voted third best airline in the world in a survey of 31,000 passengers conducted by *Holiday Which?* Although narrowly beaten by Air New Zealand and Singapore Airlines, Palmair left other British carriers, including Virgin and British Airways, on the runway. Palmair goes to show that you do not have to be big to be successful.

Source: de Bruxelles (2001) www.Lexis-Nexis.com

Question 7.1

Focus strategy

Answer Question 5 from the December 2000 Planning and Control Exam Paper on the benefits of a niche strategy to a car manufacturer and then compare your answer to the outline answer provided in the appendix at the back of the book.

Figure 7.3 compares the benefits and possible limitations of each of Porter's three generic strategies.

Type of strategy	Ways to achieve the strategy	Benefits	Possible problems
Cost leadership	• Size and economies of scale • Globalization of operations • Relocating to low cost parts of the world • Modification/simplification of designs • Greater labour effectiveness • Greater operating effectiveness • Strategic alliances • New sources of supply	The ability to: • Out-perform rivals • Erect barriers to entry • Resist the five forces	• Vulnerability to even lower cost operators • Possible price wars • The difficulty of sustaining it in the long term
Focus	• Concentration upon one or a small number of segments • The creation of a strong specialist reputation	• A more detailed understanding of particular segments • The creation of barriers to entry • A reputation for specialization • The ability to concentrate efforts	• Limited opportunities for sector growth • The possibility of out-growing the market • The decline of the sector • A reputation for specialization which ultimately inhibits growth and development into other sectors
Differentiation	• The creation of strong brand identities • The consistent pursuit of those factors which customers perceive to be important • High performance in one or more of a spectrum of activities	• A distancing from others in the market • The creation of a major competitive advantage • Flexibility	• The difficulties of sustaining the bases for differentiation • Possibly higher costs • The difficulty of achieving true and meaningful differentiation

Figure 7.3
Porter's three generic strategies

Inconsistent strategy

Porter (1980) argues that if companies fail to consistently pursue one of these generic strategies they will become 'stuck in the middle' with no discernible competitive advantage, as illustrated in Figure 7.4.

Figure 7.4
Stuck in the middle

Extended knowledge

This workbook has provided you with a brief overview of Porter's generic strategies. For a more detailed discussion refer to Drummond G & Ensor J (2001), Chapter 8, pp. 144-150.

Activity 7.1

Porter's generic strategies

Select an industry of your choice and identify an example of a company that pursues each of the generic strategies. In your opinion is there a company that is 'stuck in the middle'? To what extent does this model help companies to identify their competitive advantage?

Sustainable advantage – Davidson's approach

Davidson (1997) has identified ten ways of attaining a sustainable competitive advantage. Each of these is outlined below.

Superior product or service

This strategy is based on having a product or service that is in reality better than competitors, for example Mercedes-Benz cars.

Perceived advantage

Rather than the product *actually* being superior to competing products it is *perceived* as different. For example, when George Michael paid £1.45 million last year for John Lennon's Imagine Piano, he was not just buying a piano, he was buying a piece of history. The competitive advantage lies in the branding and perceived benefits the product delivers.

Global skills

This competitive advantage lies in the ability of companies to operate on a global basis. Coca-Cola and McDonalds have both achieved competitive advantage through their global strategies.

Low-cost producer

This equates to Porter's cost leadership strategy.

Superior competencies

Competencies, as discussed in unit 'External analysis', often take a long time to develop and can therefore be a very important source of competitive advantage. For example, Sony has superior competencies in the area of product development and innovation.

Superior assets

Assets may take the form of cash, brands or property. For example, it is now being acknowledged that brands can make a great contribution to the value of a company.

Scale advantages

In unit 'Auditing tools' you were introduced to the PIMS research, which indicated that market share was a key determinant of profitability. Therefore achieving economies of scale can be a source of competitive advantage.

Attitude advantages

The attitudes of managers and staff can be a source of competitive advantage if, for example, they have vision and commitment.

Legal advantages

A competitive advantage can be gained if a company can protect its position, for example through patents. James Dyson created a competitive advantage when he patented the cyclone technology in his bagless vacuum cleaner.

Superior relationships

Superior relationships may exist between suppliers, distributors, partners, customers, government and other opinion leaders. For example, Disney and McDonalds have a long-term promotional agreement. Boots the Chemist is developing a strategic partnership with Granada Media to launch a combined TV, Internet and broad-based health and beauty company.

Davidson suggests that some of the following sources of competitive advantage are going to increase in importance:

- Low-cost operations.
- Superior competences.
- Superior relationships.

Davidson also suggests that competitive advantage based on actual product superiority and legal advantages will decline in importance.

Extended knowledge

For a more detailed discussion of Davidson's approach to developing competitive advantage see Davidson H (1997), pp.261-269.

Competitive positions and strategy

The position that a firm holds in the market place is going to influence the basis of their competitive advantage. Kotler and Singh (1981) developed a framework that classified companies according to their position in the industry and identifies four distinct categories: market leaders, market challengers, market followers and market nichers. This framework can be compared with military strategies where competitors are regarded as the enemy, and where the fighting takes place in the market place rather than on the battlefield.

Market leaders

Market leaders are usually dominant in terms of market share. They are often the target of aggressive competitors that strive to take market share away from them. There are a number of options available to market leaders:

- **Expand the total market** by identifying new uses or users for the product or by increasing usage. This will expand the total market and as a result the leader will have a share of a larger market.
- **Expand current market share** through offensive strategies they attempt to take share away from competitors. This may include developing new products, expanding distribution channels, mergers or acquisitions or expanding into new geographical markets.
- **Defend market share:**
    - position defence
    - flank defence
    - pre-emptive defence
    - counter-defence
    - mobile defence
    - contraction defence.

These defensive strategies are illustrated in Figure 7.5.

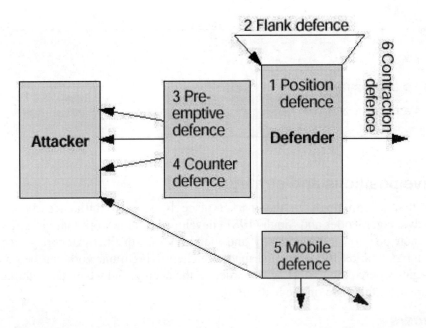

Figure 7.5
Defensive Strategies (Kotler et al, 1999)

Position defence

Position defence is concerned with blocking out competition and trying to improve current position. Market leaders have to continually look at ways to improve their business in an attempt to fend off the threat of challengers. For instance, to maintain their market leadership Microsoft is continually investing in their business to stay ahead of competition.

Flank defence

This strategy involves defending the business's non-core activities. For example, Abbey National recognized their weakness in remote access banking when they launched Cahoot.

Pre-emptive defence

This involves attacking competitors before they attack you. This strategy may employ any of the attacking strategies detailed below. For example, electricity-generating companies entered the gas market as a pre-emptive strike following de-regulation.

Counter-defence

These are largely reactive strategies where a market leader responds to an attack by a competitor. WH Smith launched an on-line bookshop in response to the threat of Internet sales operators such as Amazon.com.

Mobile defence

This is concerned with continually looking for new opportunities and moving into new areas of business in order to remain flexible. For example, easyJet has moved into car rental, financial services and Internet cafes in attempt to stay ahead of the competition.

Contraction Defence

Market leaders may find they are spreading themselves too thinly across many sectors and markets and may decide to concentrate on their core business and withdraw from other markets. Marks & Spencer is currently adopting this strategy by concentrating on UK business and withdrawing from Europe and the USA.

Market challengers

The characteristic of market challengers is that they are number two in the market and often aggressively attack market leaders in an attempt to boast them. Market leadership is seen as an attractive position due to the assumed associated benefits of economies of scale, power and status. There are number of attacking/ offensive strategies open to market challengers. These are illustrated in Figure 7.6.

- frontal (head-on) attack
- flank attack
- encirclement attack
- bypass attack
- guerrilla attack.

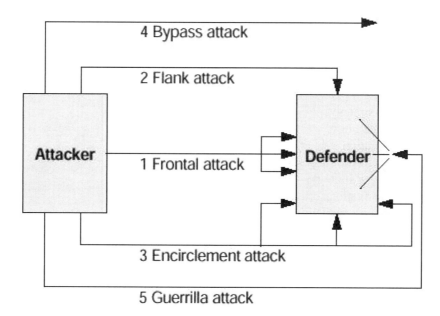

Figure 7.6
Attacking strategies (Kotler et al, 1999)

Frontal attack

Competitors are attacked head on. For market challengers to be able to sustain this type of attack, which can be very costly, they must have sufficient resources to sustain any short-term damage they may incur. For example, Virgin has taken on BA head to head in Business Class on transatlantic flights.

Flank attack

This strategy relies on the identification of a competitor's weak spots and attacking them. Ford acquired Land Rover to help attack their competitors' weaknesses in the areas of off-road vehicles.

Encirclement attack

This strategy is based on the idea of 'surrounding the enemy' and attacking on all sides. This can prove a costly option due to the additional resources necessary to serve multiple segments. The Volkswagen group offers a diverse product range that serves a wide range of segments – Skoda, Seat, Audi and Volkswagen.

Bypass attack

This strategy relies on the ability of a company to identify new opportunities in new areas. This can be achieved by identifying new market segments, new geographical markets and also technological leapfrogging. For example Royal and Sun Alliance has moved into new markets such as China.

Guerilla attack

The military similarities are apparent here because this type of attack relies on random and sporadic attacks on competitors. Tactical marketing programmes such as price promotions are used to achieve short-term gains, and it is hoped will erode market share in the longer term. Supermarket retailers often employ this attack strategy.

Market challengers have to decide not only how to attack but also who to attack:

- Market leader.
- Firms of similar size.
- Small or regional firms.

This decision will depend to a large extent on the resources that a company has at its disposal.

Specific attack strategies

All of the attacking strategies listed above refer to generic options open to market challengers. Kotler and Singh (1981) highlight many specific ways in which competitors can be attacked:

- Price discounting.
- Cheaper goods strategy.
- Prestige goods strategy.
- Product-proliferation strategy.
- Product innovation strategy.
- Improved services strategy.
- Distribution innovation strategy.
- Manufacturing cost reduction strategy.
- Intensive advertising promotion.

Market followers

These types of competitors are likely to be positioned third, fourth or fifth in the market and often duplicate the strategies of the market leader. There are obvious cost advantages in being a follower – for instance, R&D costs are lower. The extent to which a follower replicates the leader's strategy may range from counterfeiting, cloning, imitating through to adaptation. Sony is renowned for their innovative approach to consumer electronics and rival Japanese companies often follow them.

Market nichers

Market nichers do not attempt to compete against the market leaders: they identify a specialist segment and concentrate their efforts on serving the needs of this niche market. There are many current examples of niche strategies such as Ben & Jerry's ice cream, Rolex watches and Morgan cars. Market nichers can specialize by end use, vertical level specialization, specific customer specialization, quality/price specialist or channel specialist. (Kotler and Singh, 1981)

Exam hint

Offensive and defensive strategies

Some authors refer to market leader strategies as defensive strategies. In contrast, market challenger strategies are often referred to as attacking or offensive strategies. In the exam you may be asked to discuss these types of strategy. It is important that you are familiar with this terminology.

Ansoff's matrix – product/ market strategy

You should already be familiar with the Ansoff Matrix from previous studies at Advanced Certificate, particularly Marketing Operations. This will provide you with a brief overview of the model in order to refresh your memory. Ansoff (1957) developed the matrix illustrated in Figure 7.7, which provides a useful framework for identifying alternative strategies based on products and markets. It does not focus specifically on the way in which competitive advantage is gained but it does help firms to consider the different options available to them in terms of growth strategies. The matrix is based around 'new and existing markets' and 'new and existing products'. The further a firm moves away from existing customers and existing products the higher the level of risk involved. Therefore, diversification is regarded as the most risky and market penetration the least risky strategy.

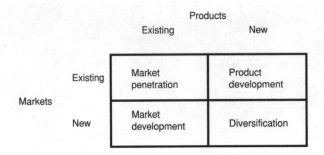

Figure 7.7
Ansoff's matrix

Market penetration

Pursuing a market penetration strategy involves selling more of the same product to the same customers. This strategy could involve:

- **Increase usage** – encourage customers to use a product more frequently (e.g. increase visits to a store by offering loyalty bonuses).
- **Convert non-users into users** – by offering incentives such as 'recommend a friend'.
- **Attract competitors' customers** – some on-line banks have enticed customers away from competition by offering incentives such as reducing their credit card balance.

This is a viable strategy if the market is not already saturated.

Product development

This involves developing new products for existing customers. For example, Boots the Chemist has developed new services such as dentistry, aromatherapy and homeopathy for their existing customer segments.

Market development

This is concerned with developing new markets for existing products and can be achieved by either targeting new segments or entering new geographical markets. With globalization, the opportunities for market development strategies are likely to increase significantly for many companies. For example, Royal and Sun Alliance adopted a market development strategy when they formed a joint venture with an Indian financial services group in an attempt to enter this potentially attractive market.

Diversification

This is probably the most risky strategy because it involves entering areas with which a firm has little or no experience. The level of risk is affected by the extent to which the new strategy is related or unrelated to existing business. Diversification into unrelated areas can be particularly risky. This strategy is often pursued via strategic partnerships or acquisition to reduce the risk. For example, the Danish toy manufacturer Lego is entering the car market by seeking a partner with a view to launching the 'ultimate family vehicle'. The car will be designed to build on Lego's goal of becoming a leading family brand.

Alliances and networks

Increasingly businesses are recognizing that to gain a sustainable competitive advantage they may have to enter into alliances with other firms. Strategic alliances are not a new phenomenon, as illustrated by the array of alliances in the car industry in the early 1990. However, the number and types of companies entering into these alliances and partnerships has proliferated in recent years and it is expected that this trend will continue. The case of IBM illustrates the growing importance of alliances to firms. In 1993 only 5% of IBM's sales outside personal computers were derived from alliances. Now IBM juggles almost 100,000 alliances, which contribute over one-third of its turnover. The company has been quoted as saying it expects these partnerships to boost sales by an extra $10 billion by 2003 (Mazur, 2001a).

Much has been written on strategic alliances and partnership. This workbook will highlight the key issues relating to alliances and networks, provide contemporary examples and provide signposts for further reading on the subject.

There are many environmental changes that are forcing firms to develop collaborative relationships. These include:

- Increasing pace of change in the environment (e.g. technological change).
- Limited resources.
- Increase in competition from both existing and new firms.

- Increased customer expectations.
- Globalization.
- Unstable and unpredictable markets.
- Increased power of certain types of companies (e.g. retailers).

Motivations for companies to enter into strategic partnerships include:

- Desire to exploit economies of scale.
- Desire to create new knowledge and increase level of innovation.
- Reduce risk.
- Enter new geographical markets.
- Exploit others assets and competencies – for example easyJet entered into a strategic partnership with Mercedes to provide cars for their car rental venture.

Types of alliances

There are many different types of alliances ranging from an informal buying co-operative to a joint venture where a legally separate company is formed. Table 7.1 illustrates the major types of alliances.

Table 7.1: Main Categories of Alliances (Adapted from Johnson & Scholes, 1999)		
Type of alliance	Characteristics	Examples
Acquisitions and mergers	Includes both co-operative and hostile takeovers. Often motivated by desire to increase efficiencies and to create synergy.	Glaxo Wellcome merged with SmithKline Beecham last year to form GlaxoSmithKline, the largest pharmaceutical company in Europe.
Consortia and joint ventures	Involves independent organizations setting up specific projects or ventures with other firms.	Eurofighter, a European collaboration consisting of four partner companies – BAE Systems (UK), Alenia (Italy), CASA (Spain) and DASA (Germany). The rationale was to reduce risk by sharing the significant development costs.
Contract or licensing	Contractual agreements where the right to a product is legally signed over to another party. This may take the form of franchising or sub-contracting.	Franchising is utilized by a wide variety of companies such as McDonalds, Ford dealerships, Hertz car rental, and the Body Shop.
Networks	Informal agreements based on co-operation rather than contractual agreements.	Many airlines have informal code sharing agreements that allow passengers to use several different airlines on the same ticket.

Factors to Consider when establishing an alliance

There are many factors to consider when seeking a partner and the process of selection can be a time-consuming process. The following identifies the key factors that organizations should consider.

Strategy

Strategy should be at the core of any alliance. The strategy should dictate why each partner and structure is better than any other option, company expectations, risk management and how the new alliance will be co-co-ordinated. According to Gomes-Casseres (2000) a coherent alliance strategy has four elements:

- A *business strategy* to shape the logic and design of alliances.
- A *dynamic view* to guide the management of each alliance.
- A *portfolio approach* to enable co-ordination among alliances.
- An *internal infrastructure* to maximize the value of collaboration.

Core competencies and strategic fit

It is important that the core competencies of each partner are complementary and that there is strategic fit. Strategic fit refers to the level of compatibility between the two organizations.

Resources

Sufficient resource allocation is a key factor on the success of a relationship.

Risk

There is a high degree of risk involved in setting up alliances. It is important that all parties are aware of these risks and have developed strategies to deal with them.

Cultural fit

It is imperative that each partner has similar goals and aspirations. Culture should play a key role in identification of suitable partners.

Flexibility

All parties must be willing to be flexible so that the alliance can respond to changes in the external environment.

Long-term Focus

Partners should not only be focusing on the short-term gains of the alliance but also on the long-term opportunities that the relationship may deliver.

There are many examples of successful strategic alliances. However, many partnerships do not deliver the predicated benefits. According to a report from KPMG and The Conference Board (cited in Mazur, 2001b), 70% of today's mergers and acquisitions fail to deliver expected business benefits, and 70% of those failures occur during post-merger integration. IMD (cited in Mazur, 2001) gives the following as reasons why alliances fail:

- Differences in vision.
- Incompatible cultures/brand fit.
- Attrition of talent and capabilities.
- Loss of intangible assets.
- High co-ordination costs.
- Synergy gridlock.
- Back-office IT disintegration.

A recurring problem for many partnerships lies in the lack of cultural fit and even what has been described as a 'culture clash'. Alliances and partnerships are one means of building a sustainable competitive advantage. However, the energy, commitment and resources needed to make them successful should not be underestimated.

Activity 7.5

Alliance examples

Scan the quality press, such as the *Financial Times*, and journals such as *Marketing* and *Marketing Week* and identify examples of strategic alliances and partnerships. Classify these according to Table 7.1 and identify the motivations for each of these partnerships. To what extent do you think they will help to gain a competitive advantage?

Case history

Manchester United and the New York Yankees

Manchester United's quest for global domination came another step closer when they announced a mould-breaking partnership with the New York Yankees baseball team earlier this year. The partnership is a marketing alliance and there are obvious benefits to both parties. The New York Yankees can give advice to the UK football club on how to conquer North America. In return Manchester United can give the Yankees a helping hand to break into Asia – where the premiership club already has a strong fan base.

In the short-term the clubs say that they want to sell their branded goods rather than their games through the partnership, although in the long-term they aim to sell their sport too.

Source www.Lexis-Nexis.com

Question 7.3

Strategic Alliance

There has been a question on strategic alliances on both of the last two Planning and Control Papers. See Question 7 on the December 2000 paper and Question 6 on the June 2000. Answer either/ both of these questions and compare your answers with the outline answers provided in the appendix at the back of the book.

Declining and hostile markets

Much discussion about strategy development and gaining a competitive advantage is concerned with the search for growing and attractive markets. However, many firms are faced not with healthy markets but ones that are mature or even declining. Many organizations assume that the most suitable strategy in this situation is one of strategic withdrawal. This is not necessarily the only strategy available to them and these markets can often be a source of opportunity if the right strategy is selected.

Declining markets

A declining market may be as a result of a variety of factors, often caused by changes in the external environment, for example:

- Development of new technology such as the Internet may replace traditional buying habits.
- Changes in Government policy such as regulations relating to financial services.
- Changing customer needs such as the increase in concern about smoking and the subsequent drop in demand for cigarettes.
- Growing interest in shopping on-line may prompt a decline for traditional retailers.

Aaker (1998), p.239, proposes four alternative strategies for firms facing a declining market:

1. Revitalize market.
2. Encourage other competitors and stay to be the profitable survivor.
3. Milk or harvest.
4. Divest or liquidate.

Revitalization

Depending on the specific market it may be possible to rejuvenate the market to extend the life of the sector. Rejuvenation can be achieved in a variety of ways, as illustrated in Table 7.2.

Method of rejuvenation	Explanation	Example
Table 7.2: Rejuvenating a declining market (Adapted from Aaker, 1998, p.241)		
Seek new markets	This can be achieved by targeting new segments or new geographical areas.	The development of mobile phones to attract teenagers.
Develop new product	New products can make existing products obsolete and speed up the replacement cycle and create growth.	Digital cameras have created a growth in this market.
Find new uses	Seek new uses for existing products to extend its usage.	Kellogg's cornflakes were promoted as suitable for meals other than breakfast.
Rejuvenate product	Changing the mix (i.e. using new methods of distribution, rebranding, promotion or new packaging) can revitalize an existing product.	Blue Nun wine (see below), Lucozade, Polo, Pepperami.
Government policy	Government can stimulate growth by changing policy.	The launch of ISAs (Individual Savings Accounts) stimulated growth in savings products.
Target growing subsegments	Despite the market declining overall it may be possible to identify sub-segments that are growing.	The brewing industry is a mature market and yet 'alcopops' and strong ales are growing segments.

Case history

Blue Nun Wine

Blue Nun is an instantly recognizable brand of wine. However, its popularity has declined rapidly since its peak in popularity in 1985. According to Fellowes (2001): 'Until recently, the mere suggestion of buying a bottle of Blue Nun was likely to induce guffaws and embarrassment.' Langguth Wine and Spirits bought the ailing brand in 1995 with the aim of relaunching and repositioning the brand and increasing global sales. Consumer research revealed that, despite the brand's outdated image, it still held very positive memories for many consumers, particularly those that bought it in the 1970s and associated it with their youth. In order to reposition the brand Langguth has made a number of changes.

- Modern consumer preferences for wine have changed. The original sweet Liebfraumilch no longer appeals and therefore the wine itself has been changed to a Qualitatswein to accommodate consumer preferences for drier wines.
- A whole new range of Blue Nun wines is being launched, including reds and sparkling wines.
- The brand is being targeted at the mainstream consumer who wants an affordable, reliable bottle of wine, not the wine connoisseur. It is positioned on the brand values of fun memories.
- Blue Nun is sold in over 80 countries including most of Europe, the USA, Australia, China, Japan, Taiwan and Singapore. To ensure consistency across countries a 'brand book' containing strict guidelines on the brand message and brand values has been developed.

The rejuvenated brand is apparently being successful. Sales in the USA have doubled in the last two years and are continuing to grow. Over 500,000 cases were sold in the UK last year, where it has been the market leader for the last two years. In the Asian markets in 2000 there was an 18% growth in sales.

Adapted from Fellowes (2001).

Profitable survivor

It may be possible to stay in the market and strengthen ones position as other competitors leave the market. This would mean that despite a shrinking market, a firm would be increasing its market share and therefore this may be a very attractive strategy.

Milk or harvest

This strategy would involve reducing investment in the market. It is likely that this will reduce sales and market share. However, the ability to invest in other more lucrative sectors outweighs this decline. The rate at which a firm milks the market will vary depending on the specific situation. Alternatively a firm may decide to adopt a 'hold' strategy that involves maintaining an adequate level of investment.

Divest or liquidate

When markets are experiencing rapid decline, margins are extremely low, other competitors have achieved a dominant position or where exit barriers can be broken down then the most likely strategy is one of withdrawal, as illustrated in Figure 7.8.

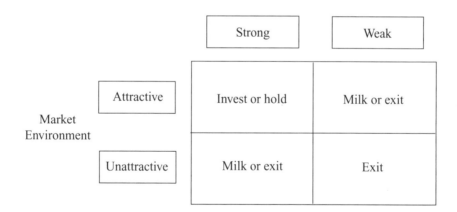

Figure 7.8
Strategies for declining markets (Adapted from Aaker, 1998, p.245)

There are many factors that will influence the choice of strategy for managing a declining market, such as:

- Predicted growth of market.
- Level and intensity of competition.
- Level of exit barriers.
- Business position within the market (strong or weak).
- Relationship with other areas of business – synergy?

147

Hostile markets

Hostile markets are those with low margins, intense competition and over-capacity. Hostile markets may result from (a) declining demand and/or (b) increase in competition. Therefore, they may even be growing markets.

The Windermere study cited in Aaker (1998), p.250-251 identified six stages of hostility as illustrated in Table 7.3.

Table 7.3: Six stages of hostility (Adapted from Aaker, 1998, p.250)	
Stages of hostility	Explanation
1. Margin pressure	This is often due to over-capacity and therefore many competitors seek profitable segments.
2. Share shifts	This may result from acquisitions or loss of share by overpriced competitors.
3. Product proliferation	Competitors try to compete for market share by improving customer value through product proliferation.
4. Self-defeating cost reduction	Due to declining margins firms may concentrate on cost reduction, which in turn may lead to decline in product or service quality.
5. Consolidation and shake-out	This may consist of downsizing, followed by mergers and acquisitions and finally the formation of international players.
6. Rescue	Many markets can emerge from hostility, often through consolidation with fewer competitors present in the market.

Hostile markets may not pass through all these stages in the same sequence. However, this model can help companies to identify and manage hostile markets.

The Windermere study (cited by Aaker, 1998 p.252) suggests that there are five possible strategies for firms operating in hostile markets:

- Focus on large customers.
- Differentiate on reliability.
- Cover broad spectrum of price.
- Turn price into a commodity.
- Have an effective cost structure.

Extended knowledge

Chapter 13 of Aaker (1998) provides a comprehensive discussion of strategies in declining and hostile markets.

Strategic wear-out

There are many examples of companies that once had a successful strategy but have failed to adapt to the changing environment and have therefore suffered from 'strategic wear-out'. Strategic wear out or strategic drift refers to the lack of fit between an organizations strategy and the needs of the marketplace (Figure 7.9). Marks & Spencer is a prime example of a company that is currently trying to overcome the problems of strategic wearout. Their successful strategy of the 1980s and early 1990s is no longer effective. They have lost market share to a new species of retailers that have a much better understanding of customer needs.

According to Davidson (1997), pp.285, there are a number of reasons for strategic wear-out:

- **Market changes**:
    o changing customer needs (e.g. increased interest in environmental issues)
    o developments in distribution such as the Internet.
- **Competition** – from either existing or new competitors.
- **Internal factors**:
    o insufficient investment
    o lack of management control of company costs
    o misguided changes to winning strategy.

Definition

Strategic wear-out

Strategic wear-out occurs when an organization no longer meets customer needs and the pursued strategy is surpassed by competitors, (Drummond & Ensor, 2001).

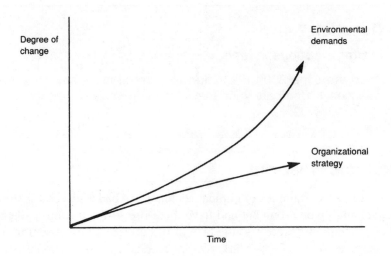

Figure 7.9
Strategic wear-out

In order to avoid strategic wearout companies should:

- Undertake regular and detailed reviews of each element that makes up the external environment
- Identify the ways in which these elements are changing
- Evaluate the impact of these changes on the organization
- Undertake an internal audit to establish the appropriateness of actions both currently and for the future to ensure that customer needs continue to be met.

Activity 7.6

Strategic wear-out

Identify two examples of firms whose strategies are suffering strategic wearout. What factors have led to this strategic drift? To what extent do you think this could be avoided? What, if any, actions are the companies taking to try to rectify their position.

Summary

- One of the greatest challenges for any organization is to develop a coherent and appropriate strategy that builds on their internal resources, exploits external opportunities and provides a distinct competitive advantage.
- Sustainable competitive advantage is not just related to how firms compete but also the basis of competition, where they compete and whom they compete against.
- Porter suggests that there are three generic forms of strategy than can provide a competitive advantage: cost leadership, differentiation or focus. Those companies that fail to consistently pursue one of these generic strategies will become 'stuck in the middle'.
- Davidson has identified ten alternative ways of attaining a sustainable competitive advantage: superior product/service, perceived advantage, global skills, low cost producer, superior competencies, superior assets, scale advantages, attitude advantages, legal advantages and superior relationships.
- Companies can be classified according to their position in the market: market leaders, market challengers, market followers and niche marketers. There are a number of offensive and defensive strategies that firms can pursue either to attack or defend their position.
- The Ansoff matrix is a useful framework for identifying the various growth strategies open to a company: market penetration, market development, product development or diversification.
- Strategic alliances are increasingly been regarded as a means of gaining a sustainable competitive advantage.
- Much writing about strategy development is focused on the search for growing and attractive markets. However, many firms are faced not with healthy markets but with ones that are mature or even declining. Firms must develop coherent strategies to deal with these declining or even hostile markets.
- Companies that once had a successful strategy but have failed to adapt to the changing environment are in danger of suffering from strategic wear-out. This refers to a lack of strategic fit between an organization's strategy and the market's needs.

Further study

Extending knowledge

Bibliography

Aaker D (1998), *Strategic Market Management*, 5th Ed, John Wiley & Sons.

Ansoff H (1957), *Strategies for Diversification*, Harvard Business Review, 25 (5), pp.113-125.

De Bruxelles S (2001), *One-plane outfit puts top airlines to flight*, The Times, 3 March.

Davidson H (1997) *More Offensive Marketing*, Penguin.

Drummond G & Ensor J (2001), *Strategic Marketing Planning and Control*, Butterworth-Heinemann

Fellowes J, (2001) *Message in a Bottle*, Marketing Business, May, pp.16-19.

Financial Times Mastering Strategy (1999), *Five Ways to Grow the Market and Create Value*, Financial Times, 18 October, p.8.

Gomes-Casseres, B, (2000), *Strategy Must Lie at the Heart of Alliances*, Financial Times, *Mastering Management Series* Part 3, 16 October.

Hooley G J, Saunders J A & Piercy N F (1998), *Marketing Strategy and Competitive Positioning*, 2nd Ed, Prentice Hall.

Jobber D (1998), *Principles and Practice of Marketing*, 2nd Ed, McGraw Hill.

Johnson G & Scholes K (1999), *Exploring Corporate Strategy* 5th Ed, Prentice-Hall, pp.13-16 and 241-244.

Kotler P & Singh (1981), cited in Kotler P (2000), *Marketing Management*, The Millennium Edition, Prentice-Hall.

Kotler P, Armstrong G, Saunders J & Wong V (1999), *Principles of Marketing*, 2nd European Ed, Prentice-Hall.

Mazur L (2001a), *The Only Way to Compete Now is with an Alliance*, Marketing, 15 February, p.20.

Mazur L (2001b), *Acquisition Activity is on a High, But In Most Cases the Deals Fail to Deliver*, Marketing, 8 February, p.26.

Porter M (1980), *Competitive Strategy: Techniques for analysing Industries and Competitors*, Free Press.

www.Lexis-Nexis.com

Objectives

By the end of this unit you will:

- Understand and be able to describe the strategic alignment process
- Understand the importance of segmentation in creating competitive advantage
- Be able to discuss the process of segmentation and the various methods of segmenting both consumer and organizational markets
- Be able to discuss the various criteria that will influence segment choice and targeting strategy
- Appreciate the importance of positioning as means of achieving competitive advantage
- Understand the role the marketing mix plays in achieving a specific positioning strategy
- Be able to discuss the various types of branding strategies
- Understand the role of innovation in achieving a competitive advantage and the methods of encouraging an innovative culture
- Understand the importance of building customer relationships
- Be able to discuss ways in which relationships can be built
- Understand the criteria by which strategies can be evaluated

Study guide

- This unit will take you about 5 hours to work through
- We suggest that you take a further 5 hours to do the various activities and questions in this unit.

Introduction

The previous unit identified a number of generic frameworks that could be used to identify various ways of achieving competitive advantage. This unit is concerned with how organizations can convert this generic advantage into a unique and sustainable advantage. A key aspect of developing a successful strategy lies in the ability of an organization to match their internal capabilities with the external market needs. This approach will be discussed and the importance of segmentation, targeting and positioning in helping to achieve a sustainable competitive advantage will be outlined. The marketing mix plays a central role in helping to achieve the desired positioning strategy. The marketing mix has been covered in detail in previous CIM modules at Certificate and Advanced Certificate in Marketing Fundamentals and Marketing Operations. It is assumed you are familiar with all aspects of the mix and therefore this workbook will only highlight the areas with which you should be familiar and concentrate on the specific issues of branding, innovation and new product development and relationship marketing. The unit will then conclude with discussion of the criteria by which organizations can select the most appropriate strategy.

Strategic alignment process

Strategy can be regarded as the matching of an organization's resources and capabilities to the environment in which it operates. This process is sometimes referred to as 'strategic fit'. It is a key step in the strategy development process and ensures that by matching markets, channels and customers with internal assets and competencies a sustainable competitive advantage is developed. It is not enough to just identify unmet customer needs. The company must have the necessary skills and resources to meet these needs. This process is referred to as the strategic alignment process and is illustrated in Table 8.1.

Table 8.1: The Strategic Alignment Process (Adapted from Davidson, 1997, p.82)		
Stage	Process	Explanation
1	Identify utilizable assets	Assets could include brands, property, patents, finance, relationships and scale advantages.
2	Identify utilizable competencies	Competencies relate to skills and may include marketing (e.g. ability to develop new and innovative products), selling (e.g. customer relationship management), operations (e.g. inventory control).
3	Select and rank business opportunities in terms of attractiveness	This involves identifying market opportunities and then developing criteria by which to measure the attractiveness of each option. Portfolio analysis can be used to identify the most attractive strategies. (This will be discussed later in greater detail in relation to segmentation.)
4	Match internal assets (stage 1) and competencies (stage 2) with market opportunities (stage 3)	This process will identify the areas in which it will be most effective for a company to compete.
5	Identify any assets or competencies that need to be strengthened	During the strategic alignment process it may be that market opportunities are identified but the firm lacks the ideal assets and competencies to capitalize on this opportunity. A firm may decide to develop or acquire the necessary competencies to exploit this market (e.g. entering into a strategic alliance, employing new staff, acquiring brands).

For a detailed discussion of assets and competencies refer to the Unit 'Internal analysis'. This process of alignment can also be used to identify suitable market segments and will be discussed further in the next section.

Segmentation, Targeting and Positioning

The process of segmentation, targeting and positioning (STP) plays a critical role in the development of any marketing strategy. Markets consist of individuals, all with different needs and wants, rather than a homogenous mass of customers. Segmentation acknowledges these differences and suggests that a marketer's role is to identify groups of individuals that have similar needs and to develop products/services to meet these needs. In some markets, such as luxury yachts or individually commissioned jewellery, it is possible to adopt the practice of one-to-one marketing where the firm can produce a customized individual product for each and every customer if they so wish. However, for the majority of companies it is not feasible to adopt this practice and therefore they seek out groups of customers that have similar needs and develop products to match their requirements. The practice of segmentation is becoming increasingly important because people today are continuously seeking individualism and looking for products/services that reinforce their own identity. This is in stark contrast to the 1960s where customers were actively seeking out mass produced products. This trend away from mass marketing has been fuelled by three major factors as illustrated in Figure 8.1. Some companies are responding to customer's need s for individuality by adopting a mass customization strategy. For example, Levi jeans offer customers the opportunity to have a customized pair of jeans made to measure. The customer selects the style and fabric, provides their measurements, and Levi tailor-makes their jeans. The challenge for firms today is to strike the right balance between mass marketing (the most cost efficient means of serving the market) and producing tailor made products (meeting individual customer needs.) This is the role of segmentation.

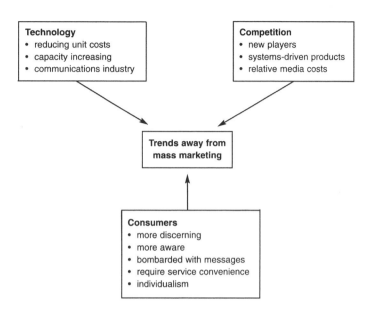

Figure 8.1
Trends away from mass marketing (Adapted from Kotler et al., 1999)

You should already be familiar with the concept of segmentation, the ways in which markets can be segmented, targeting strategies and positioning from previous CIM modules such as Marketing Operations and the Marketing Customer Interface. Therefore, this section does not attempt to provide an in-depth discussion of all the issues relating to STP. Instead, it will identify the issues with which you should already be familiar, direct you to appropriate reading to refresh your memory, highlight key topics and provide examples. There are six major steps in STP, as illustrated in Figure 8.2. Many organizations will probably not approach segmentation in such a formal and systematic manner. However, these six steps provide a structure that can help discussion of the key issues in relation to the process of segmentation.

Segmentation

1. Identify methods of segmentation (bases

↓

2. Develop profiles for these segments

↓

Market Targeting

3. Evaluate market segment attractiveness

↓

4. Select target segments

↓

Market Positioning

5. Identify positioning for each segment

↓

6. Develop marketing mix to achieve the desired positioning

Figure 8.2
Stages of market segmentation, targeting and positioning (Adapted from Kotler et al., 1999)

Exam hint

Segmentation plays an important role in understanding customer needs and identifying opportunities. It is central to any marketing strategy and has therefore featured on many of the past Planning and Control exam papers.

Segmentation

The process of segmentation involves identifying groups of customers that have similar needs and developing products to meet these needs. Doyle (1998), pp.179, identifies a number of benefits of segmentation:

- Better matching of customer needs.
- Enhanced profits.
- Enhanced opportunities for growth.
- Retention of customers.
- Targeted communications.
- Stimulation of innovation.
- Market segment share.

The first stage in the STP process is identifying the most effective means of segmenting the market. It would be possible to segment any market with any type of base. However, the base selected must relate to differences in purchase behaviour. For example, you *could* segment purchasers of coffee according to the colour of their eyes, although eye colour is not relevant to the purchase of coffee. Choice of segmentation base will also be influenced by company resources and competitor activity.

It is important to remember that markets segment themselves. Those companies that segment markets for administrate ease are in danger of failing to understand what drives customers to purchase. There are many different bases that can be used to segment both consumer and organizational markets and these are outlined below.

1. Segmentation bases

Consumer markets

The methods by which consumer markets can be segmented are closely associated with buyer behaviour (covered in Unit 'External analysis'. There are numerous ways of segmenting consumer markets and companies are continuously developing new methods in an attempt to more finely segment their markets. However, there is a general agreement that consumer markets can be segmented by customer characteristics and behavioural characteristics.

Customer characteristics

- **Demographic**- age, gender, income, occupation, education, religion, family life cycle.
- **Geographic**- country, region, county, city size, town.
- **Geodemographic**- this combines information on household location with demographic socioeconomic information e.g. ACORN, FiNPiN.
- **Psychographic**- social class, personality and lifestyle. For example VALS and Taylor Nelson's Monitor Framework are both examples of lifestyle segmentation.

Behavioural characteristics

- Benefits sought.
- Usage frequency (e.g. occasional or regular).
- Usage status (non-user, lapsed user, user).
- Purchase occasion.
- Attitude towards the product.
- Buyer Readiness stage.

It is important that you are familiar with each of these bases and are able to critique and provide examples of each. In the Analysis and Decision major case you will be expected to apply this knowledge in a practical situation. This unit will provide some examples of segmentation bases; however for a detailed discussion refer to extending knowledge for relevant sources.

Extended knowledge

Drummond G & Ensor J (2001), Chapter 4, pp. 52-69, as does Jobber D (1998), Chapter 7, pp.174-182.

Demographic – FLC (family life cycle)

Classifying consumers according to their family circumstances can be a useful method for segmenting many different types of markets. This framework can be helpful for products such as financial services. Earning potential, levels of expenditure and the need for different types of financial services will change as a person moves through this cycle. A modern family life cycle model is illustrated in Figure 8.3.

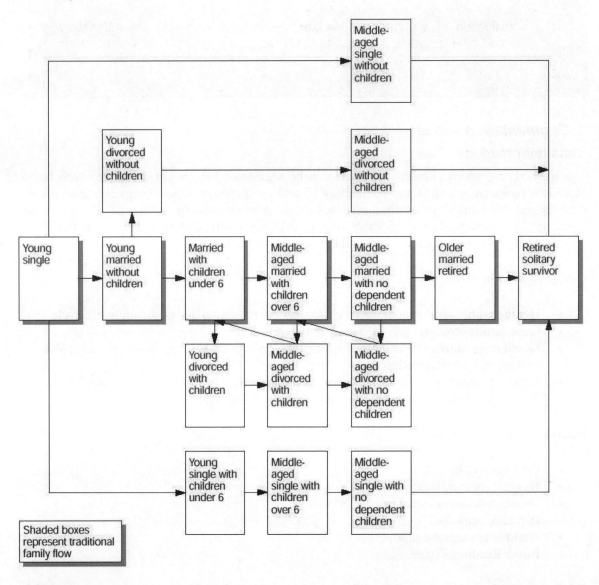

Figure 8.3
A contemporary family life cycle (Adapted from Murphy and Staple, 1979)

Geodemographics – ACORN (A Classification of Residential Neighborhoods)

Figure 8.4 illustrates the various categories into which consumers are divided according to the type of housing in which they live.

ACORN Types		% of households in GB	ACORN Groups
	ACORN Category A: THRIVING		
1.1	Wealthy Suburbs, Large Detached Houses	2.2%	1 Wealthy Achievers, Suburban Areas
1.2	Villages with Wealthy Commuters	2.8%	
1.3	Mature Affluent Home Owning Areas	2.7%	
1.4	Affluent Suburbs, Older Families	3.4%	
1.5	Mature, Well-Off Suburbs	2.9%	
2.6	Agricultural Villages, Home Based Workers	1.5%	2 Affluent Greys, Rural Communities
2.7	Holiday Retreats, Older People, Home Based Workers	0.7%	
3.8	Home Owning Areas, Well-Off Older Residents	1.5%	3 Prosperous Pensioners, Retirement Areas
3.9	Private Flats, Elderly People	1.3%	
	ACORN Category B: EXPANDING		
4.10	Affluent Working Families with Mortgages	1.8%	4 Affluent Executives, Family Areas
4.11	Affluent Working Couples with Mortgages, New Homes	1.3%	
4.12	Transient Workforces, Living at their Place of Work	0.3%	
5.13	Home Owning Family Areas	2.5%	5 Well-Off Workers, Family Areas
5.14	Home Owning Family Areas, Older Children	2.6%	
5.15	Families with Mortgages, Younger Children	1.9%	
	ACORN Category C: RISING		
6.16	Well-Off Town & City Areas	1.1%	6 Affluent Urbanites, Town & City Areas
6.17	Flats & Mortgages, Singles & Young Working Couples	0.9%	
6.18	Furnished Flats & Bedsits, Younger Single People	0.5%	
7.19	Apartments, Young Professional Singles & Couples	1.4%	7 Prosperous Professionals, Metropolitan Areas
7.20	Gentrified Multi-Ethnic Areas	1.1%	
8.21	Prosperous Enclaves, Highly Qualified Executives	0.9%	8 Better-Off Executives, Inner City Areas
8.22	Academic Centres, Students & Young Professionals	0.6%	
8.23	Affluent City Centre Areas, Tenements & Flats	0.7%	
8.24	Partially Gentrified Multi-Ethnic Areas	0.8%	
8.25	Converted Flats & Bedsits, Single People	1.0%	
	ACORN Category D: SETTLING		
9.26	Mature Established Home Owning Areas	3.4%	9 Comfortable Middle Agers, Mature Home Owning Areas
9.27	Rural Areas, Mixed Occupations	3.4%	
9.28	Established Home Owning Areas	3.9%	
9.29	Home Owning Areas, Council Tenants, Retired People	3.0%	
10.30	Established Home Owning Areas, Skilled Workers	4.3%	10 Skilled Workers, Home Owning Areas
10.31	Home Owners in Older Properties, Younger Workers	3.2%	
10.32	Home Owning Areas with Skilled Workers	3.3%	
	ACORN Category E: ASPIRING		
11.33	Council Areas, Some New Home Owners	3.7%	11 New Home Owners, Mature Communities
11.34	Mature Home Owning Areas, Skilled Workers	3.3%	
11.35	Low Rise Estates, Older Workers, New Home Owners	2.9%	
12.36	Home Owning Multi-Ethnic Areas, Young Families	1.0%	12 White Collar Workers, Better-Off Multi-Ethnic Areas
12.37	Multi-Occupied Town Centres, Mixed Occupations	2.0%	
12.38	Multi-Ethnic Areas, White Collar Workers	1.0%	
	ACORN Category F: STRIVING		
13.39	Home Owners, Small Council Flats, Single Pensioners	2.3%	13 Older People, Less Prosperous Areas
13.40	Council Areas, Older People, Health Problems	2.1%	
14.41	Better-Off Council Areas, New Home Owners	2.0%	14 Council Estate Residents, Better-Off Homes
14.42	Council Areas, Young Families, Some New Home Owners	2.7%	
14.43	Council Areas, Young Families, Many Lone Parents	1.6%	
14.44	Multi-Occupied Terraces, Multi-Ethnic Areas	0.7%	
14.45	Low Rise Council Housing, Less Well-Off Families	1.8%	
14.46	Council Areas, Residents with Health Problems	2.1%	
15.47	Estates with High Unemployment	1.3%	15 Council Estate Residents, High Unemployment
15.48	Council Flats, Elderly People, Health Problems	1.1%	
15.49	Council Flats, Very High Unemployment, Singles	1.2%	
16.50	Council Areas, High Unemployment, Lone Parents	1.5%	16 Council Estate Residents, Greatest Hardship
16.51	Council Flats, Greatest Hardship, Many Lone Parents	0.9%	
17.52	Multi-Ethnic, Large Families, Overcrowding	0.5%	17 People in Multi-Ethnic, Low-Income Areas
17.53	Multi-Ethnic, Severe Unemployment, Lone Parent	1.0%	
17.54	Multi-Ethnic, High Unemployment, Overcrowding	0.3%	

Figure 8.4
The ACORN

Question 8.1

Geodemographic segmentation

Answer the following question from the December 1999 exam paper and then compare your answer with the CIM specimen answer.

What advantages would a geodemographic segmentation approach offer a financial services organization, expanding into the insurance market, using direct marketing techniques?

Case history

FRuitS

The financial division of NOP, the market research group, and Berry Consulting, a database and modelling company, has developed a method of segmenting financial service markets according to lifestyle. They have segmented people according to a) life stage, b) financial strength and c) their pattern of purchasing of financial products, and have produced a typology based on a fruit bowl.

The FRuitS model has been developed from research that examines the financial behaviour of consumers through 60,000 interviews each year. The following segments have been identified.

Plums (10% of UK population

Typically male. Aged 44-65, living in the south, married, university educated, high income (over £35,000), homeowner with 2+ cars. Has a strong financial portfolio, 3.5 times more likely to own shares and twice as likely to have a credit card.

Pears (9% of UK population)

Slightly older than plums, more likely to be retired. Income of £7,500 to £17,500. More cautious, but twice as likely to own stocks and shares. Interested in savings, but not in the market for mortgages or bank loans.

Cherries (14% of UK population)

Around 35-54 with family, usually own their own home and 2 cars and have an income over £17,500. Prime candidates for mortgages, bank loans and credit cards.

Apples (12% of UK population)

Similar age to cherries, but income under £17,500. Likely to live in the north, Midlands or Wales, to be married, have one car, be self-employed or possibly working part-time. Moderate savings and good prospects for mortgages, loans and personal pensions, since they are less likely to be in a company pension scheme.

Dates (15% of UK population)

More likely to be female, 55+, not educated beyond age 14. Widowed or retired, they live alone as owner/occupiers or in council housing. Income up to £7,500, no car, and are more likely to have life insurance and a building society account.

Oranges (16% of UK population)

Aged 16-34. Single, most likely to be in private rented accommodation, are either unemployed or studying, with income up to £7,500. Oranges are interesting for their potential.

Grapes (13% of UK population)

Coming in bunches, they are more likely to live in households with five members or more. Aged 15 – 55 they're usually working but with relatively low incomes immediately consumed. Candidates for loans.

Lemons (11% of UK population)

Like dates, they are typically older, single or widowed, living on their own, with income below £7,500. But they are worse off, being half as likely to have household insurance, and unlikely to have loans, cards or personal pensions.

Adapted from Anon, (1996), www.Lexis-Nexis.com

Case history

Behavioural segmentation – Internet shopping

Shopping on-line is still a relatively new phenomenon. As consumers get into the swing of clicking, rather than queuing for their goods, they develop new shopping habits – habits that retailers are keen to cash in on.

Last year a survey by market analysts Datamonitor found that web consumers have habits quite different from those shopping on the high street. On-line customers fall into certain categories, exhibiting characteristics which identify them as a particular 'breed' of e-shopper.

Despite the wealth of dot.com publicity and advertisements many people are still very wary of making a purchase on-line. Although 80% of respondents had browsed the net for anything from CDs to cars, less than a third had actually taken the plunge and ordered on-line, and even fewer – just 15% – had paid over the Internet.

But, according to the report, all this is about to change. Falling prices mean that computer ownership will continue to increase, the proliferation of interactive TV, games consoles and WAP phones will all fuel the growth in on-line shopping. More than 70% of Europeans already own at least one interactive device and it is thought that, by 2004, more than three-quarters of all households with PCs will be connected to the Internet, increasing the potential on-line shopping population.

Overall, the proportion of Internet users who buy on-line is expected to rise from 25% to 70% over the next four years.

Once consumers progress from starter to expert they will inevitably spend more time, and money, on the Internet. Datamonitor spoke to a total of 12,000 people, aged from 18 upwards, in the UK, Sweden, Germany, France and Spain. According to their findings, we are all shopping animals. Which one are you?

The rhino
Not always, but mostly, elderly, with 61% of the group being over 65. Rhinos tend to belong to a relatively low income household, often due to retirement. This consumer wants to see, feel – and if possible sniff – their groceries before they hand over the ready cash. In fact, cash is the preferred method of payment and the thought of putting credit card details on to a computer and clicking on a 'mouse' which sends them to someone they've never met or spoken to is enough to send even the toughest, most thick-skinned rhino charging into the bushes for cover. Only a third of all rhinos have gone on-line at least once.

The puma
At the opposite end of the shopping jungle lies the puma. Usually young, often single, with a high income and fearless disposition, these predators want their shopping delivered yesterday and aren't afraid to try out new technology. If you can get it on-line, they'll buy it, anything from the latest Nike (or possibly Puma?) trainers to a new car. They'll even hunt for food on-line – provided it can be delivered within the hour – and can usually be relied on to try anything once. However, this big cat should remember what curiosity did and be a little more cautious when handing over their financial details if they don't want to get their claws burned.

The gazelle
Generally 30-somethings, and usually computer literate, these are the lowest spending group in the younger categories. Youthful and energetic, yes, but the gazelle has a

more timid approach to shopping on the Internet than the puma. Moving in herds, often with a young family in tow, they prefer to hang back, saving their hard-earned cash for the things they really need. They're not averse to the web, and will occasionally dip their toe in the water, but they'd rather wait to see if it's safe before wading in. Their average on-line spend in the past six months was £170.

The gorilla

Still preferring to spend most of their substantial income on the high street, this group is not as conservative as the rhinos and is open to new suggestions. They will eventually get into the swing of shopping on the Net, but only after carefully weighing up the pros and cons. Classic gorilla behaviour involves starting slowly with low-risk, familiar items – something from Amazon perhaps – and then moving on to bigger transactions as confidence builds. Despite being financially better off than rhinos only 18% of this group, had logged on to the Internet.

The jackal

This pack animal has got the Internet sussed and spends most of their day persuading other, less adventurous types, to try out the latest technology. If they're not surfing for a new coat or digging up a bargain CD, they're ordering groceries at home and breathing a contented sigh at not having to fight their way through the crowds in the high street. Around 10 years younger than gorillas or rhinos, jackals spend approximately 10 times more money on Internet shopping – an impressive average of £440 over six months.

Source: Adapted from Eames, L (2000) www.Lexis-Nexis.com

Activity 8.1

VALS

The VALS framework (values, attitudes and lifestyles) classifies consumers according to their nine lifestyle groups, as shown in Figure 8.5.

Developmental stage	Grouping (% of US population)
Need-driven	**Survivors.** This is a disadvantaged group who are likely to be withdrawn, despairing and depressed (4%). **Sustainers** are another disadvantaged group, but they are working hard to escape poverty (7%).
Outer-directed	**Belongers** are characterized as being conventional, nostalgic, reluctant to try new ideas and generally conservative (33%). **Emulators** are upwardly mobile, ambitious and status conscious (10%). **Achievers.** This group enjoys life and makes things happen (23%).
Inner-directed	**'I-am-me'** tend to be young, self engrossed and act on whims (5%). **Experientials** wish to enjoy as wide a range of life experiences as possible (7%). **Societally conscious** have a clear sense of social responsibility and wish to improve society (9%).
Nirvana	**Integrateds** are completely mature psychologically and combine the positive elements of outer and inner directedness (2%).

Figure 8.5
The VALs framework (Developed by Arnold Mitchell at the Stanford Research Institute)

Visit the VALS website at the following address, complete the mini-questionnaire and obtain the results. If possible, discuss your results with fellow students.

http://future.sri.com/VALS/VALSindex.shtml

To what extent do you think this framework is helpful in segmenting markets?
In which markets do you think this type of segmentation may be helpful?
What are the limitations of this type of framework?

Question 8.2

Lifestyle segmentation

Answer the following question from the December 1998 exam paper and then compare your answer with the outline provided in the paper.

What advantages do lifestyle segmentation techniques offer over other methods of segmenting a market? For an organization operating internationally what difficulties may they encounter using this approach?

Organizational markets

The methods used to segment consumer markets are not appropriate for organizational markets due to the complexity of purchase decisions and the decision-making group. Organizational buying behaviour was discussed in the unit 'External analysis'. Organizational markets can be segmented according to macro factors and micro factors. Figure 8.6 illustrates the major variables for segmenting organizational markets and examples of each. You must be able to discuss each of these variables. Refer to extended knowledge for relevant sources.

Variables	Examples
Macro segmentation	
■ Size of organization	Large, medium or small
■ Geographic location	Local, national, European Union, worldwide
■ Industrial sector	Retail, engineering, financial services
■ End market served	Defined by product or service
Micro segmentation	
■ Choice criteria	Quality, delivery, value in use, supplier reputation, price
■ Structure of decision-making unit	Complexity, hierarchical, effectiveness
■ Decision-making process	Long, short, low or high conflict
■ Buy class	New task, straight or modified re-buy
■ Importance of purchasing	High or low importance
■ Type of purchasing organization	Matrix, centralized, decentralized
■ Innovation level of organization	Innovative, follower, laggard
■ Purchasing strategy	Optimizer, satisfier
■ Personal attributes	Age, educational background, risk taker/adverse, confidence level

Figure 8.6
Organizational macro and micro segmentation. (Reproduced from Drummond & Ensor. 2001, p. 80)

Extended knowledge

For further discussion of the bases used to segment organizational markets refer to:

Drummond & Ensor (2001) Chapter 3, pp. 78-79

Jobber (1998) Chapter 7, pp.182-188.

2. Development of Profiles

Once the most effective bases have been identified the next step is to develop profiles of the resulting segments. In many cases companies will use not just one base for segmenting the market they may use a combination of factors.

Targeting

Targeting consists of two stages: evaluating the attractiveness of the segments and selecting a market coverage strategy.

3. Which segments to target?

Once appropriate segments have been identified the next step is to decide which of these segments to serve. There are two issues to consider: the attractiveness of each segment and the extent to which an organization can match the needs of the segment.

Segment attractiveness

According to Hooley et al. (1998) segment/market attractiveness can be assessed by the criteria illustrated in Table 8.2.

Table 8.2: Factors to consider when evaluating market segments (Adapted from Hooley et al. 1998 pp.301-307)	
Market factors	• Segment size • Segment growth rate • Stage of industry evolution • Predictability • Price elasticity and sensitivity • Bargaining power of customers • Seasonality and cyclical pattern of demand
Economic and technological factors	• Barriers to entry • Barriers to exit • Bargaining power of suppliers • Level of technology utilization • Investment required Margins available
Competitive factors	• Competitive intensity • Quality of competition • Threat of substitution • Degree of differentiation
Environmental factors	• Exposure to economic fluctuations • Exposure to political and legal factors • Degree of regulation • Social acceptability and physical environment impact

Determining organizational strengths

A market segment may be regarded as attractive, but if the company does not have the necessary resources and skills to serve this segment then it is not going to be suitable. Organizational strengths can be broken down into three areas, as illustrated in Table 8.3.

Table 8.3: Criteria for assessing company strengths (Adapted from Hooley et al., 1998, pp.309-312)	
Current market position	• Relative market share • Rate of change of market share • Exploitable market assets • Unique and valued products and services
Economic and technological position	• Relative cost position • Capacity utilization • Technological position
Capability profile	• Management strength and depth • Marketing strength • Forward or backward integration

Aligning market opportunities with company strengths

Once the attractive segments and internal company strengths have been identified it is necessary to match them in order to identify the most appropriate segments to pursue. This is the same process as strategic alignment (discussed in the last unit.) Portfolio analysis can play an important role in this process. Portfolio analysis, discussed in the Unit 'Auditing tools', has traditionally been used to summarize current business activity and, to a lesser degree, the alternative business investment opportunities open to a multi-product company. However, they can equally well be used to help identify target markets. The process is similar to that explained in unit 'Auditing tools' when discussing the plotting of strategic business units on the General Electric model:

1. Identify the appropriate criteria for measuring (a) segment attractiveness and (b) company strength.
2. Weight each factor according to its importance.
3. Evaluate each criterion (for both segment attractiveness and company strength) using a scale of, say, 1-5, where '5' is excellent and '1' is poor.
4. Calculate an overall score for (a) segment attractiveness and (b) company strength for each segment under investigation.
5. Plot these scores on a multi-factor portfolio matrix as illustrated in Figure 8.7.

(Refer to unit 'Auditing tools' for full details of this process.)

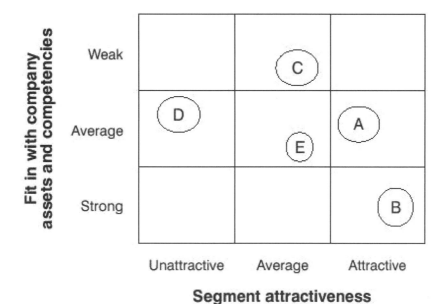

Figure 8.7
Adapted Shell Directional Policy Matrix applied to target market selection (Shell, 1975)

In reality many organizations select target markets using a more informal process than the one outlined above. In many cases there are subjective factors that that most also be taken into consideration, such as:

- Does it create a sustainable market position?
- Is it compatible with the mission statement?
- Is it consistent with organizational culture and values?
- Can the current organizational structure serve the proposed market?
- Does it facilitate an innovative approach to market entry?
-

(Adapted from Drummond & Ensor, 2001, p. 181.)

4. Market coverage strategies

Once the attractive segments have been identified it is necessary to decide which targeting strategy to pursue. Kotler et al. (1999) suggest that there are three broad approaches that can be adopted:

- **Undifferentiated marketing**: This is sometimes referred to as mass marketing and involves producing one product that is designed to appeal to all segments. In today's highly fragmented markets it is rare that this strategy is appropriate.
- **Differentiated marketing**: This involves developing a different product for each different segment. For example, Ford has identified a number of different segments with different requirements for cars and therefore produces different cars to meet the needs of each segment.
- **Focused marketing**: Companies adopting a focused strategy select one or a few segments on which to concentrate. For example, Morgan cars adopt a focus strategy concentrating on sports car enthusiasts.

Positioning

Once the target markets have been identified it is necessary to clearly position the product or service in the marketplace. The aim of a company is to identify on what basis they are to compete, and then to position their product or service clearly and uniquely in the minds of their customers. For example, Stella Artois has successfully positioned itself as 'reassuringly expensive' in the UK, despite being a relatively inexpensive lager in France. According to Kotler et al. (1999) a brand can be positioned using the following associations:

- product attributes
- usage occasions
- users
- activities
- personality
- origin
- competitors
- product class
- symbol

According to Jobber (1998) there are four factors that are critical to successful positioning:

- **Clarity**: the positioning strategy must be clear and simple – for example 'Have a break, Have a Kit Kat'.
- **Credibility**: the differential advantage must be credible in the minds of the target market.
- **Consistency**: it is important that the target market receives consistent messages about a product. Rover has been criticized for failing to identify a clear position because there has been a lack of consistency over the last few years.

Competitiveness: the basis on which a product is to be positioned must exceed what the competitors provide.

Perceptual maps can prove to be very valuable when researching customer perceptions of products and services. Perceptual maps, which are based on two axes that represent key attributes, enable a company to assess where their product sits relative to the competition. They can also identify any possible gaps in the market. Figure 8.8 illustrates a perceptual map for breakfast products and indicates that there was a gap in the market for a product that appealed to children but could be 'eaten on the hoof'. Kellogg's filled this gap when they launched their Frosties and Coco-pops cereal bars.

Sit down Breakfast

Coco-pops,
Rice Krispies, etc

Branflakes,
Cornflakes etc

Opportunity

Nutri grain
cereal bars etc

'Eaten on the hoof'

Figure 8.8
A Perceptual map of breakfast products

A number of brands have failed to establish clear positions in the minds of the customer. These positioning mistakes may be as a result of any of the following:

- **Confused positioning**: the brand fails to establish a clear position in the customer's mind relative to the competitors.
- **Underpositioning**: customers cannot see any significant advantages of this product
- **Overpositioned**: positioning of a product is so focused that customers fail to appreciate that the brand covers a wider product range.

Extended knowledge

For further coverage of positioning and perceptual maps refer to: Drummond & Ensor (2001), Chapter 9, pp. 181-188.

For an interesting overview of segmentation refer to: Doyle (1998), Chapter 3.

Question 8.4

Segmentation, targeting and positioning – mini-case

Refer to the mini-case for December 2000 – Freeplay Energy. Answer question **1b only** and then compare your answer with the outline answer provided in the appendix at the back of the book.

6. The marketing mix

The final stage of the STP process relates to the development of the marketing mix to achieve the desired positioning. You should already be fully conversant with all elements of the extended marketing mix from previous CIM Modules such as Marketing Fundamentals and Marketing Operations. This workbook is not going to discuss in detail each element of the mix. Instead it will highlight the areas with which you should already be familiar and concentrate on those aspects that are of particular relevance to the Planning and Control module.

Extended knowledge

If you wish to revisit the marketing mix refer to the following texts, which all contain separate chapters on each element of the mix.

Davidson (1997).

Doyle (1998).

Jobber (1998).

Branding

Branding has traditionally been dealt with as an aspect of 'product' within the marketing mix. However, it is increasingly being recognized that brands can be very powerful and can in fact be the driving force of a successful marketing strategy. For example, the Virgin brand has enabled Richard Branson to enter many and varied markets due to its brand equity. Richard Branson's greatest asset is probably the Virgin brand.

Definition

Brand equity

A set of assets and liabilities linked to a brand's name and symbol that add to or subtract from the value provided by a product or service to a firm and/or that firm's customers (Aaker, 1998, p.173).

Brand equity is the sum of:

- brand awareness
- brand associations
- perceived quality
- brand loyalty

(Aaker, 1998, p.173).

Benefits of branding

The benefits of branding are well documented in a wide range of sources. Doyle (1998) suggests four ways in which strong brands generate value for companies.

- Strong brands usually obtain price premiums from consumers or resellers.
- Strong brands obtain higher market shares.
- Because of customer loyalty, successful brands generate more stable and less risky earnings streams.
- Successful brands offer avenues for further growth.

Brand valuation

Many companies are beginning to realize the value of their brands and are looking for ways to quantify this value. According to Doyle (1998) there are five main methods of valuing brands:

- **Price premium valuation** – the price premium over unbranded products is used as the basis for brand valuation.
- **Incremental sales valuation** – if brands achieve higher sales than unbranded products these incremental sales can be used to value the brand.
- **Replacement cost value** – the estimated cost of developing a similar brand.
- **Stock market valuation** – the residual value once physical assets, industry factors and other intangible assets have been removed.
- **Future earnings valuation** – probably the most appropriate method. This is where the discounted present value of future earnings attributable to the brand is estimated.

No doubt the debate as to how best to value brands will continue.

Extended knowledge

For further information on valuing brands refer to: Doyle (1998), Chapter 6, p.193-194. and Hooley et al., Chapter 121, p.120-123.

Branding strategies

There are a number of alternative branding strategies that can be adopted. The four main strategies are illustrated in Table 8.4.

Table 8.4: Alternative branding strategies (Adapted from Doyle, 1998, p.167)		
Strategy	Explanation	Examples
Company brand	Firms retain the company name for their brand across their portfolio. This allows for economies of scale, strong image and provides reassurance to customers if moving into a new market. Problems may occur if a poor product detracts from brand image and organic growth can be more difficult by moving into new market segments (i.e. how far can the brand be stretched?)	Virgin Cadbury's
Individual brand names (multi-brands)	Each product has a unique brand name. This allows companies to cope with increasingly segmented markets, facilitates innovation and creative marketing. Companies can provide products of differing standards and quality without damaging their brand image. This strategy can be very costly and risky.	Proctor and Gamble with Ariel, Daz and Bold Unilever with Cif, Cha's Teashops, Persil, Domestos
Company and individual brand	This uses both the company name and an individual brand name. This strategy benefits from association with the company but enables firms to cope with increasingly segmented markets. It is difficult to enter niche segments with this strategy and the failure of one brand may impact on the overall brand image.	Vauxhall Astra, Vectra and Corsa Kelloggs Rice Krispies, Cornflakes and Coco-pops
Range branding	Products are grouped and each group has a separate brand name. This provides firms with the increased opportunity to enter new market segments with a new range brand. They can then capitalize on this brand by launching under this brand name	RHM – Sharwoods and Bisto Heinz Weight Watchers

In reality companies can use a combination of branding strategies. There are a number of factors that will influence choice of branding such as the number of products and product lines and their differential advantage, competitor strategies, target market characteristics and of course the level of available resources.

Case history

Banking on a new identity

Banks have spent decades convincing us that our money is safe. Why is it that many of them have created completely new identities for their Internet offerings? The Co-operative bank with Smile, Abbey National with Cahoot and Halifax with IF (intelligent finance) have all invested a great deal of time and money in building new brands from scratch. There are two main reasons as to why these banks have opted for a multi-brand strategy:

Attracting a different customer

By adopting a different brand name it was hoped that non-users would be attracted to the brand. Abbey National has used Cahoot to target a different, and indeed a more affluent, customer base, and the crossover between Cahoot and Abbey National customers is only 1%. Therefore they are not cannibalizing their existing sales.

Creating a different identity
Many banks have suffered from poor reputations and did not want to tarnish the image of their new operations with this reputation. For example, when the Prudential launched Egg they were left with no choice but to give it a different identity, given the problems in the financial service industry, (for example the pensions mis-selling scandal).

However, there are some limitations to this strategy:

Focus on security
The key for financial service organizations is that individuals feel they are dealing with a company that provides them with security. All the banks launching on-line banks have found the need to reassure potential customers of the link to the parent brand.

From on-line to high street
Recent reports have suggested that Egg is to establish a 'real world' presence, possibly through a concession in branches of Boots. Maybe they are recognizing that the Internet is not a market (it is a channel), and that customers want to use a variety of channels that are integrated rather than a purely Internet based offering.

Adapted from Murphy (2001), www.Lexis-Nexis.com

Brand extensions

One of the benefits of branding lies in the ability to launch new products on the back of existing ones. Traditionally brands tended to confine themselves to certain product areas. However, there are many examples of companies that are stretching their brands into unrelated areas, for example Nike is moving to consumer electronics, Virgin is selling cars and Coca-Cola has launched a new range of urban clothing. The success of these ventures will be influenced by the 'stretchability' of the brand. For example, the Virgin brand's core values appear to be transferable into a number of unrelated markets. However, if you think of Coca-Cola you think of a brown fizzy drink and it is difficult to see how these core values can be transferred into the clothing market (Tomkins, 2000). The same principle could be applied to Guiness, where the brand is also the product, and the brand is therefore less elastic. The factors to consider when thinking about brand extensions are:

- Does the brand fit the new product class?
- Does the brand add value to the offering in the new product class?
- Will the extension enhance the brand name and image?

(Doyle, 1998, p.225.)

Activity 8.2

Stretchability of the Virgin brand

Visit the Virgin website at *www.virgin.com*. Consider the wide range of markets that the Virgin brand has entered and answer the following questions:

- Why do you think Virgin has been able to successfully enter unrelated markets?
- To what extent do you think the problems associated with Virgin Trains have had an impact on the Virgin brand?

Case history

Unilever

Unilever is attempting to exploit some of its leading brands by stretching them into new markets. Unilever has set up a home-cleaning and laundry business in West London, called Myhome, whose services are branded with the Persil and Cif names. It has also launched men's barbershops in Oxford Street and Kingston that carry the name of its Lynx brand.

'Unilever's trial domestic cleansing service is a good example of the radical thinking necessary to enter new markets. It means a more intelligent understanding of what a brand's core meaning is – rather than just a literal knowledge of what it does – on the part of the marketer. Unilever seems to have come to realize that its offer is not "household cleaning products", but "clean houses". It's like the old marketing saying that Black & Decker defines its business not as selling drills, but selling holes.'

Myhome chief executive David Ball says Unilever has recognized that services will be an important part of the future for the group. The intention is to expand Myhome, which already has 150 employees, into other parts of the UK and abroad. Unilever already has a Surf Laundry Cleaning operation in India and has a company called Riverstone in the USA that provides similar services.

'People have more disposable income and as such are looking at spending it in a trade-off to create time,' says Ball. He argues that Myhome will build the standing of the Persil and Cif brands while at the same time not encroach on retail sales of the products.

The initial concept for Myhome came out of a Unilever working group on brand extensions. Given that Unilever is moving into service businesses on a number of fronts, it has what it refers to internally as a Quality Time team, drawn from the new service businesses, which shares learning and best practice.

Adapted from Gray (2001), www.Lexis-Nexis.com

Question 8.5

Branding issues

Answer question 5 on the June 2000 Planning and Control Exam and compare your answer with the outline provided in the appendix at the back of the book.

Repositioning

As markets change and new opportunities arise it may be necessary to reposition a brand to align it with the new opportunities. Brands may also require repositioning because they have been either underpositioned or over positioned or suffer from a confused positioning. Lucozade was one of the first brands that successfully repositioned its brand from a drink for unhealthy old people to an energy drink for healthy active young people. According to Doyle (1998) p188 there are a number of ways in which brands can be repositioned:

- **Real positioning** – the actual brand is changed, for example Skoda cars.
- **Psychological positioning** – the company seeks to change customer's beliefs about a brand. For example Pepperami.
- **Competitive depositioning** – firms can try to alter beliefs about competitors' products and suggest they are inferior. Many on-line banks are using this strategy.
- **Reweighting values** – buyers may be persuaded to attach a greater importance to certain values in which the brand is market leader. For example, the benefits of drinking bottled water with added calcium have been publicized.
- **Neglected values** – sometimes new choice criteria can be introduced to buyers. The Co-operative Bank is positioned on ethical issues, which in the past were irrelevant to most customers.
- **Changing preferences** – it may be possible to switch buying preferences.
- **Augmenting the product** – a brand may be enhanced by offering additional services such as warranties and after-sales service.

Case history

Apple

Apple is a good example of a brand that has successfully repositioned itself. The brand's early success was built on innovation, design and product capability. However, they became complacent and allowed Microsoft and IBM to steal their customers and market share. It deserted its core mass consumer market and lost sight of what it stood for and its customers' needs. By 1998 Apple's situation was so bad that it lost £690 million in a single quarter.

In an attempt to turn the business around the Apple founder, Steve Jobs, returned to the company and set out to undertake a fundamental review of the business and to refocus on Apple's core values. The result was the iMac, launched in 1998. 'The Internet was opening up and, as well as looking attractive and different, the iMac was a great tool to address a sector we had lost our way in' says European Marketing Communications Manager Alan Hely.

Revenue in 2001 is expected to be in the region of £4.15 billion. Market share in the UK rose from 1.5% in 1999 to 2.7% in November 2000. Apple is continuing to innovate and have realized that rarely does one product save a company.

Source: www.Lexis-Nexis.com

Question 8.6

Brand repositioning strategy

Answer Question 2 on the December 2000 Planning and Control question on the repositioning of a charity and then compare your answer with the outline provided in the appendix at the back of the book.

Global brands

Firms are increasingly adopting global branding strategies in an attempt to benefit from economies of scale and consistent messages and images throughout the world. For a detailed discussion of global brands refer to the CIM International Marketing module.

Case history

Jif to Cif

Unilever is renaming cleaning cream Jif as 'Cif' in an attempt to align the brand across the globe. The move formed part of Unilever's strategy of paring its brand range down from 1,600 to 400. The company is set to throw £1 billion behind marketing its core brands.

Jif is known as Cif in more than 80% of markets where the Lever Bros product is sold. The Jif brand until recently was available in the UK, Northern Ireland and Holland, among other markets. Jif was replaced in stores in January in the UK, and other markets will follow throughout this year. The UK launch of Cif will be supported by a £2 million TV campaign created by Lowe Lintas, as well as by direct mail and in-store activity. The product logo and range will be unchanged.

A spokeswoman for Unilever says: 'Cif is the most widely used brand name for Jif around the world. The name change brings Cif closer to becoming a global brand behind which resources can be marshalled, so enabling us to innovate better and faster to meet consumers' needs.'

Source: Marketing Week (2000), www.Lexis-Nexis.com

Question 8.7

Pan-European branding

Answer the following question from the June 1999 exam paper and then compare your answer with the outline provided in the paper.

> Your organization is a large confectionery manufacturer operating in Europe. You have been asked to write a report outlining and evaluating the various strategic options available for pan-European branding.

Question 8.8

easyJet branding strategy – mini-case

A compulsory question on branding was asked as part of the mini-case on the December 1999 Planning and Control Exam paper. Read the easyJet mini-case provided in the paper and answer the following question:

> easyJet have decided to develop a group of companies beginning with the cybercafe concept. You have been asked to provide advice on issues that need to be considered when making decisions regarding the organization's branding strategy, for the group as a whole and for the 'easycafe' concept in particular.

Now compare your answer with the CIM specimen answer.

Innovation and new product development

Innovation has been referred to as the' lifeblood' of an organization. A company must continuously seek real product and marketing improvements in order to continuously satisfy customers and fend off competitors. Innovation is most often associated with new product development. However, this is only part of the equation and innovation relates to changes in products, processes and practices. Janszen (2000) define innovations as: 'The commercialization of something new, which may be:

- A new technology;
- A new application in the form of a new product, service or process;
- A new market or market segment
- A new organizational form or a new management approach;

Or a combination of two or more of these elements.'

Many organizations are striving to develop organizational cultures that encourage innovation. For example, in 1999 Proctor and Gamble announced a major internal restructuring, sacking 13% of the workforce to streamline management and speed up decision-making. Innovation teams were set up within the company and the management of new ideas was passed to new business managers rather than existing businesses. These changes resulted in the successful launch of Swiffer, Febreze and Dryel.

Innovation is not the same as invention. There are very few 'inventors' that have successfully invented a commercial business opportunity, notable exceptions being James Dyson, Bill Hewlett and Dave Packard. 'Inventors' rarely develop innovations that change markets, make fortunes and change the way the world operates. Innovation is led by commercial application, whilst invention is led by the scientific process.

New product development (NPD)

It is apparent that new product development is a key aspect of the innovation process. The reality of new product launches is that the majority is not unique or novel. Many of the NPD launches are variations of existing products. Booz et al. (1982) identified four types of new products:

- New to the world.
- New product lines or line additions.
- Product revision.
- Reposition.

There is much risk attached to new product development. Research in the USA found that less than 1% of products launched in 1998 achieved $100 million of sales in their first year. More than two-thirds failed in their first year.

Failure of new products

There are a number of reasons that may account for the high failure rate of new products. Drummond & Ensor (2001) suggest the following:

- under-investment
- failure to deliver customer benefits
- forecasting errors
- internal politics
- industry response.

To this list could also be added

- lack of management enthusiasm
- the NPD process too slow and beaten to market by competitors.

Process

Traditionally companies adopted a linear process to NPD, as illustrated in figure 8.9. However, it is still a useful framework for ensuring that all the major factors have been reviewed and considered. Firms are facing the dilemma of ensuring that new product ideas are assessed rigorously but at the same time getting new ideas to market first. The challenge facing organizations is to develop NPD processes that are still rigorous and yet enable firms to get to market quickly. Drummond & Ensor (2001) suggest the following strategies for optimizing the NPD process.

- **Multi-functional teams** – to ensure a balanced viewpoint.
- **Completeness and evaluation** – complete all stages if the NPD process.
- **Customer Involvement –** used to evaluate possible ideas and products.
- **Parallel processing** – undertaking activities concurrently.
- **Strategic direction** – links must be made between corporate strategy and NPD.
- **Knowledge management** – the transfer of knowledge is essential to help develop a 'learning organization'.

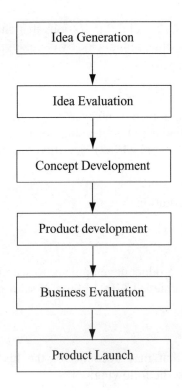

Figure 8.9
Linear new product development process (Adapted from Drummond & Ensor, 2001)

Managing innovation

Ambler (1999) suggests that if a company can get the right organizational conditions then innovation will take care of itself. The challenge to organizations is to how to create the right conditions. Generating creative ideas is only one part of the process (and often the easiest). The difficulty lies in how to convert this idea into a marketable business opportunity that adds value from a customer perspective. Drummond & Ensor (2001) suggest that to create a culture that embraces change and innovation, and an infrastructure to support this, firms should consider the enablers illustrated in Figure 8.1

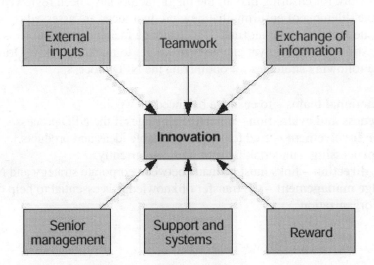

Figure 8.10
Generating innovation (Drummond & Ensor,2001)

Organizational structures can impede or assist the innovation process. Hooley et al. (1998) suggest a variety of ways in which organizations can change their structure to facilitate innovation:

- The functional approach
- A taskforce
- A project team-functional matrix
- Venture teams
- Spin-outs
- Inside-outside venture.

Extended knowledge

For a full discussion of these six approaches refer to Hooley et al. (1998) pp.386. (Chapter 16 provides a comprehensive discussion of innovation and NPD).

Drummond & Ensor (2001), Chapter 10.

Case history

BT

BT provides an excellent case to illustrate the importance of marketing's involvement in NPD. The key to successful innovation is transforming ideas into products that have commercial application. BT is sitting on up to 13,000 technology patents in its R&D centres that could be turned into new companies worth £3.7 billion by 2005. The lumbering telecoms giant is currently struggling with mountains of debt and a £57% decline in share price and yet owns the patent for what is the heart of the Internet – the software for hypertexts that allows surfers to jump from site to site. However, they only realized this last July after sitting on the patent for 14 years!

This example clearly illustrates BT's attitude to commercializing innovation. They have an incredible number of inventions that could be at the forefront of technical and scientific discoveries. However, they lack the skills, processes and culture to convert these inventions into products that are commercially viable. These inventions would provide a rich source of ideas for BT's marketers, but they are too busy trying to develop customer orientation into the somewhat inwardly looking BT culture.

Adapted from Mazur (2000), www.Lexis-Nexis.com

Question 8.9

Innovation

Answer the following question from the December 1999 exam paper and compare your answer with the CIM specimen answer.

Relationship marketing

Relationship marketing recognizes the importance of the lifetime value of a customer. The key to successful long-term business success relies not just on getting new customers but, more importantly, on encouraging customer loyalty.

Research has shown that it takes significantly more investment to acquire a new customer that it does to retain an existing one. In fact, studies have shown that it costs 5-10 times more to acquire a new customer than to retain an existing one. (Murphy, 1996). Analysts at Bain and Company Management Consultants have found that a 5% increase in customer retention can significantly increase profitability, for example by 25% in a bank (Murphy, 1996).

Therefore companies are increasingly recognizing the need to develop strategies that build customer loyalty and develop profitable relationships. The concept of relationship marketing is not limited to building relationships with customers but can equally be applied to the other markets with which a firm is associated. Building effective relationships with the various markets as illustrated in Figure 8.11 will, in the longer term, enable firms to more effectively meet their customers' needs and develop stronger relationships with their customers. The importance of developing relationships in terms of strategic alliances and partnerships was discussed in the previous unit.

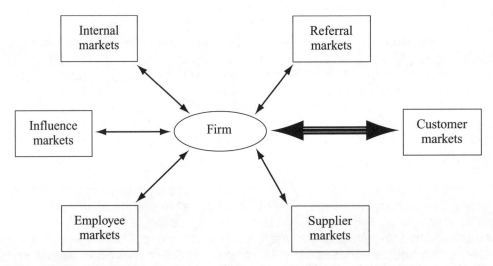

Figure 8.11
The six market model (Adapted from Christopher et al., 1994)

Definition

Relationship marketing

The purpose of relationship marketing is to establish, maintain and enhance long-term relationships with customers and other parties so that the objectives of both parties are met, (Gronroos, 1991).

Characteristics of relationship marketing

Traditional marketing techniques, often referred to as transactional marketing, view marketing and selling as one-off transactions, as opposed to relationship marketing which is concerned with the management of long-term relationships. Figure 8.12 contrasts these two approaches.

Transaction marketing	Relationship marketing
Focus on single sales	Focus on customer retention and building customers loyalty
Emphasis upon product features	Emphasis upon product benefits that are meaningful to the customer
Short timescales	Long timescales recognizing that short-term costs may be higher, but so will long term profits
Little emphasis on customer retention	Emphasis upon higher levels of service that are possibly tailored to the individual customer
Limited customer commitment	High customer commitment
Moderate customer contact	High customer contact with each contact being used to gain information and build the relationship
Quality is essentially the concern of production and no one else	Quality is the concern of all and it is the failure to recognize this that creates minor mistakes that lead to major problems

Figure 8.12
Transaction v relationship marketing (Adapted from Christopher et al., 1994)

According to De Souza (1999) customer retention has a more powerful and direct effect on profits than market share, scale advantages and other variables commonly associated with competitive advantage. This approach to marketing should not only lead to increased profitability through repeat business but should also provide opportunities for cross-selling, and the generation of positive word of mouth and new business from 'loyal' satisfied customers.

Developing relationships

Figure 8.13 illustrates the relationship marketing ladder developed by Christopher et al. (1993). This framework clearly identifies a number of stages of relationship building. The objective of relationship marketing is to move people up the ladder from prospect through to advocate and to maintain this position.

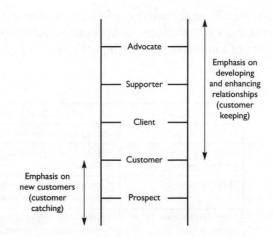

Figure 8.13
The relationship marketing ladder (Christopher, et al., 1993)

Of course, all customers are not equally profitable and worth the investment to move them up the ladder. In fact, many companies may choose to 'deselect' those that are unprofitable. Identification of various customer groupings is an important part of any relationship marketing strategy. For example, financial service companies may not want to maintain some groups of customers (e.g. those that are unprofitable – such as the 'lemons' in the FRuitS segmentation approach outlined above) (Thilo & Leventhal, 1998). Companies may choose to 'deselect' these types of customer groups. In some cases unprofitable customers are a significant group. For example, when considering the retail banking the percentage of profitable customers is 42% with 27% of customers deemed to be non-profitable (*The Banker*, May 1999).

For relationship marketing to be successful it is vital that there are obvious benefits to all parties involved. Figure 8.14 illustrates the 'cornerstones' of relationship marketing as described by Hooley et al (1998).

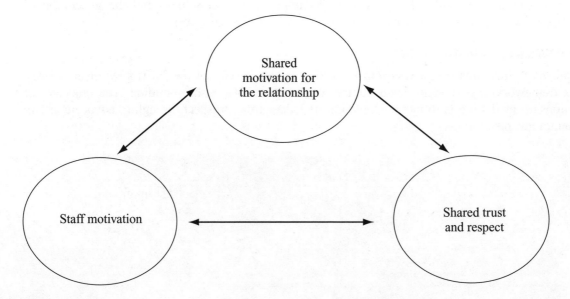

Figure 8.14
Cornerstones of relationship marketing (Adapted from Hooley et al., 1998, p.355)

The benefits for companies in developing relationships with their customers are obvious. The benefits to customers are not always as apparent. For example, customers may prefer to remain anonymous – do customers really want to develop relationships with their supermarkets, banks or DIY stores? For many customers there is a perceived lack of benefits in entering into many relationships. Supermarkets are obviously keen to retain their customers and many of these have instigated 'loyalty cards' that purport to reward loyal customers. However, many customers see very little actual benefit for the privilege of handing over a great deal of personal information that can then be used to bombard them with irrelevant and annoying direct mail. The success of the relationship also depends on the development of mutual trust between the two parties. Without the commitment of employees to deliver the expected levels of service the relationship will break down, as customers defect to other companies in search of better service.

Drummond & Ensor (2001) suggest a number of common principles of relationship marketing:

- **Use appropriately** – it is not always the best strategy.
- **Establish relationship drivers** – identify the key factors for success.
- **Build customer value** – ensure that there is real benefit to customers to enter the relationship.
- **Retain customers** – concentrate on increasing customer loyalty.

Implementing relationship marketing

The key to building successful relationship marketing strategies lies in the implementation of these programmes. Kotler et al. (1999) suggests the following stages of implementation:

- Identify key customers.
- Assign a 'relationship manager' to each of them.
- Develop clear job descriptions.
- Appoint a manager to supervise relationship managers.
- Develop long-term plans for developing relationships.

This list is not exhaustive and may not apply in all situations. However, it does highlight the importance of effective management of the relationship. Many organizations have restructured their sales force based on relationship management.

Day (1998), in an article in the *FT Mastering Marketing* series, suggested that for relationships to be successful they should focus on:

- **Delivering superior value** – continually develop ways to add value for your customer.
- **Demonstrating trustworthiness** – the firm must gain and maintain their customers trust.
- **Tightening the connections** – make it more attractive for the customer to remain loyal.
- **Co-ordinating capabilities** – all activities should be co-ordinated.
- **Engage the entire organization** – both hearts and minds – the company culture must support this strategy.
- **Tighten organizational alignment** – identify any weak links and strengthen them.
- **Make learning a priority** – continually seek ways to improve.
- **Refresh and maintain databases and records** – this is a time-consuming but essential task.

Extended knowledge

For further coverage of relationship marketing refer to: Hooley et al (1998), Chapter 15, (in particular pp.354-355) and Day (1998).

Strategic evaluation

Once an organization has identified the various strategic options available, it is then necessary to evaluate them in order to identify the 'best' strategy that will gain the best source of competitive advantage. In reality many companies do not adopt formal processes and instead rely on 'gut feel'. However, there are a number of approaches that can be adopted to assess strategies.

Criteria

Johnson & Scholes (1999, pp.355) suggest a list of criteria by which companies can evaluate alternative strategies:

- **Suitability** – does it:
  - o Exploit strengths and competencies?
  - o Rectify weaknesses?
  - o Deflect threats?
  - o Seize opportunities?
- **Feasibility** – can it be implemented?
  - o Sufficient finances?
  - o Deliver the goods?
  - o Deal with competitor's response?
  - o Access to technology etc?
  - o Time?
- **Acceptability**:
  - o To stakeholders?
  - o Legislation and environmental impact?

Aaker (1998), p.30, provides a slightly different list of criteria to that of Johnson & Scholes and in particular highlights the importance of how the proposed strategy fits with existing strategies.

1. Consider in the context of environmental opportunities and threats
2. Sustainable competitive advantage?
   1. Exploit strengths or competitor's weaknesses?
   2. Neutralize weaknesses or competitor's strengths?
3. Consistent with vision/objectives?
   1. Achieve long-term ROI?
   2. Compatible with vision?
4. Be feasible:
   1. Need only available resources.
   2. Be compatible with the internal organization.
5. Relationship with other strategies:
   1. Balanced portfolio?

2. Consider flexibility?
3. Exploit synergy?

Use of portfolio analysis in strategy evaluation

The use of portfolio analysis is assessing target markets was discussed earlier in this unit. This technique can be used to assess alternative strategic options. The resulting matrix will identify those strategies that would be the most attractive to pursue and those which a company should avoid.

Summary

- Successful strategies rely on strategic fit between an organization's resources and capabilities and the environment in which it is operating. This process is referred to as the strategic alignment process.
- Segmentation, targeting and positioning all play a critical role in the development of any successful marketing strategy. Segmentation is concerned with identifying groups of customers with similar needs and developing marketing mixes to satisfy these needs.
- Consumer markets can be segmented by: customer characteristics (demographic, geographic, geodemographic and psychographic) and behavioural characteristics (benefits sought, usage frequency, usage status, purchase occasion, attitude towards the problem and buyer readiness stage).
- Organizational markets can be segmented by macro factors (organizational size, geographic location, SIC, end market served) and micro factors (choice criteria, buy class, level of innovation, etc.)
- Once appropriate segmentation bases have been identified and profiles developed for each segment it is necessary to select those segments to target and those to avoid. In order to do this two issues need to be considered: the attractiveness of the segment and the extent to which an organization can match the needs of the segment.
- Positioning is the final stage of the STP process and is concerned with clearly and uniquely positioning a product or service in the minds of the customers. This can be achieved through the marketing mix.
- It is increasingly being recognized that brands can be very powerful and in fact can be the driving force of a successful marketing strategy. The importance of brands is being reflected by the inclusion of brand values on the balance sheet.
- There are four main branding strategies that can be adopted: company brand, individual brand names, company and individual brand and range branding.
- Companies are increasingly using their brands to stretch into related or new market sectors. The success of this will depend on the 'stretchability 'of the brand.
- Many brands are being repositioned in the hope that they will be aligned with new market opportunities or to achieve a clearer positioning in the minds of the customers.
- Many companies are developing global brands in an attempt to benefit from economies of scale and to achieve a consistent brand image.
- Innovation is more than just developing new products. It relates to changes in products, processes and practices. Innovation has been referred to as the lifeblood of an organization and companies are increasingly looking for ways to improve their level of innovativeness.
- The new product development process has traditionally been regarded as a linear process. In order to speed up the development of new products it is increasingly being recognized that companies have to develop techniques such as parallel processing to increase the pace of development.
- Firms need to concentrate on creating the right organizational conditions and culture in order to facilitate effective innovation. This can be achieved by considering the following factors:

1. Senior management, external inputs, teamwork, exchange of information, reward systems and support systems.
2. Relationship marketing is concerned with developing long-term relationships with profitable customers rather than achieving one off transactions. Research has shown that it is more profitable to retain existing customers than to gain new ones.
3. Once an organization has identified various strategic options it must evaluate them in order to identify the 'best' strategy. Some firms may rely on 'gut feel' others develop criteria by which to evaluate the alternative strategies.

Further study

Extending knowledge

Bibliography

Aaker D (1998), *Strategic Market Management*, 5th Ed, John Wiley & Sons.

Ambler, T (1999), *Sorting through the innovations to find real gold*, Marketing, 11 February, p.7.

Anon (1996), *Juicy prospects for finance products*, Financial Times, 16 May.

Booz, Allen & Hamilton (1982), *New Product management for the 1980's*, Booz, Allen and Hamilton.

Christopher M, Payne A & Ballantyne D (1993), *Relationship Marketing*, Butterworth-Heinemann.

Davidson H (1997), *More Offensive Marketing*, Penguin.

Day G (1998), *Building relationships that last*, Financial Times Mastering Management series, 28 September.

De Souza (1999), *Rules of Attraction*, Financial World, February pp.28-31.

Doyle P (1998), *Marketing Management and Strategy*, 2nd Ed., Prentice-Hall.

Drummond G & Ensor J (2001), *Strategic Marketing Planning and Control*, Butterworth-Heinemann.

Eames, L (2000), *Consumer Shopping animals: so what kind of Internet consumer are you – a gazelle or a gorilla?*, The Guardian, 25 May

Gray, R (2001), *Products stretch out into services – brands can build reputations by creating experiences for customers*, Marketing, 1 March.

Hooley GJ, Saunders JA & Piercy NF (1998), *Marketing Strategy and Competitive Positioning*, 2nd Ed, Prentice Hall.

Janszen F (2000), *The age of Innovation*, FT Prentice-Hall.

Jobber D (1998), *Principles and Practice of Marketing*, 2nd Ed, McGraw Hill.

Johnson G & Scholes K (1999), *Exploring Corporate Strategy*, 5th Ed, Prentice-Hall.

Gronroos, C (1991), *The Marketing Strategy continuum, towards a marketing concept for the 1990's*, Management Decision, 29:1, pp. 7-13.

Kotler P, Armstrong G, Saunders J, & Wong V (1999), *Principles of Marketing*, 2nd European Ed, Prentice-Hall.

Mazur L (2000), *Good inventions need marketing to come real*, Marketing, 14 December.

Murphy D (2001), *Banking on a new identity – why do banks adopt separate on-line brands?*, Marketing, p.33.

Murphy J (1996), *Customer Loyalty: happy customers add directly to the bottom line*, Financial Times, Mastering Management series, 1 November.

Murphy PE & Staples W (1979), *A Modernised Family Life Cycle*, Journal of Consumer Research, June.

Thilo P & Leventhal B (1998), *The Use of Market Segmentation in Customer Management*, MRS Conference Papers.

Tomkins R (2000), *Stretching a selling point*, Financial Times, 26 May.

Objectives

By the end of this unit you will:

- Be aware of, and be able to discuss, barriers to implementation of marketing plans
- Understand the importance of internal marketing
- Be able to develop an internal marketing plan
- Understand the importance of leadership and project management in the implementation of plans
- Know the dimensions of an effective marketing feedback and control system
- Identify suitable control mechanisms for measuring the success of plans

Study guide

- This unit will take you about 3 hours to work through
- We suggest that you take a further 3 hours to do the various activities and questions in this unit.

Introduction

The last three units have concentrated on the development of marketing strategies that help to achieve competitive advantage. This unit, in contrast, is concerned not with the development of plans, but with the implementation and control of them. The challenge of marketing lies not only in the ability to produce a winning marketing strategy but also more importantly, in transforming this plan into commercial reality. The implementation of plans is probably one of the most difficult tasks facing marketers. These difficulties arise because marketers have to rely on other people, some of whom may be in a different department, another city or even another country, to implement these plans. There are many barriers within organizations that can hamper implementation. In order to overcome these barriers there is a need for strong leadership and vision, effective management, sufficient resources and effective systems. This unit will highlight the techniques that marketers can use to facilitate effective implementation.

The second part of the unit will concentrate on aspects of control. Control is a vital component of any planning process. It is necessary in order to measure the success of the plan and to also inform future strategies. A range of financial and non-financial control measures is discussed.

Implementation

Marketing implementation is concerned with translating marketing plans into action. The marketing plan is the vehicle for communicating the strategy within the organization and addresses the issues of 'what' should happen and 'why' is should happen. Implementation is concerned with 'how' the strategy should be carried out, 'who' is to be responsible, 'when' things will take place and 'where' things will happen. Too often in organizations the implementation stage is overlooked and as a result a 'good strategy' can fail. It is important that organizations devote as much time and energy to the implementation of plans as they do to creating marketing strategies.

Strategy success

There are two factors that contribute to the success of a strategy:

- The strategy itself.
- The ability to implement the strategy.

Bonoma (1984) suggested that the various combinations of these factors would lead to four alternative business outcomes, as illustrated in Figure 9.1.

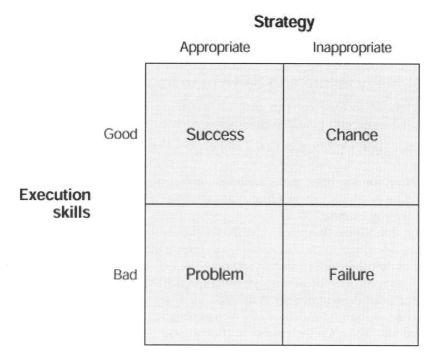

Figure 9.1
Strategy and execution (Adapted from Bonoma, 1984)

Success

This is the most desirable situation where an effective strategy is well implemented.

Chance

In this situation the strategy is weak. However, if the strategy well implemented there could be a chance that it will be successful.

Problem

This occurs often. A strong strategy has been developed but is poorly executed, resulting in problems. It is interesting to note from this model that it is probably better to have an inappropriate strategy that is effectively implemented than a good strategy that is poorly implemented.

Failure

This is the least desirable outcome – a strategy is neither appropriate nor effectively implemented.

Obviously this is a simplified model that will vary depending on the specific situation and the degree to which strategies are inappropriate. However, it does present a graphical representation of the importance of implementation in the planning process. The next section will identify the reasons why strategies are often ineffectively implemented.

Marketing strategy failure and barriers to implementation

There are a variety of factors that can lead to marketing planning failure. One of the major contributions to failure occurs at the implementation stage. So why do plans fail?

According to Aaker (1998), p.299, there are a number of pitfalls of the planning process:

- **Spreadsheet mode** – many plans are based on income statements and balance sheets that are therefore internally driven. Often plans are an extension of last year's plans rather than being driven by external factors.
- **Focus on short-term financial objectives** – the results of this often involve under investment in critical areas to improve short-term financial performance.
- **Annual cycle constraints** – threats and opportunities do not coincide with annual planning cycles. Managers often breathe a sigh of relief once they have submitted their annual plans and forget about them until next year.
- **Plans without souls** – the danger of a formal planning process is that the resultant plan can lack creativity, and often the emotional commitment needed for successful implementation is missing.
- **Rigid plans** – firms are operating in dynamic environments and therefore plans should be flexible.
- **Lack of commitment to the final plan** – this can be a major problem. The strategic plan has little relevance to actual operations or the link between strategy and operations is not clear. There maybe also be a lack of commitment because people have not 'bought into' the plan.

The following could also be added to the list:

- **Lack of time and other resources** – in some cases plans are developed but little thought is given to how they are to be financed or staffed.
- **Separation of planning from management** – this can result in a lack of commitment to the plan because those responsible for implementing the plan have not been involved in the planning process.
- **Implementation is recognized too late and is bolted on at the end** – implementation converts ideas into reality and requires planning. However, in many situations this is not recognized.
- **Lack of fit with organizational culture** – culture can have a major affect on the success of plans.
- **Does not fit well on the existing organizational structure** – new plans may crossdepartmental boundaries and therefore there can be conflict about ownership and budgets.

The major problem with implementation of plans lies in the failure of companies to manage change successfully. Inevitably a new strategy is going to result in the need for change. Many people are resistant to change because they are familiar with the status quo and fear the consequences of change. Therefore any new marketing strategy is going to be met with suspicion, unless the company can engender a culture that not only accepts change but also welcomes it. Marketing managers need to be aware of the internal barriers that exist, and then need to develop strategies to overcome these barriers. Organizations need to learn how to effectively manage change.

Activity 9.2

Internal barriers

Critically review the internal barriers to successful implementation that exist in your organization. What barriers exist, why are they present and how might they be overcome?

Managing change

The development of a culture that embraces change is an essential ingredient in the successful implementation of marketing strategy. The transition curve can help in understanding how people adapt to change (see Figure 9.2).

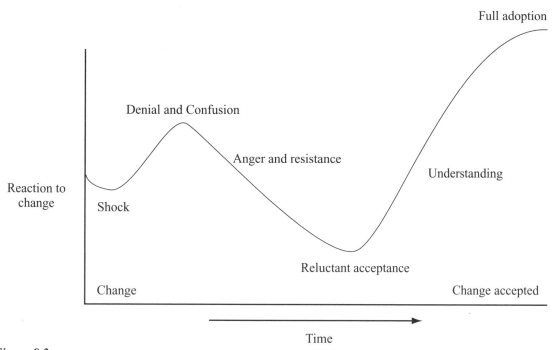

Figure 9.2
Reaction to change (Adapted from Wilson, 1993)

This model is useful because it illustrates that eventually people will internalize the new status quo (or will have left the organization). Adapting to change can be a very painful process and the expression of anger and frustration is a natural part of this adaptation. The implication for marketers is that the acceptance of major changes in working practices and responsibilities will take time.

Implementation process

The development of a market orientation is a key ingredient of successful implementation. Without a customer-centred philosophy it is likely that any new strategy will encounter problems. The development of a market orientation is a key task of the marketing department. However, this is often a difficult process due to the inherent conflicts that exist within organizations. Market orientation is discussed in Unit 'Market-led planning and the strategic marketing process'. Jobber (1998), p.568 suggests the following process for ensuring the successful execution of the marketing plan:

1. Gain the support of key decision makers and overcome the opposition of others.
2. Gain the required resources such as people, time and budget.
3. Gain commitment of individuals and departments in the company who are involved in front-line implementation.
4. Gain the co-operation of other departments needed to implement the plan.

Internal marketing, discussed below, can be used to facilitate this process.

Drummond & Ensor (2001) identify a number of factors that will contribute to the successful implementation of plans illustrated in Table 9.1.

Table 9.1:	Factors in successful implementation (Adapted from Drummond & Ensor, 2001, p.251)
Factor	**Comment**
Leadership	A strong and effective leader that is able to motivate and build teams is an essential ingredient for successful implementation.
Culture	Culture refers to the shared values and beliefs. If a plan goes against the dominant culture it is likely the plan will fail, unless support is gained via internal marketing.
Structure	Organizational structures not only denote levels of responsibility but also facilitates communication. Communication is a key aspect of implementation and organizations must ensure that the structures do not act as barriers to effective communication.
Resources	Appropriate levels of resources should be available – time, money and staff
Control	Effective controls should be established to measure the progress and success of plans.
Skills	Skills necessary for successful implementation include: technical/marketing skills, HRM skills and project management skills.
Strategy	An appropriate and relevant strategy must be communicated to all participants.
Systems	Effective systems should be in place. For example, marketing information systems that generate relevant and timely information.

These factors are embodied in the 7-S model developed by McKinsey and Co as illustrated in Figure 9.3. This model consists of two categories of factors:

- **Soft or HRM aspects** – style, staff, shared values and skills.
- **Hard or process aspects** – Strategy, structure and systems.

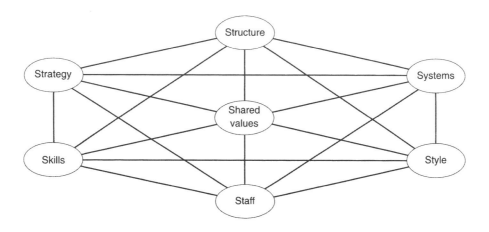

Figure 9.3
McKinsey 7-S framework (Adapted from Drummond & Ensor, 2001)

Internal marketing

According to Berry (1986), 'The most important contribution the marketing department can make is to be exceptionally clever in getting everyone else in the organization to practice marketing'. This is essentially what internal marketing is concerned with.

Definition

Internal marketing

Has the goal of developing a type of marketing programme aimed at the internal marketplace in the company that *parallels* and *matches* the marketing programme aimed at the external marketplace of customers and competitors (Piercy 2000, p.592).

Internal marketing can play a key role in the implementation of plans. It is concerned with adopting the principles and practices of external marketing to the internal market. Figure 9.4 illustrates that in fact there are three types of marketing that occur within an organization. The success of external marketing lies in the ability of the organization to satisfy the needs of the customer. Organizations are dependent on their staff to achieve this, particularly in high customer contact service businesses. Therefore, successful internal marketing is increasingly being seen as a prerequisite for effective external marketing.

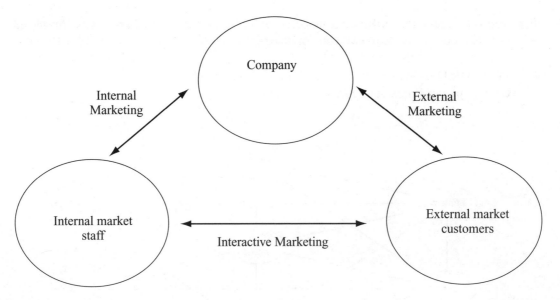

Figure 9.4
Three types of Marketing (Adapted from Kotler et al., 1999)

Internal marketing suggests that employees should be treated as internal customers and marketing plans need to be 'marketed' internally to gain acceptance and to ensure that employees understand the rationale behind the plans, can see how they can contribute to the success of the plan and importantly, 'buy into' the plan. This is not an easy task. A survey of employees in British companies with 1000 people or more, published by the Marketing & Communications Agency (MCA) and MORI, shows the scope of the challenge. The majority of employees said they feel undervalued, uninvolved and lack confidence in their organizations' leaders and vision (Mazur, 1999). Employees that lack motivation and confidence in their organizations are unlikely to buy into new ideas readily.

Increasingly organizations are recognizing that one of their greatest untapped assets is their own employees and that getting staff to act as brand ambassadors is one of the few things competitors cannot directly copy. Research among marketers at last year's Marketing Forum found that almost half the delegates now had a dedicated budget for internal marketing (Mazur, 1999).

Internal marketing is therefore not only important to ensure that staff buys into plans. It can also be used to transfer employees themselves into source of competitive advantage.

Case history

Richer Sounds

Julian Richer the founder of Richer Sounds embraces the concept of internal marketing wholeheartedly. He is probably unaware that this is what he is doing but the result is the same. Richer refers to this as the Richer Way: 'make sure your staff are happy in order to give good customer service, increase turnover, reduce complaints, cut theft and absenteeism'. Richer Sounds consists of 27 hi-fi stores located in the cheaper ends of towns and specializes in end of line equipment. In the London Bridge shop the average sales per square foot are £5,500 compared with £630 at PC World and £520 at Currys. The general philosophy of these stores is to 'pile 'em high, sell them cheap but also have great customer service'. Richer Sounds' competitive advantage is its staff. Julian Richer realized that if staff was happy and motivated they were more likely to provide a better service to the customers. His methods of creating a happy workforce are numerous and legendary, including free access for staff to seven holiday homes in the UK and Paris (regardless of sales performance), trips on

The internal marketing plan

The internal marketing plan should take the same format as an external marketing plan with objectives, strategy, market segmentation, marketing mix programmes and evaluation.

Internal market segmentation

Internal markets could be segmented in a number of different ways such as by job function, role or location. However, these methods may not be the most appropriate. It may be useful to segment according the extent to which people are likely to accept the proposed change. Jobber (1998) suggests that three different segments can be identified:

- **Supporters** – likely to gain from the change.
- **Neutrals** – will neither gain nor lose.
- **Opposers** – likely to lose from the change or are traditional opponents.

A separate marketing mix can then be developed for each of these segments. It may also be possible to identify influential individuals that are opinion leaders.

Internal marketing mix

Product

The internal product can be viewed as the marketing plan, the company itself or even the individual's own job or function. Employees need the benefits of the 'product' communicated to them.

Promotion

This is a crucial element of the mix and refers to any medium that can be used to communicate with the target groups. The promotional mix could include newsletters, discussion groups, presentations, workshops, and the use of the company Intranet etc. It is also concerned with the message that is being transmitted. A key aspect of internal communication is that it is two ways. It is important to include staff in the process from the beginning rather than just telling them what is going to happen.

External communication is also an important feature of an internal communication plans. It is essential that any external communication be in line with the messages being transmitted internally. This will ensure that staff is receiving consistent messages from all sources. In the worse-case scenario external communication can even alienate staff. This is exactly what happened to Boots, when its staff complained about a TV campaign that portrayed Boots' staff as incompetent.

Distribution

This refers to the places where the product and communication will be delivered to internal customers such as seminars, meetings, away days, informal conversations, company Intranet, etc. There is some overlap between distribution and communication mediums.

Price

Price relates to the price the staff has to pay as a result of accepting the plan. Change may result in change of job role, loss of status, office moves etc.

Internal marketing execution

Successful execution of the internal plan is reliant on three key skills (Jobber, 1998, p.576):

- **Persuasion** – the ability to develop a persuasive argument and to support words with action.
- **Negotiation** – it is likely that some negotiations will have to take place so that all parties are happy.
- **Politics** – organizations are made up of people, all with their own personal agendas. Therefore it is essential that the sources of power are identified and used to help implement the plan.

Internal marketing evaluation

In order to evaluate the success of internal marketing programmes appropriate measured have to be used, such as:

- The extent of support of key players.
- Employee satisfaction levels.
- Reduced customer complaints.
- Higher customer satisfaction scores.

Many companies are now conducting regular surveys to monitor levels of staff motivation, acceptance of the marketing concept and perceptions of the organization. In addition, it could be argued that if internal marketing is being effective then it should be having an impact on external marketing. By measuring levels of customer satisfaction and numbers of customer complaints it may give an indication of the success of internal marketing programmes.

Potential problems

There are a number of potential problems associated with internal marketing. For example:

- Opposers create convincing counter arguments.
- Insufficient time to implement effective internal plans.
- High staff turnover that causes problems in ensuring all staff is involved.
- Low-paid shop (front-line) staff – this may result in a 'why should I bother?' attitude.
- Cost – internal marketing programmes can be costly and many organizations are still slow to recognize their importance.

Question 9.1

Internal marketing

Answer the question below from the December 1998 exam paper and then compare your answer with the CIM specimen answers.

As the Marketing Manger for a chain of hotels, you have decided to develop an internal marketing programme. Prepare a briefing paper for your Managing Director outlining the key elements of an internal marketing programme, how such a programme might be developed and implemented, and the nature of any problems that are likely to be encountered.

Project management

The ability to manage projects effectively is a key aspect of implementing plans. Project management is concerned with the achievement of predetermined goals within a certain timescale and with a limited amount of resources. The skills associated with project management are the same in whatever context they are being used. They are highly applicable to the implementation of marketing projects that are often complex, involve, and impact on, a wide variety of people from different areas of the business. It is inevitable that project managers will have to deal with 'opposers' and overcome other barriers to implementation. It is essential that project managers acquire the necessary skills to integrate activities, motivate participants, and develop a sense of teamwork and monitor progress. Drummond & Ensor (2001) suggest five common tasks of project management Table 9.2.

Definition

Project Management

Project management involves achieving unity of purpose and setting achievable goals within given resources and timescales. Drummond & Ensor (2001)

Table 9.2
Common tasks in project management (Adapted from Drummond & Ensor, 1998, p.261)

Task	Comment
Objective setting	It is important that objectives are SMART (Specific, Measurable, Acceptable, Realistic and Timebound).
Planning	This involves breaking down the project into manageable tasks, co-ordinating activities and monitoring progress.
Delegation	The key to successful management is the recognition that you cannot do everything yourself.
Team building	An essential skill for a project manager is the ability to build a successful team.
Crisis management	There will be times when things do not go to plan and urgent action is required. In order to try to anticipate likely problems, scenario planning can be used.

Question 9.2

Overcoming internal barriers

Answer the question below from the June 1999 exam paper and then compare your answer with the CIM specimen answers.

Many organizations wish to build or maintain a high degree of market orientation or customer focus. How can they overcome the internal cultural barriers that may oppose this approach?

Control

The marketing planning process would not be complete without some form of evaluation of performance and assessment as to whether the marketing objectives have been achieved. There are three main components of control:

1. Setting targets/objectives against which performance can be measured.
2. Measurement of performance.
3. Corrective action.

A key aspect of control is that it should lead to corrective action. Failure to meet targets may be as a result of (a) unrealistic objectives (and therefore targets may have to be reviewed) or (b) poor performance of individuals (and therefore additional training, advice, etc., may have to be offered). If targets are met then individuals should be rewarded and objectives may also have to be reviewed for the future.

Definition

Control

Control consists of verifying whether targets have been achieved. Its purpose is to identify any problems or errors in order to rectify then and prevent recurrence. It operates on everything: things, people and actions.

Evaluation of marketing plans can also be used to inform future marketing decisions. Therefore, the planning and control cycle is a continuous feedback loop. The objectives and control measures must be fully integrated to ensure that what is intended to happen is in fact what is evaluated. The balanced scorecard is a useful framework for ensuring that objectives are linked to performance measures. The balanced scorecard also highlights the importance of ensuring that a balanced range of objectives has been developed. The balanced scorecard is discussed in the unit on strategic intent.

Effective Control Systems

The most obvious question, yet one that is frequently overlooked is, 'What is it that we seek to control?'. Too often marketers focus on what is easy to measure rather than what is important. Therefore much effort is put into measuring quantifiable processes such as market share, efficiency of sales staff or number of hits on the website rather than important issues such as customer satisfaction. Control measures can broadly be categorized into financial and non-financial measures.

The linkage between control and the planning process, and the different types of control which may result, is summarized in Figure 9.5

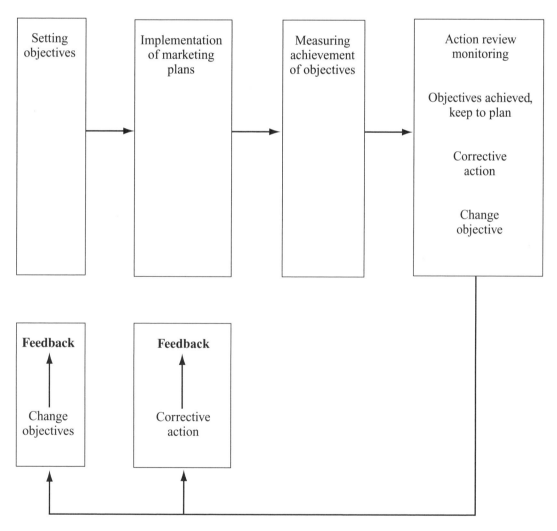

Figure 9.5
The control process

Factors influencing control measures

The marketing control process has been referred to as 'closing the (planning) loop'. Most marketing practitioners have experienced a planning situation where considerable effort has been placed on the planning activity but people have been 'too busy' to review and change the plan, an activity frequently left to the end of the marketing plan year, by which time it is too late. Control issues have moved towards the top of the marketing agenda. The specific control measures selected will depend on:

1. Hierarchy – i.e. the hierarchical level within the organization that is being considered.
2. Whether it is an interim or final control.
3. Whether control is being used to monitor the efficiency or effectiveness.

Hierarchy

The place of the marketer in the organizational hierarchy has a large influence on the type of marketing planning which is undertaken and consequently on the planning and implementation controls. The level of focus and the time horizon are two of the main differences that result from hierarchy. Control measures for long-term time horizons for the whole organization (strategic corporate marketing planning) are very different to those which are required for tactical planning for a product division.

Interim or final control

Final controls are those that are linked to the planning cycle, usually one year. Such controls are usually directly linked to marketing objectives, e.g. increase market share by 6 percentage points. Control in this case is straightforward, whether or not the marketing objective has been met. Interim controls are more complex. For example, how can we tell that we are on target to achieve a 6 percentage points increase in market share over the year? This is highly unlikely to occur in terms of an increase of 0.5 percentage points each year.

Use to monitor efficiency or effectiveness

This is measured by the ratio of inputs over outputs and was discussed in the Unit 'Financial analysis and techniques for developing a view of the future'. Writers often make the distinction between efficiency (which indicates how well resources are used) and effectiveness (whether particular actions should be taken, i.e. is the business moving in the correct direction?). In the context of control, efficiency tends to be measured, while effectiveness is analyzed and considered in formulating marketing objectives and strategy following analysis of the marketing environment. It is essential that control measures focus on both effectiveness and efficiency.

Definition

Efficiency and effectiveness

Efficiency (doing things right) How well utilized are the inputs? Do we make maximum use of finance, minimize cost and operate at optimal levels of capacity? **Efficiency (doing things right)** Are we doing the right things? This relates to actual performance and will include sales revenue, profit, market share and measure of customer satisfaction. (Drummond & Ensor, 2001)

Characteristics of effective control systems

In order to develop effective and meaningful control measures it is essential they are flexible and adhere to the following principles (suggested by Drummond & Ensor, 2001):

- **Involvement** – participants in the control process should be involved in the development of the control measures. If not, there is a danger that staff will fail to take ownership of the measures.
- **Target setting** – objectives should be quantifiable and achievable.
- **Focus** – recognize the difference between the source and the symptoms of the problem.
- **Effectiveness** – ensure that what is being measured is the right thing: 'what gets measured gets done'
- **Management by exception** – develop tolerance zones and take corrective action if results fall outside this zone.
- **Action** – effective control systems should promote action rather than just identifying problems.

Developing relevant and effective control systems is a challenging task for marketers. They can be costly and it is important that the benefits of the system outweigh the costs. Rigid control measures have also been blamed for stifling creativity because people have to conform to pre-set targets. A further problem of control methods is that they can encourage a culture of inspection rather than of development and continuous improvement.

There are a variety of ways of classifying the various forms of control. For the purpose of this text control measures will be categorized as either financial or non-financial.

Financial control measures

Financial control measures are an essential part of the control process. There are two main types of financial control that are employed: ratios and budgets.

Ratios

Financial ratios are commonly employed as a means of control. Ratios are a simple and effective means of measuring performance. However, they should not be viewed in isolation. Ratios can be used for two main purposes:

- **Trend analysis** – comparisons can be made over time.
- **Comparative analysis** – ratios can be compared with industry standards or the competition.

Ratios can be classified into four main categories:

- **Profitability ratios** – concerned with measuring a firms ability to produce profit.
- **Liquidity ratios** – concerned with the ability of a company to remain solvent.
- **Debt ratios** – concerned with a firms ability to manage debt.
- **Activity** – relates to the effectiveness of a firm to generate activity.

For further discussion of ratios refer to the Unit 'Financial analysis and techniques for developing a view of the future'.

Budgets

These are the most commonly applied means of control. Forecasts are translated into budgets in an attempt to ensure that key financial targets are achieved. Budgets therefore translate the marketing strategy into financial terms. All plans, whether marketing, production or HRM, are translated into financial terms in the form of a budget. It is then possible to co-ordinate the activities of all departments into a single master plan. Budgets can be set in a variety of ways:

- **Based on the past** – many organizations develop budgets based on previous budgets taking into account inflation, etc.

- **Objective and task (zero-based)** – budgets are based on the cost of achieving a set of given objectives.
- **Activity related** – for example budgets are set as a percentage of forecasted sales
- **Competitive parity** – budgets are based on what the competition are spending.

Budgets are an essential control measure but their value depends to a large extent on the appropriateness of the methods by which they have been set. Many companies are now recognizing that the budgeting system is perhaps the greatest barrier to change. Budgets tend to reinforce command and control management and undermine attempts at organizational change. The annual budgeting cycle can be inappropriate for companies facing rapidly changing markets. Budgets tend to encourage incremental thinking, the extrapolation of existing trends with little vision of the future and can even stifle breakthroughs in improvement.

Non-financial controls

Non-financial controls can be applied at all levels within an organization – strategic, operation and tactical. The advantages and disadvantages of non-financial controls are summarized in Tables 9.3 and 9.4 (adapted from Ittner & Larcker, 2000).

Table 9.3	Advantages of non-financial measures in providing improved control criteria.
Alignment to long-term organizational strategies	Financial control measures tend to be aligned with annual or shorter term accounting measures. These are not directly linked to key competitive issues such as competitive strength or customer alignment.
Closer linkage to the drivers of industry success	Drivers of success in many industries are linked to factors that cannot readily be measured in a company account. These include, for example, innovativeness, intellectual capital, and organizational culture.
Non-financial indicators provide improved indicators of future financial performance	The only financial indicator of investment into customer loyalty programmes, or in research and development activities, is a reduction in the current year's profits. Financial measures provide no indication of the potential future, beneficial impact. Non-financial measures can indicate improvements in customer loyalty levels and in customer perception of products.
Measures beyond management control	Financial measures are generally assumed to be within management control. However, much is beyond management control and of great impact on the business. Non-financial measures can provide vital information on the marketing environment on 'uncontrollable areas', e.g. changes in the economy, in social values, in legal decisions etc.

Disadvantages/ problems of non-financial measures include:

Table 9.4	Disadvantages/problems of non-financial measures
Time and cost	Financial measures are relatively inexpensive control mechanisms in contrast to many non-financial measures, which require, in some cases, specially commissioned research to implement – for example consumer attitude measurement.
Problems of comparison	A variety of measures are possible which creates problems of comparison. In addition, when confronted by many measures, which measures should be considered more important where measures indicate conflicting conclusions (e.g. customer satisfaction versus market share versus repeat purchases).
Lack of clear causal links	Lack of clarity in matching non-financial measures to tangible objectives. Xerox, for example, placed greater weighting on customer satisfaction surveys and spent a lot on them. Implicit in this is that customer satisfaction is linked to financial performance. Research found this not to be the case: consequently Xerox changed their emphasis to customer loyalty, which was found to be correlated with financial performance.
Lack of rigor	One criterion against which to judge measures is statistical rigour, i.e. that results are repeatable and have assigned probabilities. Non-financial measures are frequently statistically unreliable and can potentially report random events.

Benchmarking

Benchmarking is a technique in which individual processes within the value chain are compared between organizations. The objective is to compare performance with that of market leaders with a view to identifying best practice and continual improvement. Benchmarking assesses small processes within the organization; consequently very different organizations may be used in the comparison. For example:

- An airline may benchmark on food preparation and serving processes against a leading fast-food restaurant.
- A restaurant chain may benchmark on inventory management against a leading supermarket group.
- A large legal consulting firm may benchmark on customer relationship marketing against a leading financial services organization.

Definition

Benchmarking

A systematic and ongoing process of measuring and comparing an organization's business processes and achievements against acknowledged process leaders and/or key competitors, to facilitate improved performance. (Drummond & Ensor, 2001)

Benchmarking may be considered in five stages:

1. The specification of the precise processes which are to be benchmarked and how these are to be measured.

2. Selection of the organization against which to benchmark, i.e. the leading organization in the processes of interest.
3. Identification of the differences in performance and the reasons for under-performance.
4. Planning of how improvements are to be made to achieve best practice.
5. Setting up of a monitoring and assessment programme to control the delivery of improved performance.

Case history

Benchmarking in practice

Plastic Engineering, based in Leamington Spa, Warwickshire, sells £8.5 million of safety systems such as brakes and steering columns to the motor industry each year. It has been under increasing pressure to cut prices to remain competitive against overseas manufacturers. The company decided to use the Benchmarking Index to give an objective measure of their performance against the opposition. The company provided all the relevant data and information and then received a Benchmarking report that compared the company's performance with that of 200 other plastic companies on a wide range of indicators such as delivery times, stock turn, productivity per worker and wastage rates. It also measured against a wider sample in areas such as customer and staff satisfaction.

The results confirmed much that the company already knew, but did not have the courage to face. They were in the best 25% of companies in the survey in the areas of product quality and customer satisfaction. However, the firm did not score well on management/staff communication, stock turn and productivity per worker.

As a result of these findings the company made major changes to its working practices. The old assembly line was replaced by team working. Functional divisions were replaced by cell manufacture, investment in training was doubled and exchange visits were organized with companies achieving best practice in areas targeted for improvement.

The changes brought valuable benefits. Plastic Engineering reduced its stock of raw materials by 19% by encouraging suppliers to deliver just in time. The shopfloor was less cluttered and the capital tied up in stock was cut from £240,000 to £200,000. Better housekeeping resulted in a 5% decline in wastage. The business improved its on-time delivery rate from 60% to 98% in six months. The Benchmark Index cost the company £400 and the managing director believed this was the best investment they ever made.

Source: Sumner Smith (2000), www.Lexis-Nexis.com

Balanced scorecard

The balanced scorecard is a framework, developed by Kaplan and Norton (1992) that acknowledges the various perspectives of different stakeholder group, whilst at the same time linking objectives with performance measures. This model was outlined in the Unit 'Strategic intent'. However, it is worth revisiting it at this stage to highlight its role in the control stage of the planning cycle. Refer to Figure 6.5 for an overview of the various performance measures that may be used. The model suggests that objectives and subsequent performance measures should relate to four distinct areas: the customer perspective, the financial perspective, the internal perspective and innovation and learning. This approach highlights the importance of developing a balanced set of objectives and ensures that organizations do not place all their emphasis in one area, such as finance.

Marketing performance control

Kotler et al. (1999) identify four main types of controls for marketing activity:

- **Annual planning** – this involves evaluating the performance of the previous years marketing activities such as sales, market share, customer satisfaction.
- **Profitability** – profitability is a major concern of any marketer. Profitability can be calculated not only by product but also by distribution channel, market segment of even individual customer.
- **Efficiency control** – this is concerned with optimization of assets. For example, return on promotional spend. Figure 9.6 illustrates some of the various measures that can be used to evaluate the marketing mix.
- **Strategic control** – it is imperative that marketing activity is ultimately helping to achieve organizational goals. This can be undertaken in the format of the marketing audit that will review all marketing activity.

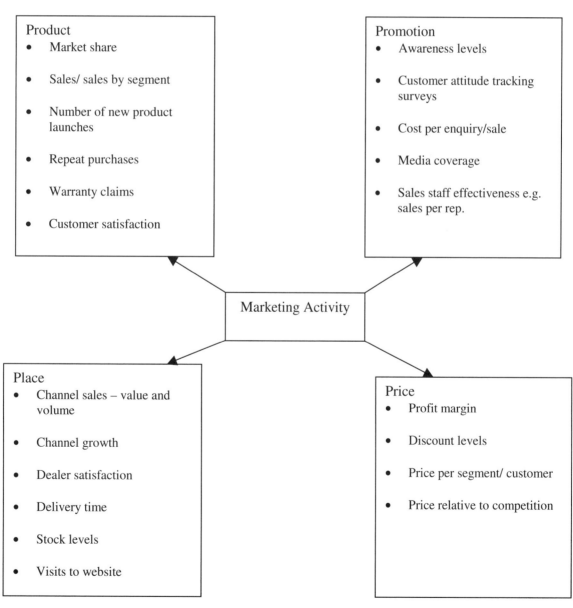

Figure 9.6
Controlling the marketing mix (Adapted from Drummond & Ensor, 2001)

Extended knowledge

For further reading on control refer to: Drummond G & Ensor J (2001), Chapter 14.

Question 9.3

Control systems

Answer the following question from the December 1996 exam paper and then compare your answer with the outline answer in the paper.

It is increasingly being recognized that marketing managers often pay more attention to planning than to the control process. Explain why this should be the case, the probable consequences, and how an effective marketing control system might be established.

Summary

- Marketing implementation is concerned with translating marketing strategy into action. This very important stage is often overlooked by many organizations. In some cases plans fail, not because they are inappropriate plans, but because they are poorly implemented.
- There are many barriers that exist to successful implementation of plans such as mechanistic planning cycles, focus on the short-term, rigid plans, lack of commitment to the plan, lack of time and other resources and lack of fit with organizational culture and structure.
- The development of an organizational culture that welcomes change is a key ingredient in the successful implementation of marketing plans. Managers need to be familiar with the process of change and the impact it has on people in order to effectively manage change.
- The development of a market orientation is an essential task of the marketing department. Without a customer-centred philosophy it is likely that any new plans will encounter problems.
- In order to achieve successful implementation of plans it is necessary to consider leadership, organizational culture, organizational structure, available resources, control mechanisms, skills, the strategy itself and the systems.
- Internal marketing is concerned with applying the principles and practices used for external marketing to the internal marketplace. This will ensure that internal marketing programmes will mirror those of the external marketplace. Internal marketing can play an important role in facilitating the successful implementation of plans.
- The skills associated with project management, such as objective setting, planning, delegation, team building and crisis management, are all skills that can help to implement often complex marketing projects.
- The final stage of the marketing planning process is the development of control mechanisms to monitor the success of marketing plans. The outputs of these measurements should be linked to action, in the form of either corrective action or the revisiting of marketing objectives. The results can also be used to inform future decisions.
- Control mechanisms should be developed that measure not only efficiency but also effectiveness. Control measures can be categorized into either financial or non-financial control mechanisms.

- Financial controls generally include the use of ratios and budgets. Non-financial controls can be applied at any level within the organization.
- Benchmarking is a key non-financial control technique where organizations measure their performance i.e. benchmark, against other organizations in an attempt to identify 'best practice'.
- There are four main types of controls for marketing activity: annual planning, profitability, efficiency control and strategic control.

Further study

Extending knowledge

Bibliography

Aaker D (1998), *Strategic Market Management*, 5th Ed, John Wiley & Sons.

Beenstock S (1998), *Ninety five percent of this man's staff says they love working for him. What's his secret?*, Management Today, April

Berry (1986), *Big Ideas in services marketing*, Journal of Consumer Marketing, Spring.

Bonoma T (1984), *Making your Marketing Strategies Work*, Harvard Business Review, 62:2, pp. 68-76.

Drummond G & Ensor J (2001), *Strategic Marketing Planning and Control*, Butterworth-Heinemann,.

Ittner C and Larcker D (2000), *A bigger yardstick – Company financial data has limitations as a measure of company performance*, Financial Times, Mastering Management Series, 16th October.

Jobber D (1998), *Principles and Practice of Marketing*, 2nd Ed, McGraw Hill.

Kaplan RS & Norton DP (1992), *The Balanced Scorecard: Measures that drive performance*, Harvard Business Review, 70:1, pp. 71-79.

Kotler P, Armstrong G, Saunders J, & Wong V(1999), *Principles of Marketing*, 2nd European Ed, Prentice-Hall.

Mazur L (1999), *Unleashing employee's true value*, Marketing, 29 April.

Piercy N (2000), *Market-Led Strategic Change*, 2nd Ed, Butterworth-Heinemann.

Sumner Smith D (2000), *Firms get ahead by measuring themselves against the best*, Sunday Times, 15 October.

Wilson G (1993), *Making Change Happen*, Pitman.

Preparing for your examination

You are now nearing the final phase of your studies and it is time to start the hard work of exam preparation.

During your period of study you have been used to absorbing massive loads of information, trying to understand and apply aspects of knowledge that are very new to you, while information provided may be more familiar. You may even have undertaken many of the activities that are positioned frequently throughout your text, which have enabled you to apply your learning in practical situations. Whatever the position is of your knowledge and understanding and level of knowledge application, do not allow yourself to fall into the trap of thinking you know enough, you understand enough or even worse, thinking you can wing in on the day.

Never underestimate the pressure of the CIM examination, getting into the examination hall, and wishing it had all been different, that indeed you had revised and prepared for this big moment, where all of a sudden the Senior Examiner becomes an unrelenting question master!

The whole point of preparing this unit for you is to ensure that you never take the examination for granted, and that you do not go into the exam completely unprepared for what you find what might come your way for three hours at a time.

One thing for sure, is that there is no quick fix, no easy route, no waving a magic wand and finding you know it all.

Whether you have studied alone, in a CIM study centre, or through distance learning, you now need to ensure that this final phase of your learning process is tightly managed, highly structured and objective.

As a candidate in the examination, your role will be to convince the Senior Examiner for this subject that you have credibility. You need to demonstrate to the examiner that you can be trusted to undertake a range of challenges in the context of marketing, that you are able to capitalize on opportunities and manage your way through threats.

You should prove to the Senior Examiner, that you able to apply knowledge, make decisions, respond to situations and solve problems. The list of solutions you will need to provide to prove your credibility could be endless.

Very shortly we are going to look at a range of particular revision and exam preparation techniques, methods, time management issues and encourage you towards developing and implementing your own revision plan, but before that, lets look a little bit a the role of the Senior Examiner.

A bit about the Senior Examiners!

You might be quite shocked to read this, or even find it hard to understand, but while it might appear that the examiners are 'relentless question masters', but they actually allow you to be able to answer the questions and pass the exams. In fact they would derive no satisfaction or benefits from failing candidates, quite the contrary, they develop the syllabus and exam papers in order that you can learn and utilize that learning effectively in order to pass your examinations. Many of the examiners have said in the past that it is indeed psychologically more difficult to fail students than pass them.

Many of the hints and tips you find within this unit have been suggested by the Senior Examiners and authors of the workbook series, therefore you should consider them carefully and resolve to undertake as many of the elements suggested where possible.

The Chartered Institute of Marketing has a range of processes and systems in place within the Examinations Division to help to ensure that fairness and consistency prevail across the team of examiners, and to ensure that the academic and vocational standards that are set and defined are indeed maintained. In doing this, CIM ensures that those who gain the CIM Certificate, Advanced Certificate and Postgraduate Diploma, are worthy of the qualification and perceived as such in the view of employers, actual and potential.

Part of what you will need to do within the examination is be 'examiner friendly' and you will need to ensure that they get what they ask for, doing this will make life easier for you and for them.

Hints and tips for 'examiner friendly' actions are as follows:

- Show them that you understand the basis of the question, by answering precisely the question asked, and not including just about everything you can remember about the subject area.
- Read their needs – how many points is the question asking you to address?
- Is the question asking you to take on a role? If so, take on the role and answer the question in respect of the role. If you are asked to be a Marketing Manager, then respond in that way. For example, you could be positioned as follows:

  'You are working as a Marketing Assistant at Nike UK' or 'You are a Marketing Manager for an Engineering Company' or 'As Marketing Manager write a report to the Managing Partner'.

  These are actually taken from questions in past papers, so ensure you take on board role-play requirements.

- Deliver the answer in the format requested. If the examiner asks for a memo, then provide a memo, likewise if the examiner asks for a report, then provide a report. If you do not do this, in some instances you will fail to gain the necessary marks required to pass.
- Take a business-like approach to your answers. This enhances your credibility. Badly-ordered work, untidy work, lack of structure, headings and subheadings can be offputting. This would be unacceptable in work; likewise it would be unacceptable in the eyes of the Senior Examiners and their marking teams.
- Ensure the examiner has something to mark, give them substance, relevance, definitions, illustration and demonstration of your knowledge and understanding of the subject area.
- See the examiner as your potential employer, or ultimate consumer/customer. The whole purpose and culture of marketing is about meeting customers' needs. Try doing this, it works wonders.
- Provide a strong sense of enthusiasm and professionalism in your answers, support them with relevant up-to-date examples and apply them where appropriate.
- Try to differentiate your exam paper, make it stand out in the crowd.

All of these points might seem quite logical to you, but often in the panic of the examination they 'go out of the window', indeed out of our minds, therefore it is beneficial to remind ourselves of the importance of the examiner. They are the 'ultimate customer' – and we all know customers hate to be disappointed.

As we move on some of these points will be revisited, and developed further.

About the examination

In all examinations, with the exception of Marketing in Practice at Certificate Level and Analysis and Decision at Diploma level, the paper is divided into two parts.

- Part A – the Mini-case study = 40 per cent of the marks
- Part B – Option choice questions – choice of three questions from seven = 60 per cent of the marks.

Let's look at the basis of each element.

The mini-case study

This is based on a mini-case or scenario with one question possibly subdivided into between two and four points, but totalling 40 per cent overall.

In essence, you, the candidate, are placed in a problem-solving role through the medium of a short scenario. On occasions, the scenario may consist of an article from a journal in relation to a well-known organization, for example in the past, Interflora, EasyJet, Philips, among others, have been used as the basis of the mini-case. Alternatively they will be based upon a fictional company, which the examiner has prepared in order that the right balance of knowledge; understanding, applications and skills are used.

Look at the examination papers at the end of this book and see the mini-case.

Approaches to the mini-case study

When undertaking the mini-case study there are a number of key areas you should consider.

Structure/content

The mini-case that you will be presented with will vary slightly from paper to paper and of course from one examination to the next. Normally the scenario presented will be between 400-500 words long and sometimes will centre on a particular organization and its problems or may even specifically relate to a particular industry.

The length of the mini-case study means that usually only a brief outline is provided of the situation and the organization and its marketing problems, and you must therefore learn to cope with analysis information and preparing your answer on the basis of very limited amounts of information.

Time management

Your paper is designed in order that you are assessed over a three-hour period. With 40 per cent of the marks being allocated to the mini-case, it means that you should dedicate somewhere around 70-75 minutes of your time to write up the answer, on this mini-case, plus allowing yourself approximately 20 minutes reading and analysis time. This takes you to around 95 minutes, which is almost half of your time in the exam room.

Do not forget that while there is only one question within the mini-case it can have a number of components. You must answer all the components in that question, which is where the balance of times comes in to play.

Knowledge/skills tested

Throughout all the CIM papers, your knowledge, skills and ability to apply those skills will be tested. However, the mini-cases are used particularly to test application, i.e. your ability to take you knowledge and apply it in a structured way to a given scenario. The examiners will be looking at your decision-making ability, your analytical and communication skills and depending on the level, your ability as a manager to solve particular marketing problems.

When the examiner is marking your paper, he/she will be looking to see how you really differentiate yourself, looking at your own individual 'unique selling points' and to see if you can personally apply the knowledge or whether you are only able to repeat the textbook materials.

Format of answers

On many occasions, and within all examinations, you will most likely be given a particular communication method to use. If this is the case please ensure that you adhere to the requirements of the examiner. This is all part of meeting customer needs.

The likely communication tools you will be expected to use are as follows:

- A memorandum
- A memorandum/report
- A report
- Briefing notes
- Presentation
- Press release
- Advertisement
- Plan

Make sure that you familiarize yourself with these particular communication tools and practise using them to ensure that on the day you will be able to respond confidently to the communication requests of the examiner. You may look back at the Customer Communications Text at Certificate level to familiarize yourself with the potential requirements of these methods.

By the same token, while communication methods are important, so is the meeting the specific requirements of the question. **Note the following carefully.**

- **Identify** – select key issues, point out key learning points, establish clearly what the examiner expects you to identify
- **Illustrate** – this means the examiner expects you to provide examples, scenarios, and key concepts that illustrate your learning.
- **Compare and contrast** – look at the range of similarities between the two situations, contexts or even organizations. Then compare them, i.e. ascertain and list how activities, features, etc. agree or disagree. Contrasting means highlighting the differences between the two.
- **Discuss** – questions that have 'discuss' in them offer a tremendous opportunity for you to debate, argue, justify your approach or understanding of the subject area- *caution* it is not an opportunity to waffle.
- **Briefly explain** – This means being succinct, structured and concise in your explanation, within the answer. Make your points clear and transparent and relevant.
- **State** – present in a clear, brief format
- **Interpret** – expound the meaning of, make clear and explicit what it is you see and understand within the data provided
- **Outline** – provide the examiner with the main concepts and features being asked for and avoid minor technical details. A structure will be critical here; or else you could find it difficult to contain your answer.
- **Relate** – show how different aspects of the syllabus connect together.
- **Evaluate** – This means review and reflect upon an area of the syllabus, a particular practice, an article, etc, and consider its overall worth in respect of its use as a tool or a model and its overall effectiveness in the role it plays.

Your approach to mini-cases

There is no one right way to approach and tackle a mini-case study, indeed it will be down to each individual to use their own creative minds and approaches to the tasks which are presented. What you will have to do is use your initiative and discretion about how to best approach the mini-case. However having said this, there are some basic steps you can take.

- Ensure that you read through the case study at least twice before making any judgements, starting to analyse the information provided, or indeed writing the answers.
- On the third occasion read through the mini-case and, using a highlighter, start marking the essential and relevant information critical to the content and context. Then turn your attention to the question again, this time reading slowly and to carefully assess what it is you are expected to do. Note any instructions that the examiner gives you, and then start to plan how you might answer the question. Whatever the question ensure there is a structure: a beginning, structured central part of the answer and finally, always closing with a conclusion.
- Always keep in mind the specifics of the case and the role which you might be performing, and keep these contexts continually in mind.
- Because there are limited materials available, you will sometimes need to make assumptions. Don't be afraid to do this, it will show initiative on your part. Assumptions are an important part of dealing with case studies and it can help you to be quite creative with your answer. However, if you do use assumptions, please explain the basis of them within your answer so that the examiner understands the nature of them, and why you have arrived at your particular outcome. **Always ensure that those assumptions are realistic.**
- Now you are approaching the stage where it is time to answer the question, tackling the problems, making decisions and recommendations on the case scenario set before you. As mentioned previously, these will often be best set out in a report or memo type format, particular if the examiner does not specify a communication method.
- Ensure that your writing is succinct, avoids waffle and responds directly to the questions asked.

Part B

Again, with the exception of the Analysis and Decision case study, each Part B is comprised of six or seven, more traditional questions, each worth 20 per cent. You will be expected to choose three of those questions, to make up the remainder of the 100 per cent of available marks.

Realistically, the same principles apply for these questions, as in the case study. Communication formats, reading through the questions, structure, role-play, context, etc. everything is the same.

Part B will cover a number of broader issues from within the syllabus and will be taken from any element of it, the examiner makes the choice, and no prior direction is given to students or tutors on what that might be.

As regards time management in this area, you should have approximately one and a half hours left, i.e. 90 minutes. If you do have, this means you should give yourself seven minutes to read the question and plan out your answers, with 22 minutes to write and review what you have put within your answer.

Keep practising – use a cooker timer, alarm clock or mobile phone alarm as your timer and work hard at answering questions within the timeframe given.

Specimen examination papers and answers

To help you prepare and understand the nature of the paper, you will find that the last two CIM examination papers and specimen answers are included at the end of this unit. During your study, the author of your book may have on occasions asked you to refer to these papers and answer the questions, providing you with a specimen answer for guidance. Please utilize every opportunity to undertake and meet their requirements.

These are vital tools to your learning. The specimen answers are not always perfect, as they are answers written by students and annotated by the Senior Examiners, but they will give you a good indication of the approaches you could take, and the examiners provide annotation to suggest how these answers might be improved in the future. Please use them. You can also access this type of information through the Virtual Institute on the CIM web site using your student registration number as an access code.

Other sources of information to support your learning through the Virtual Institute are 'Hot Topics'. These give you scope to undertake a range of associated activities related to the syllabus, and study areas, but will also be very useful to you when you are revising.

Key elements of learning

According to one Senior Examiner, there are three elements involve in preparing for your examination.

- Learning
- Memory
- Revision

We are going to look at what the Senior Examiner suggests, by examining each point in turn.

Learning

Quite often, as students, we can find it difficult to learn. We passively read books, look at some of the materials, perhaps revise a little and regurgitate it in the examination. In the main this is rather an unsatisfactory method of learning. It is meaningless, useless and ultimately leaves us mindless of all that we could have learned had we applied ourselves in our studies.

For learning to be truly effective it must be active and applied. You must involve yourself in the learning process by thinking about what you have read, testing it against your experience by reflecting on how you use particular aspects of marketing, and how you could perhaps improve your own performance by implementing particular aspects of your learning into your everyday life. The old adage goes something like 'learning by doing'. If you do this, you will find that passive learning does not have a place in your study life.

Below are some suggestions that have been prepared to assist you with the learning pathway throughout your revision.

- Always make your own notes, in words you understand and ensure that you combine all the sources of information and activities within them.
- Always try to relate your learning back to your own organization
- Make sure you define key terms concisely, wherever possible
- Do not try to memorize your ideas, but work on the basis of understanding and most important, applying them.
- Think about the relevant and topical questions that might be set – use the questions and answers at the back of each of your workbooks to identify typical questions that might be asked in the future.
- Attempt all of the questions within each of your workbooks since these are vital tests of your active learning and understanding.

Memory

If you are prepared to undertake an active learning programme then your knowledge will very probably be considerably enhanced, as understanding and application of knowledge does tend to stay in your 'long-term' memory. It is likely that passive learning will only stay in your 'short-term' memory.

Do not try to memorize parrot fashion, it is not helpful and even more important, examiners are experienced in identifying various memorizing techniques and therefore, will identify them as such.

Having said this, it is quite useful to memorize various acronyms such as SWOT, PEST, PESTLE, STEEPLE, or indeed various models such as Ansoff, GE Matrix, Shell Directional, etc., as in some of the questions you may be required to use illustrations of these to assist your answer.

Revision

The third and final stage to consider is 'revision', which is what we are now going to concentrate on.

Revision should be an ongoing process rather than a panic measure that you decide to undertake just before the examination. You should be preparing notes throughout your course, with the view to using them as part of your revision process. Therefore ensure that your notes are sufficiently comprehensive that you can reuse them successfully.

For each concept you learn about, you should identify, through your reading and your own personal experience at least two or three examples that you could use; this then gives you some scope to broaden your perspective during the examination. It will of course, help gain you some brownie points with the examiners.

Knowledge is not something you will gain overnight, as we saw earlier, it is not a quick fix; it involves a process of learning that enables you to lay solid foundations upon which to build your long-term understanding and application. This will benefit you significantly in the future, not just in the examination.

In essence you should ensure that you do the following prior to the real intensive revision process commencing.

- Ensure that you keep your study file well organized, updated and full of newspaper and journal cuttings that may assist you formulate examples in your mind for use during the examination.
- Practise defining key terms and acronyms from memory
- Prepare topic outlines and essay answer plans
- Read your concentrated notes the night before the examination.

Revision planning

You are now on a critical path, hopefully not too critical at this time, with somewhere in the region of between four and six weeks to go to the examination. Hopefully the following hints and tips will help you plan out your studies.

- You will, as already explained, need to ensure that you are very organized and therefore before doing anything else, put your files, examples, reading material in good order, so that you are able to work with them in the future and of course, make sense of them.
- Ensure that you have a quiet area within which to work. It is very easy to get distracted when preparing for the examination.
- Give up your social life for a short period of time, as the saying goes 'no pain – no gain'.
- Take out your file along with your syllabus and make a list of key topic areas that you have studied and which you now need to revise. You could use the basis of this book to do that, by taking each unit a step at a time.
- Plan the use of your time carefully. Ideally you should start you revision at least six weeks prior to the exam, so therefore work out how many spare hours you could give to the revision process and then start to allocate time in your diary, and do not double-book with anything else.
- Looking at each of the subject areas in turn, identify which are your strengths and which are your weaknesses. Which areas have you really grasped and understood, and what are the areas that you have really struggled with. Split you page in two and make a list on each side of the page. For example:

Planning and control	
Strengths	Weaknesses
Audit – PEST, SWOT, Models	Ratio analysis
Portfolio analysis	Market sensing
	Productivity analysis
	Trend extrapolation
	Forecasting

- However many weeks you have left, break down your list again and divide the points of weaknesses, giving priority in the first instance to your weakest areas and even prioritizing them by giving them a number. This will enable you to master the more difficult areas. Up to 60 per cent of your revision time should be given over to that, as you may find you have to undertake a range of additional reading and also potentially gaining tutor support, if you are studying at a CIM Accredited Study Centre.
- The remaining time should be spent reinforcing your knowledge and understanding of the stronger areas, spending time testing yourself on how much you really know.
- Should you be taking two examinations or more at any one time, then the breakdown of your time and managing of your time will be critical.
- Taking a subject at a time, work through your notes and starts breaking them down in to subsections of learning, and ultimately down into key learning points, items that you can refer to time and time again, that are meaningful and that your mind will absorb. You yourself will know how you best remember key points. Some people try to develop acronyms, or flowcharts or matrices, mind maps, fishbone diagrams, etc. or various connection diagrams that help them recall certain aspects of models. You could also develop processes with that enable you remember approaches to various options.

(But remember what we said earlier about regurgitating stuff, parrot fashion.)

You could use the type of bomb-burst in Figure A1.1 as a way of remembering how the key components of STEEPLE break down in your learning process.

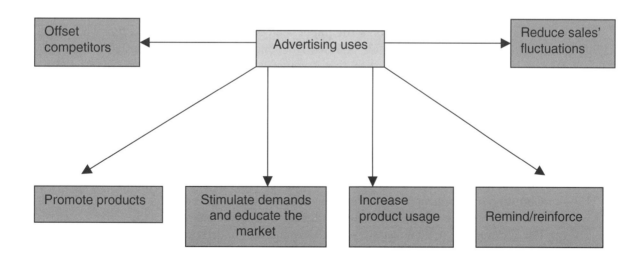

Figure A1.1

Figure A1.1 is just a brief example of how you could use a flow chart diagram which, in this case, highlights the uses of advertising. It could be a very helpful approach to memorizing key elements of learning.

- Eventually you should reduce your key learning to bullet points, from which you can revise. For example: imagine you were looking at the key concepts of Time Management – you could eventually break them down into a bullet list which contains the following key points in relation to 'Effective Prioritization:'
    1. Organize
    2. Take time
    3. Delegate
    4. Review

Each of these headings would then remind you that you need to discuss elements associated with the subject area.

- You should avoid getting involved in reading too many textbooks at this stage, as you may start to find that you are getting a little confused overall.
- Now refer to the end of this book and look at some of the exam questions listed, and start to observe closely the various roles and tasks they expect you to undertake, but more importantly the context in which they are set.
- Without exception, find an associated examination question for the areas that you have studied and revised, and undertake it, more than once if necessary.
- Without referring to notes or books, see if you can draft a answer plan with the key concepts, knowledge, models, information, that are needed for you to successfully complete this answer and list them. Then refer to the specimen answer to see how close you are to the actual outline presented. Planning your answer, and ensuring that key components are included, and that the question has a meaningful structure is one of the most beneficial activities that you can undertake.
- Having done this, now write the answer out in full, time constrained and in hand written not with the use of IT. At this stage, you are still expected to be the scribe for the examination and present your hand-written work. Many of use find this increasingly difficult as we spend more and more time using our computers to present information. Spidery handwriting is often offputting to the examiner.

When you are ready to write your answer in full – ensure you do the following.

- **Identify and use the communication method** requested by the examiner
- **Always have three key parts to the paper** – an introduction, middle section where you will develop your answer in full, and finally a conclusion. Where appropriate ensure that you have an introduction, main section, summary/conclusion and if requested or helpful – recommendations.
- **Never forget to answer your question in the context or role set.** If you answer the question void of either of these, then you will fail to gain marks.
- **Always comply with the nature and terms of the question**
- **White Space** do not overcrowd your page – make sure there is white space. There is always plenty of paper available for you to use. Make sure you leave space between paragraphs, and that your sentences do not merge into one blur.
- **Count** how many actions the question is asking you to undertake and double-check at the end that you have met the full range of demands of the question.
- **Use Examples** – to demonstrate your knowledge and understanding of the particular syllabus area. These can be from journals, the Internet, the press, or your own experience – this really helps you add value to your answer.
- **The Senior Examiner is your customer** – or indeed future employer, as we have previously said. Consider carefully what is wanted to satisfy their needs and do your best to deliver. Impress them and show them how you are a 'cut above the rest'. Let them see your vigour and enthusiasm for marketing.

- **Use the specimen exam papers and specimen answers** to support your learning and see how you could actually improve upon them.

Practical actions

The critical path is becoming even more critical now as the exam looms. The following are vital points.

- Have you registered with CIM?
- Do you know where you are taking you examination – CIM should let you know approximately one month in advance.
- Do you know where your examination centre is? If not find out, take a drive, time it – whatever you do don't be late!
- Make sure you have all the tools of the examination with you. A dictionary, calculator, pens, pencils, ruler, etc. Try not to use multiple shades of pens, but at the same time make your work look professional. *Avoid using red and green as these are the colours that will be used for marking.*

Summary

Many of the hints and tips here are very generic and will work across most of the CIM. However we have tried to select those that are most helpful, in order that you take a sensible planned approach to your study and revision.

The key to your success is being prepared to give it the time and effort required, planning your revision, and equally important, planning and answering your questions in a way that will ensure that you pass your examination on the day.

The hints and tips presented are there to guide you from a practical perspective, the syllabus content guidance and developments associated to your learning will become clear to you while you work through this workbook. Each of the authors have given subject specific guidance on the approach to the examination and how to ensure that you meet the content requirements of the question, in addition to the structuring issues we have been discussing throughout this unit.

Each of the authors and Senior Examiners will guide you on their preferred approach to questions and answers as they go. Therefore where you are presented with an opportunity to be involved in some activity or exam question either during or at the end of your study units, do take it, as it helps you learn in an applied way, but also prepares you for the examination.

Finally as a reminder

- Ensure you make the most of your learning process throughout
- Keep structured and orderly notes from which to revise
- Plan your revision – don't let it just happen
- Provide examples to enhance your answers
- Practise your writing skills in order that you present your work well and your writing is readable
- Take as many opportunities to test you knowledge and measure your progress as possible
- Plan and structure your answers
- Always take on the role and context of the question and answer in that context
- Adhere to the communication method selected by the examiner
- Always do as the question ask you
- **Do not leave it until the last minute!**

The writers and editorial team at Butterworth-Heinemann would like to take this opportunity to wish you every continuing success as you endeavour to study, revise and pass your examinations.

Butterworth-Heinemann and Karen Beamish would like to acknowledge Mike Worsam's contribution to this unit.

Introduction

The secret of success when taking any examination is preparation. With this important thought in mind, The Chartered Institute of Marketing has asked the Senior Examiners to produce these specimen answers to the actual questions set.

The answers are for your guidance and should not be seen as perfect solutions. In marketing, there is never one entirely correct solution. Whatever the style adopted, the format and the content of these answers should be indicative of what the examiners want to see.

It is hoped that you will find these specimen answers, and the examiners' comments, useful and informative. However, it is regretted that no correspondence can be entered into regarding the subject matter. We advise students to practise past questions and to use their tutors for guidance and feedback.

The copyright of all The Chartered Institute of Marketing examination material is held by the Institute. No Case Study or Questions may be reproduced without its prior permission which must be obtained in writing.

Exam material

Weetabix

The breakfast cereal market in the UK is estimated to be worth around £1 billion a year and has been growing at around 2%-3% a year in terms of value. Consumers in the UK eat 17 lbs of breakfast cereal a year, more than in any other country in the world. The nearest rivals are consumers in the United States of America, who eat 10 lbs a year. This sector of the UK market is highly competitive with both Kellogg's and Nestlé – two of the world's biggest food companies – being actively involved ('Cereal Partners' being Nestlé's joint venture with General Mills). The market share breakdown is shown in Table 1.

Table 1: Share of the UK Breakfast Cereal Market by Company	
Company	**Market share (%)**
Kellogg's	43.5
Weetabix	15.2
Cereal Partners	12.0
Others	29.3

Source: Marketing

As well as having major global players active in the market, retailer own-label brands have been growing in strength. In the last three years alone retailers' own-label brands have increased their share of the market from 22% to 33%.

Weetabix is a medium-sized company employing 2,000 people in the UK. Yet, against this market background in the year ending February 1999 Weetabix's turnover had risen 12% from £274 million to £308 million. Pre-tax profits had grown 23% to £52 million from £42 million. In fact

221

Weetabix has shown steady growth for a number of years. Back in 1982 Weetabix had a turnover of just £55 million with profits of just over £1 million.

Weetabix (the product) was developed in Australia around 1900. It is a sugarless flaked wheat biscuit with a consistency that turns into a soft pulp once milk is poured over it. When eaten this biscuit delivers nourishment in the form of a strong mix of complex carbohydrates. Due to its soft consistency it can be eaten by any age group. In particular, it is ideal for weaning babies. It is currently the number two brands in the UK breakfast cereal market (see Table 2). Unlike the other leading brands, no other retailer or manufacturer has managed to launch successfully a 'me-too' product. The majority of own-label flaked wheat biscuits are actually manufactured by Weetabix.

Weetabix (the company) has six major products, which are: Weetabix (plus a variation, Frutibix), Alpen, Crunchy Bran, Weetos, Ready Brek and Advantage. This gives the company some advantages in concentrating investment and management effort over a small range of products. Some observers see this situation arising because Weetabix is poor at innovation and see the company as having a conservative new product development policy. This is especially noticeable given that the other major players in this market have launched a number of minor variations on their basic breakfast cereal products in recent years.

Table 2: The UK Breakfast Cereal Market

Position	Brand	1998 Listing (£m)	% Change on previous year	Company
1	Kellogg's Corn Flakes	Over 90	-7.8	Kellogg's
2	Weetabix	75-80	0.7	Weetabix
3	Kellogg's Frosties	60-65	-5.9	Kellogg's
4	Nestlé Shredded Wheat	45-50	14.2	Cereal Partners
5	Kellogg's Rice Krispies	35-40	-6.2	Kellogg's
6	Kellogg's Crunchy Nut Corn Flakes	35-40	-3.7	Kellogg's
7	Kellogg's Healthwise Bran Flakes	30-35	-5.2	Kellogg's
8	Kellogg's Special K	25-30	0.9	Kellogg's
9	Quaker Sugar Puffs	25-30	8.8	Quaker
10	Kellogg's Optima Fruit 'n' Fibre	25-30	-2.5	Kellogg's

Source: AC Nielsen MEAL

Weetabix does not compete in every segment of the market and does not have multiple products in each category. However, it does tend to dominate the categories where it chooses to compete. For instance, Alpen is the brand leader in muesli, Ready Brek created and still dominates the hot cereal sector and Weetabix leads the wholewheat biscuit category.

Table 3: Advertising Spend, Cereals	
Company	**Advertising Spend in £m (April 1998-March 1999)**
Kellogg's	55
Cereal Partners	19
Weetabix	15
Quaker Oats	107
Others	202
Total	**92.9**

Source: Media Monitoring Services

One of Weetabix's key strengths is its high level of service. The Federation of Wholesale Distributors awarded the company a gold medal for service levels in 1995. Weetabix has a reputation of having products in stock, of delivering when they say they will deliver and of offering merchandising and marketing support. This is in an industry where wholesalers are used to being let down on as many as one in ten orders.

At the end of 1998 Kellogg's decided to increase its advertising expenditure by 40%. At the same time it cut its prices on six of its leading brands by 12%. This price war was started in retaliation to the growth of the own-label brands – however, it has obvious implications for Weetabix. The chairman of Weetabix said in February 1999 that he was 'concerned that the tactics of our major competitors may harm the whole breakfast cereal sector'.

Trends are also changing in the breakfast cereal market. Fewer consumers are having a sit down breakfast and are instead eating food such as croissants that can be eaten while travelling. A number of manufacturers have developed products to address this market (see Table 4). Kellogg's in particular has been active in this area of product development. Kellogg's Nutri-Grain is a bar high in fibre that the company is branding as a 'morning bar'. This product is now being extended with the addition of Nutri-Grain Twists containing separate sections of yoghurt and fruit purée that are twisted into the Nutri-Grain bar. Kellogg's is also extending three of its breakfast bar brands into cereal bars. The Kellogg's brands of Frosties, Coco Pops and Smacks are all being launched in a cereal and milk bar format. Cereal and milk bars are bound together with dried milk and are claimed to contain the equivalent amount of milk as in a traditional bowl of breakfast cereal.

Table 4: Estimated Manufacturers' Shares in the UK Cereal Bar Market in 1997		
	£m	**%**
Kellogg's	14.1	25
Jordan	13.9	25
Mars	11.4	20
Quaker	6.2	11
Other brands	0.8	1.5
Own label	9.8	17.5
Total	**56.2**	**100**

Source: Mintel

This mini case study has been prepared from secondary sources.

PART A

Question 1

As a consultant, write a report to Weetabix outlining and evaluating the strategic options open to the company in responding to the developing price war initiated by Kellogg's.

(20 marks)

Weetabix has decided to review the company's innovation activities.

Prepare a report advising the board of Weetabix on the auditing process necessary to undertake this analysis successfully.

(20 marks)

(40 marks in total)

Marking scheme

Question 1a

Candidates should point out that price wars are extremely dangerous and contagious. The results are often that margins decline and the product/service becomes a commodity sold on price alone. Kellogg's may be embarking on a price war because it believes:

- Consumers are highly responsive to prices.
- Competitors cannot meet price cuts.
- The organization is the lowest cost producer and can sustain low prices long-term.

Candidates should outline that it is important, before considering the options available for Weetabix, to firstly analyse its competitors, particularly Kellogg's. The strength of the competitors needs to be assessed by analysing:

- Size of company.
- Financial state of company.
- Reasoning behind the initiation of price war.
- Resources involved.
- Company aim – long and short-term strategy.
- Previous patterns of behaviour in other markets.

By building up a clear view of the competitive situation, Weetabix can assess the options available. Candidates may then go on to discuss the theoretical approaches to a price discounter, which are as follows.

Weetabix could follow Kellogg's prices if:

- Costs are falling.
- There is excess supply.
- Customers are price-sensitive.
- A price fall is compatible with brand image.
- The company has a build or hold market share objective.

Weetabix should resist cutting prices if:

1. The 'do nothing' option is risky. Even though Kellogg's is not competing with like-for-like products, consumers may still switch between products in response to a price-based offer.
2. Weetabix could respond with a promotional offer such as on-pack coupons for a special offer. This method is known to be successful in the cereals sector. It also has the advantage of encouraging loyalty to Weetabix for the duration of its special offer and for the duration of Kellogg's price cuts.
3. One of the reasons for Kellogg's price cutting is in response to own-label brands. As Weetabix manufactures many own-label brands it will need to work with retailers to ensure these products remain competitive. One option would be for retailers to cut their own-label prices whilst Weetabix maintained the prices of its branded products. Weetabix would also need to consider whether retailers would then demand lower prices from Weetabix or whether retailers would bear the cost of the price reductions.
4. The loyalty of customers to particular brands would also need to be investigated. Even though customers may switch to Kellogg's for the duration of the promotion they may switch back in the long-term. This would mean that Weetabix would only experience a short-term reduction in market share.

Longer Term Options

Price wars are generally short-term in nature as they are uneconomical in the long-term. In order to be able to maintain prices and compete with Kellogg's, Weetabix has several options for competing in the longer term.

Porter identifies three options:

- Cost leadership – not possible for Weetabix as it does not have the range of products required nor the size of production facilities to benefit from economies of scale.
- Differentiation – this involves creating a product sufficiently different from the competition with attributes that consumers are willing to pay more for.
- Focus strategy – involves focusing on one or more segments of the market and employing either a cost leadership or differentiation strategy – or both. Essentially this is the direction that Weetabix is taking.

Conclusion

Given that Weetabix has fewer resources available than Kellogg's, the following offensive strategies would not be suitable:

- Frontal attack – would need three times as many resources as Kellogg's to be successful.
- Surrounding attack – this is a very long-term option and would involve matching Kellogg's in all areas, e.g. cereal bar market, etc.
- Guerrilla attack – involves small-scale one-off attacks, e.g. public relations activities. However, these can be quite negative in nature.

The following offensive strategies would be acceptable.

- Flanking attack – this would involve occupying a geographic area or segment not yet occupied by Kellogg's, but which will be of future importance.
- By-pass attack – this involves innovating in completely new products or markets not occupied by the competition. This will be addressed in the report in Question 1b.

These options would enable Weetabix to develop its strengths without jeopardising its profits.

Senior Examiner's Comments

The student answer obtained an A grade. It answered the question, taking a strategic focus. The answer also specifically addressed the price war element of the question and the specific situation of Weetabix described in the mini case.

Answer – Question 1b

Report

To: Board of Weetabix

From: Consultant

Subject: Weetabix's Innovation Activities

Introduction

Innovation can be in:

- Products.
- Processes.
- Practices.

It is vital to long-term sustainable profits. Products can be:

- Imitated.
- Improved.
- Innovative/new.

Competitors are improving on/imitating Weetabix's products in recent times.

Innovation

Weetabix is viewed as lacking innovation and quite rapidly is reviewing its innovation activities.

Process

The process for the innovation audit should cover:

- Innovation climate.
- Actual innovation performance (hard measures of).
- Policy/strategies for innovation.
- Balance of senior management cognitive styles.

Innovation Climate Survey

This examines aspects such as:

- Attitude to innovation.
- Atmosphere/provision of time to innovation.
- Idea generation methods.
- Exchange of information.
- Support from senior management.
- Systems, structure generating innovation climate.
- Technology deployed.

A good way to interview/communicate with employees is by means of metaphors.

Actual Performance

For example, a number of new products generated in last year. Number of pioneer products re pioneers, migrators, etc.

In my previous company the vice president set a target of increasing conversion rate of R&D spend to new products by x% in 3 years.

Policy/Strategies

What is the corporate policy on innovation?

Balance of Cognitive Styles of Senior Management

E.g.

- Intuitive.
- Thinking.
- Feeling.
- Sensing.

This will affect the objectives set, choice of strategy (whether innovative-based or not).

Review Processes for NPD

- Idea generation.
- Idea evaluation.
- Concept development.
- Business evaluation.
- Product development.
- Product launch.

This should be checked (covered partly in Section 'Climate').

Conclusion

Regular systematic review is needed of the firm's innovation activities if the firm is to compete effectively in the long-term in the increasingly competitive environment it faces when going forward.

Senior Examiner's Comments

This student answer obtained a B grade. It answered the question taking a broad definition of innovation rather than merely New Product Development (NPD). The answer covers all aspects of an innovation audit. It could have been improved by relating this more directly to Weetabix. For instance, Weetabix's service delivery appears to be first class, suggesting it is product rather than service innovation that it has neglected.

PART B

Answer THREE Questions Only

Question 2

Write a report critically evaluating the usefulness of the value chain in analysing an organization's capabilities and in the formulation of marketing strategies.

(20 marks)

Marking scheme

Defining the value chain

The value chain is made up of primary activities:

- Inbound logistics.
- Operations.
- Outbound logistics.
- Marketing.
- Service.

These are aided by support activities:

- Procurement.
- Technology development.
- Human resource management.
- Organizational infrastructure.

An organization's capabilities are made up of its assets and competencies

Davidson suggests these assets will come from such areas as:

- Scale advantages.
- Processes.
- Customer franchises.
- Working capital.
- Sales and distribution network.
- Relationships with other organizations.
- Property.

Competencies will come from areas such as:

- Marketing.
- Selling.
- Operations.

Candidates should then debate the usefulness of the value chain in identifying an organization's areas of unique capabilities. A good answer may go on to discuss the fact that in most industries a single organization rarely undertakes all the value activities from product design through to delivery to the final customer. Therefore any analysis should recognize this wider value system.

Answer – Question 2

Value Chain Analysis

To: Marketing Director

From: Marketing Manager

Introduction

The value chain takes a 'systems approach' to evaluating the activities of a firm. Michael Porter developed this tool.

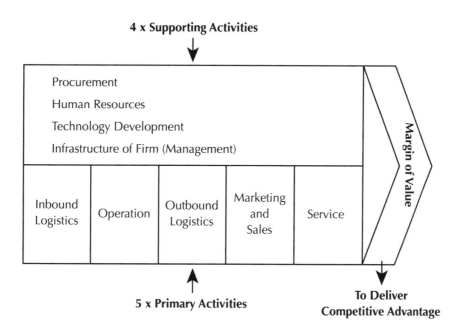

4 x Supporting Activities

Procurement

Human Resources

Technology Development

Infrastructure of Firm (Management)

Inbound Logistics

Operation

Outbound Logistics

Marketing and Sales

Service

Margin of Value

5 x Primary Activities

To Deliver Competitive Advantage

Figure 1
The Value Chain

Analysing organizational capabilities

The value chain is designed to analyse the activities in the firm. It is hard to apply to a Services Company and works best with product based companies.

In this way, it is possible to see which aspects the firm is carrying out well and which are areas of weakness. It also shows where supporting activities complement primary activities and the linkages between them.

Assets and competencies

Capabilities are made up of assets and competencies.

Assets – organizational:

- Finance.
- Operations.
- Marketing.
- Legal.

Competencies – organizational:

- Strategic.
- Operational.
- Functional.
- Team.
- Individuals.
- Corporate.

Marketing assets:

- Alliance-based.
- Customer-based.
- Internal.
- Distribution.

The value chain certainly helps to identify areas from the above list. It is a useful tool to determine which activities are generating value, and areas where the activities could be optimized.

Linkages between activities are vital forms of competitive advantage.

Formulation of marketing strategies

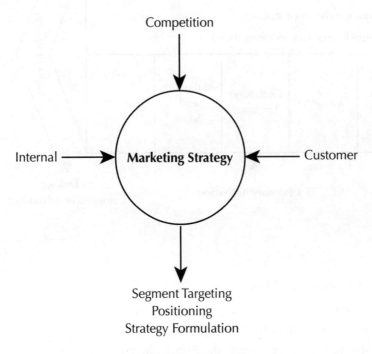

Marketing Strategy

Figure 2
Marketing strategy

The value chain can be considered with Porter's earlier analysis 'generic strategy' to consider strategic competitive options:

- Cost leadership.
- Differentiation.
- Differentiation/cost focus.

The value chain helps uncover sources of cost leadership and differentiation.

Competitive strategy

- Identify competitive advantage.
- Learning/experience curves.
- Generic strategy.

Industry position

- Market position.
- Offensive/defensive strategies.

Product/market strategies

- Ansoff.

Value chain analysis certainly helps with competitive strategy formulation.

Value chain also helps in merger/acquisition analysis:

- Sometimes pooling of assets does not lead to efficient generation of value. Rather capabilities should 'complement' one another. Many mergers have failed or not done as well as hoped originally because of this phenomenon.
- A good knowledge of internal capabilities helps formulation of a competitive position, if the market needs are understood and competitor capabilities (which can be analysed to some extent by the value chain) are assessed effectively.

Summary of a few aspects

Advantages: good to identify sources of competitive advantage which determine value creation and value destruction.

Disadvantages: Hard to use, not very suitable for service organizations and needs to be used alongside other tools.

Conclusion

The value chain is a popular, but difficult, auditing tool to use properly. It is best used in conjunction with other auditing tools, e.g. PIMS, PLC, Portfolio Analysis, Cost Efficiency Analysis, in order to assess capabilities, match with competition and deliver (ultimately) value and satisfaction sustainability to the user/customer.

Senior Examiner's Comments

The student answer obtained an A grade. It answered the question, taking a strategic focus. The answer covers all aspects of the question. It clearly defines the value chain and assets and competencies. The answer then goes on to show how the tool can be used to develop strategy. The uses of diagrams saves the candidate time in describing the value chain and yet adds clarity to the answer. Finally, the candidate also highlights some weakness of the tool.

Question 3

Having undertaken a market analysis, a company that designs female clothing in Hong Kong is considering launching a new range of garments. What criteria would you advise them to use in evaluating which potential target market or markets to enter?

(20 marks)

Marking scheme

The main criteria for judging this potential target market or markets will be the attractiveness of the market segment and its fit with the organization's assets and competencies.

Criteria for evaluating the market segment attractiveness are:

- Segment size.
- Segment's rate of growth.
- Segment's profitability.
- Customer's price sensitivity.
- Stage of life cycle.
- Predictability.
- Pattern of demand.
- Quality of competition.
- Potential to create differentiated position.
- Likelihood of new entrants.

- Power of supplier.
- Power of customers.
- Barriers to entry/exit.
- Impact of changes in the external environment on the segment.

Criteria for evaluating organizational capabilities are:

- Assets, such as:
    o Advantages of scale.
    o Production processes.
    o Customer franchises.
    o Working capital.
    o Sales/distribution network.
    o Relationships with other organizations.
    o Property.
- An organization's main competencies will fall into three key areas:
    o Marketing – NPD, brand management, market research techniques, etc.
    o Selling – Supply change management, account management, customer service, relationship development, etc.
    o Operations – Motivation and control, inventory control, industrial relations, etc.

The clothing company will need to match its assets and competencies to the potential target markets it judges to be most attractive.

Both the value chain and an adapted Shell Directional Policy Matrix would play a useful role in this process.

Answer – Question 3

Introduction

Following the market analysis, the company should have an idea of the key issues affecting the industry, including social trends. Presumably the market analysis would have included a Porter's 5 forces analysis to determine:

- Buyer power.
- Supplier power.
- Threat of substitute.
- New entrants.
- Competitive rivalry.

Assuming there is demand for the product, the company needs to look at the following:

Segmentation

Who do these garments appeal to?

- Young females.
- Older females.

How are they going to segment the market?

- Lifestyle, age, socio-economic status.
- Are they luxury goods or everyday wear?

When looking at segments they need to determine:

- Profitability.
- Demand.
- Sustainability of the segment in the long-term.
- Accessibility (for example will they market abroad?)
- Measurability (can we measure the profitability?)
- Achievability.
- Segment size (is it large enough?)
- Market size.
- Potential for growth.
- Effect of external trends on the demand for these items (especially if they are high fashion items).

Competitor capabilities: The company needs to look at competitors in the market:

- What are their objectives and strategies?
- What are their capabilities in terms of:
  - Products?
  - Innovation?
  - Financial strengths?
  - People and management expertise?

Distribution: When determining which market to enter, the company should look at:

- Distribution channels available – Are they fragmented? Do they allow concentrated selective and intensive distribution? This should be related back to the organizational objectives.
- Power of competitors over a distribution channel. Some competitors, if they are large enough, will have a hold over the channel that would mean that the Hong Kong retailer will not be able to use this channel. For example, Coca-Cola's power over McDonald's prevented Irn Bru being distributed through McDonald's outlets in Scotland.

International markets: The company needs to decide if it is going to market solely in its home market or abroad. If abroad it needs to decide:

- Who is going to distribute.
- Who is going to provide service and sales support.
- Should it get involved in Joint Ventures partnerships or buy a branch abroad? This would depend on its level of commitment to this market.

It also needs to be sure that these fashion garments appeal to the culture of the people in the international market. Is its product global? Does it have mass market appeal or should it follow a niche marketing strategy?

Align with core competencies and assets

Once the company has looked at the market, competitor activity and segmentation, it needs to align this with its own assets and competencies. In particular:

- Does it fit with the strategy and mission of the organization? For example, if it were a provider of luxury goods, would launching a range of cheap garments fit with its strategy?
- Does it have the distribution systems and technical knowledge to compete in the chosen segment or target market?
- What is the level of brand awareness in its chosen market?
- Are its brands competing?

- Can it compare and sustain competitive advantage against the key competitors?

Conclusion

Once the company has carried out the audit, it needs to look at its assets and competencies and match these to particular target markets. It also needs to analyse external factors such as distribution, competitor activity and segment profitability. Evaluation against Johnson and Scholes's sustainability, feasibility and accessibility will provide a useful framework.)

Senior Examiner's Comments

This answer obtained a B grade. Its strength is that it specifically addresses the scenario outline in the question. To have obtained an A grade this answer would have needed a stronger structure and a slightly more strategic focus.

Question 4

Evaluate the usefulness to organizations of the balanced scorecard approach as advocated by Kaplan and Norton.

(20 marks)

Marking scheme

Candidates should start with a definition of the 'balanced scorecard.'

In the balanced scorecard approach, Kaplan and Norton suggest that at the same time as a balanced set of objectives is created; a coherent set of performance measures is also developed.

Candidates should outline that the balanced scorecard approach advocates that managers should look at their business from four key perspectives:

- Customer perspective.
- Internal perspective.
- Innovation and learning perspective.
- Financial perspective.

Having these four perspectives leads to a wider set of objectives and measures being employed by an organization rather than purely financial measures.

Candidates should then illustrate this point with some examples of appropriate objectives and measures for each of the four perspectives (see Figure 3 for examples).

Evaluation of usefulness

Candidates should then go on to discuss the usefulness of this approach:

- Widens the view managers have of a business rather than concentrating on financial data.
- Forces managers to understand the complex relationships underlying the traditional functional structures.
- Ensures consistency between objectives.

Problems

- Can be difficult to operate in practice as objectives are formed not only in a range of areas but at different levels and on different timescales, i.e. both vertically and horizontally through the organization.

	Strategic Objectives	Strategic Measures
Financial	F.1 Return on capital F.2 Cash flow F.3 Profitability F.4 Profitability growth F.5 Reliability of performance	→ ROCE → Cash flow → Net margin → Volume growth rate vs. industry → Profit forecast reliability → Sales backlog
Customer	C.1 Value for money C.2 Competitive price C.3 Customer satisfaction	→ Customer ranking survey → Pricing index → Customer satisfaction index → Mystery shopping rating
Internal	I.1 Marketing • Product and service development • Shape customer requirement I.2 Manufacturing • Lower manufacturing cost • Improve project management I.3 Logistics • Reduce delivery costs • Inventory management I.4 Quality	→ Pioneer percentage of product portfolio → Hours with customer on new work → Total expenses per unit vs. competition → Safety incident index → Delivered cost per unit → Inventory level compared to plan and output rate → Rework
Innovation and Learning	I.L.1 Innovate product and services I.L.2 Time to market I.L.3 Empowered workforce I.L.4 Access to strategic information I.L.5 Continuous improvement	→ Percentage revenue from pioneer products → Cycle time vs. industry norm → Staff attitude survey → Strategic information availability → Number of employee suggestions

The Balanced Scorecard
(Source: Adapted from Kaplan and Norton 1992, 1993)

Figure 3
The balanced scorecard

Answer – Question 4

To: Managing Director

From: Marketing Manager

Subject: The Balanced Scorecard

Introduction

In the majority of firms in many sectors there is a conflict between short-term profit objectives and other longer term objectives. Managers and decision makers tend to focus on the former at the expense of the latter. The 'Balanced Scorecard' is an attempt to help managers escape this blinkered, short-termist approach and adopt more of a 'stakeholder view'.

The balanced scorecard looks at aspects such as:

- Customer (perspective).
- Financial.
- Innovation/learning.
- Internal.

It establishes a set of performance measures against these types of parameters. Therefore it acts as an alternative tool for monitoring performance against pre-set objectives, and facilitates control by enabling subsequent alteration of objectives and strategies.

An example of a possible balanced scorecard:

Table 5	
Objective	**Performance Measure**
1. Financial ROCE, profitability, etc.	Profit/QTR, etc.
2. Innovation/Learning Increase % of sales due to new products developed between R&D and marketing to 20%. Increase marketing orientation through learning.	Sales turnover due to additions to product line. Number of staff in each function doing CIM Diploma in Marketing.
3. Customer Increase customer satisfaction.	Customer satisfaction ratings, number of product return, number of complaints.
4. Internal Increase team competencies.	Number of team building courses held.

3. Summary of advantages and disadvantages

Advantages:

- Enables a balanced view of the business.
- Widens the management view.
- Helps to ensure horizontal integration.
- Helps to ensure vertical integration.
- Aids removal of barriers across functions.
- Supports monitoring and control activities.
- Helps build objectives that are consistent and self-supporting.
- Can aid the development of an innovation culture.

Disadvantages:

- Adds to managers' activities list.
- Won't always get buy-in from everyone.
- Conflicts with 'empire-builders'.
- Needs top-down support.
- Everyone (managers) has to be involved.

4. Conclusion

The balanced scorecard widens the view of management and supports the longer term view of Marketing Philosophy – generating value and satisfaction through meeting customer needs, via development of relationships. It helps businesses develop more innovation based strategies, not just follower/me-too approaches, which are not always good for the economy in the longer term.

Senior Examiner's Comments

This student answer obtained an A grade. It discussed all aspects of the question, outlined very clearly the Balanced Scorecard approach and went on to give an evaluation of its usefulness.

Question 5

A Western European soft drinks company is negotiating an agreement with a bottler and distributor in the Russian market. In its own domestic Western European market, the brand is seen as non-conformist and slightly maverick in nature. You have been asked to write a report to the Marketing Director advising the soft drinks company of the branding issues they need to consider before finalising any agreement.

(20 marks)

Marking scheme

Candidates should begin with a general statement on the importance of branding. They should emphasize that the overall aim of branding decisions is to create an identity for the product that is distinctive and also in line with the targeting and positioning decisions already taken.

Before entering any agreement the drinks company will need to assess the likely target market for its brand in the Russian market by evaluating:

- Actual and potential market size.
- Likely market growth.
- Market profitability.
- Distribution systems.
- Market trends.

It will also need to analyse the Russian bottler and distributor with regard to:

- Current performance.
- Reputation.
- Company culture.

Candidates should go on to discuss the key issues that affect the branding decisions. These are likely to be cultural issues affecting consumer behaviour in the Russian market. Examples of some of the issues they should go on to discuss are:

- How will Russian consumers perceive this UK brand?
- Is there currently any awareness of this brand in Russia?
- Will the current brand position in Western Europe of being non-conformist and slightly maverick translate into the Russian market?
- Do Russians use this product in the same way as Western European customers?
- Is the potential target market in Russia similar in its behaviour and attitudes to the current Western European segment?

Candidates should point out that the decision about positioning of the brand in Russia will depend on the organization's long-term strategic objectives – i.e. whether or not it aims to develop a standardized global brand.

Answer – Question 5.

Report

To: Marketing Director

From: Brand Manager

Re: Branding Issues on Entering the Russian Market

Background

We have been in discussion with a Russian bottler and distributor to allow entry into the Russian market.

In our current market the brand is seen as non-conformist and maverick. This report will cover the branding issues before licensing the agreement and entry into the Russian market.

Branding Issues

Russian Market Segment

In Western Europe our brand occupies a distinct market niche. We need to ensure that this niche is available within the Russian market. In other words, we need to know the competition in this segment. It may be that our proposed brand positioning is already occupied within the Russian market.

By having this, and the structure of the Russian soft drinks market, we will have the background for our branding strategy within the Russian market.

Will the Current Branding Work in Russia?

Our current brand has distinct elements in Europe that set it apart. We need to know whether our brand and its current values will be accepted within the Russian market.

This will involve a significant amount of qualitative research e.g. focus groups, but will give us the direction for our branding strategy. If the current brand values will succeed within the Russian market we need to establish objectives and communication programmes.

Brand Objectives

For any strategy, objectives are essential. Branding strategy is no exception to this. We need to set out objectives for the brand in terms of awareness and consideration among the target market within 1, 2 and 3 years of the launch. By doing this we will have the bedrock for any reviews and remedial action (if required).

Communication of Brand

This is essential for us to establish a brand within the Russian market that will support sales volume. If we assume that we will use current positioning within the Russian market we need to establish a programme of advertising, sales promotion and PR which will:

- Generate awareness.
- Embody values into the brand.

By doing this we will be able to create the necessary differentiation within the market. I would suggest that a heavy investment is required in brand development.

Brand values don't succeed in the Russian market

If the research suggests that current brand values will not create differentiation and drive sales within the Russian market then we need to investigate the market. This should explore those values and elements that will give sufficient advantage for launch and drive sales volumes in the long-term.

It is essential that whichever brand values are chosen, they provide a sustainable differentiation for the long-term within the Russian market.

If new brand values are devised then a similar programme to that devised in the previous section needs to be created to establish the brand in the new market.

Review

It is essential that we establish a review programme to monitor the progress of the brand. We need to ensure that there are facilities within the Russian market to create a regular brand trading facility. We will then be able to see the progress towards the objectives, perceptions of the brand and the remedial action, if any, that is required.

Summary

A move into a new market creates a range of branding issues. The main issues, which need to be addressed, are:

- Will existing brand values drive sales volumes in Russia?
- Will the new market accept the brand values?
- What communications are required to build the new brand in Russia?
- How do we review the progress to achieve branding and marketing objectives?

Senior Examiner's Comments

This answer obtained a B grade because it answers the question directly in a very applied manner. Its strength is the fact that it directly focuses the answer to the scenario outlined in the question. To have obtained an A grade it would have needed to have a slightly more theoretical background and have taken a rather more strategic view. However, this was a very solid answer and benefited from a very clear structure.

Question 6

A major bank is considering a strategic partnership with a mobile phone operator to provide customers with a package that offers home banking, bill paying and smart cards. Discuss the bank's motivation for such a move and assess the issues that are likely to be critical to a successful alliance.

(20 marks)

Marking scheme

The bank's motivation for pursuing a strategic partnership with a mobile phone operator is likely to be to maintain competitive advantage. In this case the bank aims to maintain competitive advantage through erecting new barriers against competitors. The alliance offers the possibilities of a broad product line, large sales and extensive service capabilities – all of which are examples of effective barriers. The bank, by forming an alliance, can achieve greater sales – but at less cost – through this partnership rather than trying to offer this spread of services by itself.

There are four key types of marketing alliance:

- Product and/or service alliances.
- Logistics alliances.
- Promotional alliances.
- Pricing collaborations.

The likely success of any strategic alliances will be dependent on three key issues:

- Strategic compatibility.
- A long-term focus.
- Flexibility.

Answer – Question 6

Background

The financial services sector is driven by innovation. There are constant developments in terms of technology, which create customer improvements. The bank is considering a strategic partnership with a mobile phone operator. This would affect home banking, bill payment, etc. for the bank's customers. This note outlines the bank's motivation for the alliance and issues critical for its success.

Motivation

Customer Retention

It is much easier and cheaper to retain customers than attract new ones, especially in very competitive marketplaces. The alliance should help increase the loyalty of customers to the bank.

Perception of Brand Values

Banks always have a poor reputation. This alliance will help reposition the bank's image with values such as innovation, modernity and customer focus. These are very desirable brand values in the banking sector.

Improve Customer Access

As technology develops, customers are demanding better access to their finances. Recent examples of this are the introduction of telephone and Internet based banking. The development of mobile phone banking gives customers increased access to their accounts and this extends one of the major trends in the marketplace.

Cost Cutting

The introduction and development of technology has allowed banks to reduce transaction costs. Removing people from branches and onto mobile phone transactions will serve to reduce these costs even further.

Product Attractiveness

The addition of this development to the bank's product/access range helps to improve the attractiveness of its offerings and create a major point of differentiation. As the market is very fast moving and competitive, the ability to create an element of differentiation is vital.

Attract New Customers

The addition of this development to the bank's product/access range also helps customer recruitment, which is a vitally important issue.

PR Benefits

This alliance provides ammunition with which to gain a PR advantage. It thus needs to be extensively used to gain maximum advantage.

Issues Critical to the Success of the Alliance

Take-up of Phones

This is essential if the phone company and the bank are to achieve their targets, e.g. cost cutting, increased profits, product take-up etc. Targets should be set by both companies in conjunction with each other. The targets should be mutually beneficial to the companies.

Customer Communications

These are vital if take-up targets are to be achieved. The party picking up the costs must be agreed in advance. This also applies to the positioning. Branding etc. must be agreed in advance. The decision on this will have a major impact on the acceptance by customers of the offer.

The rationale for the alliance must also be carefully communicated to the customer. It must be spelt out that the rationale is to improve customer access. Should the customer feel the rationale is to be cost cutting and branch closures, then the offer is likely to be received badly.

Commitment of Both Sides

It is essential to have the full commitment of both parties. The lack of commitment from one of the parties, such as poor customer service, will have a negative impact.

Pricing

Customers should feel they are getting a good deal. Discounted phone calls and line rental charges would be a good tactic. Failure to do this could seriously jeopardize the success of the venture.

Branding Implications

If both companies feel that the impact on their brands has been positive then they are likely to see the venture as a success.

Failure of fulfilment, customer service issues, etc. could easily create negative implications for the branding of both companies.

Behaviour Change

Both parties hope to see a behaviour change. The banks would like to see more remote electronic transaction. The phone company would like to see increased phone usage. If these behavioural changes are achieved then both parties will view the alliance as a success.

Summary

The bank's motivations for the alliance are largely: cost cutting, increasing customer loyalty/retention and creating product/brand differentiation. The main issues critical to the success of this alliance are the commitment of both parties, a discounted pricing structure, achieving the necessary take-up of the offer and an effective communications programme.

Senior Examiner's Comments

This student answer obtained a B grade. It answered all aspects of the question, both motivation for the alliance and the critical success factors. The paper also dealt specifically with the scenario outlined in the question. To have obtained an A grade it would have needed to refer to the background theory on alliances and take a slightly more strategic view. However, this was a competent answer that gained clarity through a very strong structure.

Question 7

The Marketing Director of an academic book publishing company has asked you to write a report evaluating the use of scenario planning in helping their organization to develop an understanding of how this sector of the market may develop in the future.

(20 marks)

Marking scheme

Candidates should begin by describing the essence of scenario planning and its difference from other forecasting techniques – namely, the idea of identifying a diverse range of potential futures. Good answers will emphasize that there is no aim to assign probabilities to the likelihood of any scenario happening.

They should then go on to outline the four key stages in the development of simple scenarios:

- Identify the critical variables.
- Develop possible strings of events.
- Refine the scenarios.
- Identify the issues arising.

Candidates should then illustrate the benefits of scenario planning to an organization in the academic book publishing industry. Given the dynamic environment this industry is facing with the emerging Internet revolution, these benefits are likely to include:

- Helping managers to understand the critical issues that lie at the heart of the future of the organization.
- Creating a framework within which to understand events as they actually evolve.
- Preparing managers for the possibility of discontinuities in the external environment.
- Helping to place fundamental strategic issues on the management agenda.

Answer – Question 7

Report

To: Marketing Director

From: Marketing Manager

Subject: Evaluation of Scenario Planning

Introduction

Scenario planning is one of a family of forecasting tools: trends, modelling, individual (genius) forecasting, consensus (Jury & Delphi) market sensing and scenario planning.

Background

Scenario planning was originally a military strategic tool. Large companies then employed it successfully in the 1970s; Shell used it to anticipate and be ready for falls in demand for oil. It was important to Shell because of high fixed costs involved in capacity planning. In the 1990s Ericsson used it successfully to foresee/embrace the possibility of mobile/wireless telephones, took the lead in standards development and helped Europe dominate the world with GSM.

What It Can Do

Scenario planning is about possibilities and not forecasts. It is therefore suitable for complex and uncertain markets where change is rapid and forecasts are impossible. It provides an insight into the dynamic variables/interactions in the industry.

Process

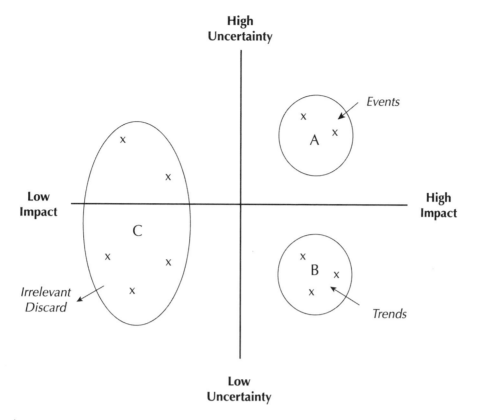

Figure 4
Matrix

- Identify problems relevant to the business.
- Brainstorm change drivers relevant to the problem.
- Filter suggestions by placing on matrix.
- Collect events A.
- Collect trends B.
- Discard C.
- Develop themes (uses a simplistic 'thematic' approach – in my experience the best!)
- Make trends consistent across themes.
- Make internally consistent.
- Check relevance to initial problem.

Porter suggests scenarios are only useful if you make them relevant to the firm's microenvironment.

The Team

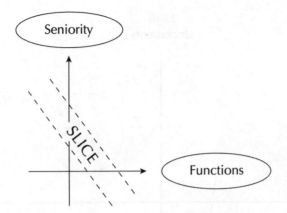

Figure 5
Slice

- Take a diagonal slice across the firm:
- Include dissidents/mavericks/devil's advocates; they are creative and help avoid the dreaded 'groupthink'.
- Take about three months to build scenarios; not so long that people get bored.
- Do activity off-site/undisturbed.
- Have fun (in the author's experience it is fun if it is done properly).

What to do with the Output

- Use the range of possible futures to develop a flexible corporate strategy.
- Monitor key events to find which future we are heading for!
- Build a war room (optional) which everybody can input to.

Advantages of Scenario Planning

- Gives insight into industry.
- Sensitizes staff to key areas.
- Helps monitor activities.
- Good for complex markets/rapidly changing.
- Helps with contingency planning.
- Good for senior managers.

Disadvantages of Scenario Planning

- Time-consuming.
- Expensive.
- Needs skilled facilitators.
- People can become bored.
- Need right mix of people.
- Will not provide a forecast.
- May not be made relevant to the firm.
- Can turn into a jokey but ineffectual exercise, considered an 'off-line' activity and ignored by busy operational staff.

Academic Book Publishing

First we need to understand the industry – industry analysis is necessary, e.g. supply chain.

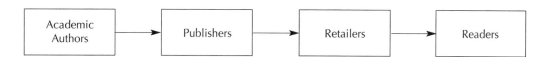

Figure 6
Supply chain

And decide ultimately (maybe) how this might change.

Some Change Drivers

- Internet retailing.
- Relationship marketing.
- Out of town retailing.
- Demise of the high street.
- Expansion (i.e. horizontal integration) of firm into book selling etc.

A theme can then be developed which uses these key drivers.

Conclusion

Scenario planning is an excellent tool for gaining insight into a fast-moving industry. It can also be used for strategic planning. It is time-consuming and expensive, but if done properly is well worth the effort.

Senior Examiner's Comments

This student obtained an A grade. The answer covered all aspects of the question and was in report format, which added clarity to the answer. The paper outlines the scenario planning process, evaluates the usefulness of the tool and then discusses it in relation to an academic book publishing company.

Introduction

The secret of success when taking any examination is preparation. With this important thought in mind, The Chartered Institute of Marketing has asked the Senior Examiners to produce these specimen answers to the actual questions set.

The answers are for your guidance and should not be seen as perfect solutions. In marketing, there is never one entirely correct solution. Whatever the style adopted, the format and the content of these answers should be indicative of what the examiners want to see.

It is hoped that you will find these specimen answers, and the examiners' comments, useful and informative. However, it is regretted that no correspondence can be entered into regarding the subject matter. We advise students to practise past questions and to use their tutors for guidance and feedback.

The copyright of all The Chartered Institute of Marketing examination material is held by the Institute. No Case Study or Questions may be reproduced without its prior permission which must be obtained in writing.

Exam material

Freeplay Energy

In the early 1980s Trevor Bayliss, the British inventor, developed the concept of a self-powered radio. Electricity for the radio would be provided by an integral wind-up generator. Bayliss's idea was that this self-powered radio would allow people in remote villages across Africa to gain access to news and information from around the world. In 1994 the South African based BayGen Power company (later renamed Freeplay Energy) signed an exclusive agreement with Trevor Bayliss to develop and commercialize the product.

Although Trevor Bayliss no longer has an active involvement with Freeplay Energy, the partners who run the company are still driven by the desire to improve the lives of individuals in the developing world. The company's Cape Town factories are co-owned by local charities that represent the disabled, single mothers and former offenders. Around one third of the company s employees are from these disadvantaged groups.

The first commercial version of the wind-up radio was the FPR1 and this was distributed to villages by aid agencies. Very early on, it became apparent that the radio was too heavy, too fragile and more crucially too expensive for its intended market. Villagers appeared to be more willing to spend £2 to £3 a month on batteries, than an initial £29 on a radio that did not require battery replacements. The product however began to develop sales in more affluent markets. In the UK the Design Council awarded the wind-up radio Millennium Product status. One national newspaper went as far as naming it the most significant invention of a generation.

Freeplay Energy began to realize that volume sales could be developed by concentrating on the European and North American markets. Sales growth in these markets has allowed Freeplay to invest further in the technology, and as a result develop products that are smaller, lighter, more durable and less expensive. The FPR1 had to be wound for 20 seconds in order to produce 30 minutes of playing time. The FPR2, which Freeplay launched in 1997, weighs less, is more compact and supplies an hour of playing time after being wound for 20 seconds.

In 1999 the company added to the radio range with the launch of a new model, the Freeplay S360. The company also launched the 20/20 flashlight, which contains an integral energy storage unit to generate power for instantaneous or later use.

Currently Freeplay Energy has a £30m turnover and is forecast to produce around 1.2 million units in the year 2000. Around 70% of its sales are in the United States of America and 25% in Europe, with Africa and the Middle East making up the balance. The company's promotional budget is around £3m.

Through market research the organization has identified that the product is positioned differently in the various overseas markets. In Germany the product appeals to the consumer's strong environmental consciousness. In the United States of America and Japan, where there is a strong outdoor culture, the product is bought as a component of tornado or earthquake survival kits. In the UK, the company's biggest market per capita, the general public is proud of the fact that the product was invented there.

The company still has an aspiration to create products that will bring modern forms of communication to individuals in remote rural villages. However they believe that entering into the European and North American markets has allowed them to develop much larger manufacturing volumes which in turn has enabled them to gradually lower prices.

Freeplay Energy has a number of new product ideas under investigation. One initiative is the concept of a satellite telephone that can be charged with energy provided by a self-powered generator rather than costly disposable batteries. The company believes this product would overcome some of the problems faced by African economies. African states cannot afford to develop the landlines and other facilities needed for a modern telecommunications infrastructure. This approach would allow these states to make a technology leap and allow individuals access to the global communications network. Other product ideas include self-powered pull cord lights, water purification systems and even foetal heartbeat monitors.

The company's philosophy is to attempt to create a range of products that will help improve communication across the developing world. This is reflected in its tagline, 'Powered by You'.

The company now has to consider how it plans to develop over the next five years. There are a number of strategic choices to be made. It could move away from making its own products or it could carry on some manufacturing but licence out its technology to mobile phone manufacturers such as Nokia, Ericsson and Motorola.

This mini-case study has been prepared from secondary sources.

PART A

Question 1

The managers of Freeplay Energy have asked you to write a report advising them of the issues they need to consider when developing the organization's mission, goals and objectives. This report should specifically address Freeplay's unique situation and its current stage of development.

(20 marks)

The managers of the company have also asked you to write a report outlining the process the company should follow in order to undertake successfully market segmentation, targeting and positioning. This report should specifically discuss the segmentation variables that would be applicable in this market.

(20 marks)

(40 marks in total)

Outline Answer – Question 1a

Defining Mission versus Goals and Objectives/Influences on Mission and Objectives

- Corporate governance.
- Stakeholders.
- Business ethics.
- Cultural context.

Specific Internal and External Influences

Internal:

- Management style, i.e. risk averse.
- Organization culture, e.g. not responsive to change.
- Internal stakeholder expectations, e.g. Shareholders, Employees, Trade Unions.
- Internal resources, e.g. poor cash flow situation.

External:

- Microenvironmental, e.g. customers, competitors, the market.
- Macroenvironmental, e.g. political factors, economic factors, legal factors, social factors, technological factors.
- External stakeholders, e.g. general public, pressure groups.

Trade-offs

- short-term versus long-term.
- Profit margins versus competitive position.
- Profit versus non-profit objectives.
- Related versus non-related growth opportunities.
- Market penetration effort versus market development effort.
- Growth versus stability.
- Risk avoidance versus risk taking.

These issues need to be discussed in the context of the organization in the question.

Answer – Question 1a

Report on Freeplay Energy

To: The Management Team, Freeplay Energy

From: The Marketing Consultant

Date: 7th December, 2000

Subject: Freeplay Energy

Contents

1. Executive summary.
2. Introduction.
3. Definition of mission, goals and objectives.
4. Issues to be considered in determining mission, goals and objectives:
    1. Determining Mission.
    2. Determining the Goals.

3. Determining Objectives.

1. Executive Summary

Freeplay Energy is a successful technologically advanced company with an ethical philosophy. It is faced with growing expectations and subsequent need for change.

In the light of this background I have been requested to advise you on issues to be taken into account in developing organizational goals, missions and objectives.

2. Introduction

There is a trend in today's business world towards strategic planning. This entails amongst other things the definition of one's mission, goals and objectives.

3. Definition of Mission, Goals and Objectives

A mission is a company's reason for practising business. It answers the questions: What are we in business for? What are we trying to achieve?

Goals

A goal is a broad aim of what is to be achieved, normally qualitative in nature.

Objectives

Objectives are quantified goals of what is to be achieved. These should be specific, measurable, achievable, realistic and given a timescale.

4. Issues to be considered in determining mission, goals and objectives

i) Determining Mission

As addressed above, the mission determines the overall direction of the company and its resources. In determining mission the following issues are considered:

a. Vision

This is where the organization sees itself years from now. It is evident that Freeplay Energy sees itself as a technological champion making the lives of people in less developed countries better through innovations, like self-powered communications. This determines the base of your mission.

b. The Company Philosophy

This is to create a range of products that will help improve communications across the developing world. This too feeds into the mission statement.

c. The Products or Services

The products and services – communication products in your case – feed into the mission.

d. The Shareholders

Companies when determining a mission take note of the shareholder's needs, which could be to make profit or involve qualitative needs like making the world a better place.

e. The Customer

In marketing the customer is king. In other words decisions and actions are geared towards satisfying customers' needs; this also determines the mission.

f. The Macro Environment

Issues in the macroenvironment also help determine the mission. These include political stipulations, social, legal and technological trends.

g. Social Responsibility and Ethics (Stakeholders)

Besides having responsibility for one's immediate environment a company has responsibility for stakeholders. For instance, in Freeplay's case this is to improve the lives of the disabled, single mothers and the less developed world.

h. Employees

Freeplay's responsibility to its employees also feeds into the mission statement.

ii) Determining the Goals

The goals are subsequent to the mission statement and the issues to be considered include:

- The company resources and capability.
- The market.
- The competitors.
- The internal culture.
- The political, legal, economic and technological trends.

Whilst the goals are a follow-on from the mission, they have to be worked on within the confines and stipulations of the company mission (some schools of thought believe it limits one to think within the box).

Company Resources and Capability

The goals projected should take note of a company's strengths and weaknesses. These are determined by conducting a positional audit encompassing all functions: marketing, finance, human resources, R&D, and production. The competitive advantage should be able to fulfil the required goals. For instance:

- Adequate resources – human, financial, etc.
- Adequate skills, knowledge, etc.

The Market

The goals should be determined after having observed the consumer/customer segments. By observing the segment's needs and wants we then set out to fulfil them. For instance, in Freeplay's case the needs of, say, the USA, Europe, Africa and the Middle East should help determine our goals.

The Competitors

Our competitors and other original equipment manufacturers' activities impinge on the goals of the organization. In particular: their capabilities or sources of competitive advantage.

The Internal Culture

What culture exists in Freeplay Energy? Is it product or customer-focused? It is evident that there is a tendency towards being market-led.

PEST Factors

The goals should be determined, taking note of the trend of the macro factors – say, technological advancement or legal regulation.

iii) Determining Objectives

As stated earlier, objectives should be specific, measurable, achievable, realistic and given a timescale. In developing objectives Freeplay should take note of the following:

- The company's resources and capability. For instance, do we have the competitive advantage to survive in the aggressive communications industry?
- The culture as noted under Goals.
- The customer's profile: ability to pay, trends, segments etc.
- The competitors' activity – their market share, strategies, resources.
- The macroenvironment.
- Time constraints.

Senior Examiner's Comments

This student answer obtained an A grade. As you can see it goes into a great deal of detail, discussing the factors that should influence Freeplay's mission, goals and objectives. The answer could have been improved if it had discussed the tension between Freeplay's current mission and its actual markets.

Outline Answer – Question 1b.

Criteria for Identifying Market Segments

- Homogeneous.
- Exclusive.
- Substantial.
- Accessible.

Segmentation Variables

- Profile variables.
- Behavioural variables.
- Psychographic variables.

Assessing Attractiveness of Segments/Matching to Assets and Competencies

- Market factors.
- Competition.
- Environmental factors.

Positioning

- Credence.

- Competitiveness.
- Consistency.
- Clarity.

These issues need to be discussed in the context of the organization in the question.

Answer – Question 1b

Report

To: Managers of Freeplay Energy

From: Marketing Consultant

Date: 7th December, 2000

Subject: An Outline of the Process of Market Segmentation, Targeting and Positioning for Freeplay Energy

Introduction

Further to my earlier report, this paper details how Freeplay can segment its market, select targets and position itself in the minds of consumers.

Segmentation

There is an enormous potential market for Freeplay products. We all at some point in the week (if not each day) listen to the radio. We all at some point need a torch and increasingly, we can't go anywhere without a mobile phone.

However, to use its resources efficiently, Freeplay must decide which segments of the market it will focus its attentions on.

Freeplay needs to choose segments which are attractive to it and ones which match the organization's competencies.

Factors to consider in determining the 'attractiveness' of a market segment include:

- Is it reachable?
- Can Freeplay measure it?
- Is the segment stable or changing?
- Is it big enough to be profitable?
- Will all members of the segment react in the same way to the marketing mix?
- Will the segment react in a different way to stimuli compared with other segments?

For segments to be considered for selection, Freeplay needs to ensure it can answer 'yes' to the above questions.

Segmentation Variables

There are various 'classic' segmentation bases in the consumer market. These include segmenting on the basis of demographics (age, sex, etc.), geographics (where people live), psychographics (how people think), what stage of the family life cycle they are in (bachelor, married no children, retired no children, etc); lifestyle; buyer behaviour.

For Freeplay, some are more relevant than others and these are detailed here.

Geographic

Freeplay sells its products all over the world so segmenting the markets by country or continent is an obvious one. This would provide measurable, reachable groups of consumers. It would also mean that a promotional strategy would be easier to segment as language and cultural considerations in promotional campaigns could be taken into account when targeting each segment. Distribution could also be easily structured around a geographic segmentation process.

Usage

Freeplay could segment the market on the basis of how people use its products.

It has already identified different uses for its 20/20 flashlight torch. Some groups have purchased this as part of an emergency kit for when earthquakes or tornados strike.

I am sure that the UK's love of camping and caravanning would identify another use for this product if researched as an essential camping kit accessory.

Benefits

Freeplay could also consider segmenting the market by the perceived benefits customers get from owning a Freeplay product.

In Germany it has already identified that people like to think of the environmental aspects of owning the 20/20 flashlight.

In the UK people feel their country is benefiting from the proliferation of a home grown invention.

The benefits derived in Africa are entirely different once again.

Targeting

Once Freeplay has decided how it wishes to segment the electrical products market it needs to choose one of three different approaches.

- Undifferentiated – using the same marketing mix for each product.
- Differentiated – developing different mixes for each segment.
- Customized – choosing one segment and concentrating effort. One mix would be developed and executed.

Positioning

Positioning is in the minds of the customer. Freeplay needs to position its products to differentiate its offering from those supplied by competitors.

Issues for Freeplay to consider here relate to which factors to base the positioning on. Commonly in consumer markets, positioning can be centred on:

- Attitudes to the product benefits derived from the product (this would fit well if benefits segmentation were chosen).
- Use of the product (again very appropriate for Freeplay's unique feature).
- Quality/value of the offering.
- Price is also a possibility.

An ideal way to formulate a positioning offer is in the use of perceptual maps. Here, two variables (in Freeplay's case maybe quality and price) are used and products plotted accordingly, (see Figure 1.).

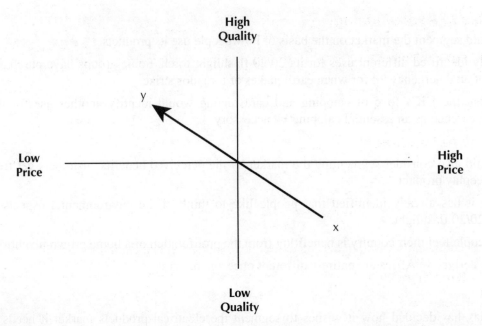

Figure 1

N.B. 'x' represents the initial reaction of African consumers with 'y' the position Freeplay should be aiming for

The Next Steps

Following the positioning process. Freeplay must translate all this data and considerations into a compr   udgets attached and responsibilities assigned. Only then can the marketing plan be fully actioned.

My services are at your disposal for this next crucial stage, to assist Freeplay in implementation and control of the marketing plan if needed.

Senior Examiner's Comments

This student answer obtained an A grade. The answer outlines the segmentation, targeting and positioning process in some detail. Its strength comes from the fact that it also specifically discusses segmentation approaches that Freeplay Energy could apply.

PART B

Answer THREE Questions Only

Question 2

Prepare a report advising a leading charity which promotes nature conservation, on how to select and implement a brand repositioning strategy.

(20 marks)

Outline Answer – Question 2

Why Reposition?

- Under-positioning.
- Over-positioning.
- Confused positioning.

Approaches to Repositioning

- Image repositioning.
- Market repositioning.
- Product/service repositioning.
- Total repositioning.

Approaches to Positioning

- USAP versus ESP.
- Brand associations.
- Attributes, benefits, users, activities, usage occasion, etc.

These issues need to be discussed in the context of the organization in the question.

Answer – Question 2

To: Marketing Director

From: Marketing Consultant

Subject: Repositioning Brands

Date: 7th December, 2000

Introduction

Repositioning brands involves changing a product or service without altering its core elements.

The key criterion is perception. This report will evaluate the issue regarding repositioning this charity.

Repositioning – Attitude Change

This involves changing people's attitudes towards:

- The charity.
- The service.
- How it is perceived by the stakeholders.

Essentially there is a need to promote a change in the affective attitude; the beliefs element. Consideration also needs to be given to the cognitive and perhaps more importantly connotative element to change behaviour as well as beliefs.

The above issue will be incorporated into the charity's promotional activity, especially advertising.

Establishing Current Perceptions

Market research will establish how the charity's stakeholders currently perceive the organization.

If the charity has a competitor/rival charity, this perception must also be understood.

Perceptual Mapping

The attribute established through research should then be plotted to establish:

- Where the charity is currently positioned.
- Where the charity wishes to be positioned.
- Where the nearest competitor is positioned.

The charity can then see if any gaps exist in order to reposition.

When the charity has established which position to adopt, the implementation can begin.

Implementation

McKinsey's 7Ss framework can be used as a guideline to implementing the strategy.

- Strategy – clear objectives: i.e. to reposition, the charity must be established and communicated internally to ensure 'buy-in'.
- Staff – must understand the mission and objectives and support the repositioning.
- Shared values – this is particularly important due to the nature of the organization and the need to change.
- Systems – will need to be utilized to facilitate the change needed.
- Structure – the strategy will require top down and cross-functional support.
- Style – a unique image will be required in order to promote the change and alter existing attitudes.
- Skills – at every level internal and external (if there is a need to utilise agencies and market research).

Monitor and Control

Once the repositioning strategy has been implemented, the need to monitor its reception is imperative.

Feedback should be encouraged and actively pursued from stakeholders in order to establish if a change in perception has occurred.

These results should be compared with the objectives in order to assess success.

Conclusion

Brand repositioning involves internal and external commitment and awareness.

Senior Examiner's Comments

This student answer obtained an A grade. It covers the key issues in a practical way and in the context of the organization outlined in the question. The paper is in report format. This has the advantage of providing conciseness but at the same time adding clarity to the answer.

Question 3

The marketing director of a cosmetics company has asked you to undertake a competitor analysis. Outline the content and structure of such an analysis. Illustrate the relevance of each aspect of the analysis in informing strategic decisions.

(20 marks)

Outline Answer – Question 3

All aspects of the answer have to relate to how they inform strategic decision-making.

Criteria to Identify Strategic Groups

- Size of company.
- Assets and skills.
- Scope of operation.
- Breadth of the product range.
- Choice of distribution channel.
- Relative product quality.
- Brand image.

Competitor's Objectives

- Whether the competitor's current performance is likely to be fulfilling its objectives. If not, the competitor may initiate a change of strategy.
- Investment is more likely from companies that have objectives which are long-term in nature, such as market share and sales growth, rather than organizations under pressure to produce short-term profitability.
- Non-financial objectives, such as gaining technology leadership, outline the likely future direction of the competitor's strategy.

Competitor's Current and Past Strategies

- Identification of the current markets, or market segments.
- Identification of the way it has chosen to compete in those markets.
- Direction in which the competitor is moving.
- Strategies that have failed in the past.

Competitor's Capabilities

- Management capabilities.
- Marketing capabilities.
- Innovation capabilities.
- Production capabilities.
- Financial capabilities.

Competitor's Future Strategies and Reactions

- Certain retaliation.
- Failure to react.
- Specific reactions.
- Inconsistent.

Problems in Identifying Competitors

- Overlooking smaller competitors.
- Focusing on established competitors.
- Concentrating on current domestic competitors.

Answer – Question 3

Outline of Competitor Analysis for a Cosmetics Company

Introduction

An analysis of competitors is a key aspect of the external audit. Other elements which need examination here are the market, the consumers and the industry as a whole. This paper outlines the content and structure of a competitor analysis.

Who are our Competitors?

This may seem an obvious question, but the term 'competitor' can mean many different types of company.

In our case, competitors are the cosmetics companies addressing the same market segment. Alternatively they may be other cosmetics firms targeting any segment, or they could be other firms trying to acquire our target market's spending power. These could include producers of magazines, hosiery, accessories, toiletries or perfumes.

It is important to decide who we are competing with, as we will need to gather data on these firms to feed into our MkIS. This will also help us with benchmarking analysis.

Their Goals and Objectives

Once we have determined with whom we are competing, we need to find out what their goals and objectives are.

This can help us in developing our own objectives: either to move in the opposite direction or attack them head-on. This will help us determine our competitive position.

Their Strengths and Weaknesses

An audit of their strengths and weaknesses will identify areas where they are weakest. We could then adopt a 'flank attack' here.

We also need to know where their strengths lie. This information could help us with our new product development – either by producing a similar product to one of their stronger offerings (there is obviously a market for them) or consolidate our offering to avoid confrontation.

If we establish their weak product areas, our new product development strategy could exploit this and we could be first to market with a new product – taking advantage of a weak area in their product portfolio.

Their Strategies

As with their objectives and goals, by finding out their strengths we can decide how we will compete with them.

If their corporate strategy is to be the cost leader then we should avoid following this route – there can be only one in each industry. If their strategy is focus, to whom are they targeting? And if they are choosing to differentiate, which branding, CRM or promotional strategies are they adopting? All this information will help us decide how we should counter their plans.

By understanding how they are positioning themselves, we can spot if there is an unexploited niche position into which we should strive to move – if profitable.

How are they Likely to React?

We should also try to establish how they are likely to react to our marketing plans. Four styles of competitive reaction have been identified:

- Laid-back – no reaction.
- Tiger – react aggressively to all competitors.
- Selective – react selectively to competitors.
- Stochastic – unpredictable reactions.

By understanding this, we can be prepared with a counter-attack if necessary.

Other Models to Consider

We could also plot the sales history on a product life cycle chart. This would help us assess the competitor's cash flow and from it we may be able to second-guess when new products are likely to be released.

We should also consider compiling a Boston Consulting Group matrix to assess how balanced the competitor's product portfolios are. We could use this to help us identify unexploited product areas.

All this data should be fed into our MkIS and SWOT analysis to help future marketing plans.

Research Data

All this analysis will be based on secondary data. I realize that some of this will be difficult to obtain – in particular goals, objectives and strategies.

However, a rigorous competitor analysis together with the other external analyses outlined in the introduction will be vital for us to sustain competitive advantage without marketing plans.

Senior Examiner's Comments

This student answer obtained an A grade. The answer could have been stronger when outlining the content of a competitor analysis. However it clearly demonstrated the relevance of each aspect of analysis in informing strategic decisions and this was its strength.

Question 4

Write a report comparing and contrasting the effectiveness of the Boston Consulting Group matrix and the Shell Directional Policy matrix in portfolio analysis to a chemical company organized into several operational divisions.

(20 marks)

Outline Answer – Question 4

Candidates should begin by describing the BCG

- It is essential that they refer to relative market share.

Weaknesses of BCG Approach

- It is overly simplistic to use only relative market share and growth as the key factors.
- It ignores factors such as developing sustainable competitive advantage.
- Cash flow is only one criterion by which to make investment judgements. Consider also ROI, market size, competitors, assets, cost, competencies, etc.

The Shell Directional Policy Matrix

Uses a range of weighted criteria in place of relative market share and growth in order to overcome the simplistic nature of the BCG. Prospects for sector profitability is on one axis and enterprise's competitive capabilities on the other.

Prospects for sector profitability are assessed on a range of weighted criteria including:

- Market size.
- Market growth rate.
- Strength of competition.
- Profit potential.
- Social, political and legal factors.

Enterprise's competitive capabilities:

- Market share.
- Potential to develop differential advantage.
- Opportunities to develop cost advantages.
- Channel relationships.
- Brand image/reputation.

These issues need to be discussed in the context of the organization in the question.

Answer – Question 4

To: JKL Chemicals

From: Miss J. Morris

Subject: The Effectiveness of Portfolio Planning Tools

Introduction

A diversified organization needs to assess the 'balance' of its activities in order to succeed. Portfolio planning tools (including BCG and Shell Directional Policy Matrix/GE) have been used to assist in two key decisions:

- The selection of strategy and allocation of resources.
- To assess the balance in the organization in terms of future growth, cash flow and risk.

The effectiveness of any tool depends on the success to which it achieves these objectives.

This report will first focus on the BCG matrix and drawing on its weaknesses, move on to discuss the Directional Policy Matrix (as a means of overcoming the criticisms). Finally, the strengths and weaknesses of portfolio planning in general will be discussed.

The Boston Consulting Group (BCG) Matrix

The BCG matrix focuses on two key measures:

- Market growth.
- Relative market share.

Market growth is related to cash flow and cash use/requirement and is intended as a proxy for the more difficult measure of product life cycle. The assumption is that in the early stage, considerable cash is required to support the introduction/development of a product. As the product progresses through the life cycle to maturity and decline, cash requirements reduce.

Relative market share is assumed as a proxy for cash generation. This is based on the idea of the experience effect, and has since been supported by the PIMS study. The assumption is that the higher the market share, the stronger the cash generation. Low market share equals lower cash generation. Experience areas are linked to market share by a cycle of virtue. This higher market share results in lower unit costs, higher profits and more investment in R&D and so the cycle goes on.

The Implication for Strategy of the BCG Matrix

Combining the two dimensions – cash generation and cash use – the BCG matrix offers managers of diversified businesses a useful way in which to access all businesses within their portfolio. This offers in a simple way guidance on strategy for each area of operation.

Relative Market Share

	High	Low
High	Star Build	Question Mark Support or Divest
Low	Cash Cow Hold	Dog Divest

The Strategy Implications of the BCG

Figure 2
The BGG Matrix

Whilst the BCG matrix's strengths lie in its simplicity and its ability to produce strategic guidance and provide an easily applicable tool for management, its simplicity is indeed one of its downfalls. The BCG matrix has been criticized due to:

- Cash flow being only one measure that firms use in assessing success.
- Other factors aside from market growth and relative market share contribute to cash flow.
- The basic assumptions of the model are flawed – small firms with low share can make profit, cash cows do not always create cash surplus, and price wars can reduce it.
- It is often difficult to define segments/markets, reducing the effectiveness of the BCG matrix.
- The model does not tell you how to develop new business nor how to compare existing businesses.

The Shell Directional Policy Matrix was developed specifically to address two key weaknesses of the BCG matrix by using:

- ROI as a basis.
- A number of measures in assessing an enterprise's competitive capabilities and the prospects for sector profitability.

The Shell Directional Policy Matrix

The Shell DPM recognizes that market growth is just one measure of the prospect for sector profitability. Others include competition, distribution strength, technology and economic considerations. Also, relative market share is just one measure of an enterprise's competitive capabilities (others include product quality, culture and management).

The strength of this model is that it requires management to select the factors that it feels are right for the firm's own circumstances. For example, a commodity player might emphasize low cost operations.

Management is required to assign a score to each selected factor, weigh the importance of each and combine into an overall assessment of the prospects for sector profitability and of an enterprise's competitive capabilities. This is, however, both a strength and weakness. A strength is that it is tailored to the firm and requires discussion and debate internally, but it is a weakness due to its subjective nature.

The Implications for the Shell Directional Policy Matrix

Like the BCG matrix, the Shell DPM provides managers with an indication of the most appropriate direction for strategy, in the form of a 3x3 matrix, shown in Figure 3:

Figure 3 {NOTE FROM FIGURE "isbn0750649267pap02fig03.pdf"}The Shell Directional Policy Matrix

Portfolio Planning Tools in General

Portfolio planning models are extremely useful to management in providing guidance for the product market strategic decisions. However, there are inherent weaknesses in all models:

- Do not take into account risk.
- Assume market is given.
- Require high amounts of data to achieve output.
- Ignore the opportunity to 'create' segmentation.

Conclusion

In conclusion, given that the BCG matrix is focused on cash flow and the Shell DPM on ROI , there probably is a case for using the models in tandem to enhance usefulness of any analysis. The inherent weaknesses of portfolio planning tools in general must be born in mind, however, in application.

Senior Examiner's Comments

This student answer obtained an A grade. As you will see, it answered all aspects of the question – i.e. comparing and contrasting the BCG matrix and Shell DPM. It also went on to discuss the weaknesses and merits of portfolio models in general. The report format helped the answer to be both clear and concise.

Question 5

A venture capitalist company aims to turn around the fortunes of a car manufacturer in decline by following a focus or niche strategy and concentrating on the production of specialist sports cars. What are the benefits of a niche strategy to this company and in which circumstances is it likely to be most effective?

(20 marks)

Outline Answer – Question 5

The answer should start by defining what is a niche/focus strategy in terms of Porter's model.

How does this create competitive advantage?

Reduces Direct Competition

- Reduces pressure from substitutes.
- Customers needing specialist products have less bargaining power.
- Suppliers of specialist equipment have less bargaining power.

Circumstances in which it is Likely to be Effective

- The relative costs of the focuser are unlikely to increase and offset the cost advantages or differentiation achieved.
- The requirements of the target market and those of the whole market are unlikely to converge.

- Competitors are unlikely to invade particularly lucrative sub-markets within the strategic target; i.e. 'out-focus' the focuser.

Problems

- Success might attract new entrants to the market niche.
- High development costs may not be recoupable from smaller market niche.

Answer – Question 5

To: The Manager

From: Marketing Consultant

Date: 7th December, 2000

Subject: Niche Strategy

Introduction

Niche strategy involves identification of a specific target audience and serving it with a given strategy. As put forward by Porter, one can either focus differentially or cost focus.

Options

A niche company may have several options to create a niche. These could be geographical, product type or end-user options.

Benefits of Niche Strategy

- Niche strategy is ideal for a company with meagre resources.
- Niche markets are normally serviced by few players since they are unattractive to large players. For instance, Ford looks towards large markets.
- Niche markets are easier to control as the market is small.
- It is possible to implement one-to-one marketing for the car business. This can be done through customer relationship marketing. With vehicle markets, which are highly competitive, loyalty building enhances competitive advantage.
- Niche markets are beneficial in that the consumers' needs can be met ideally at a profit. For instance, with the market being small you can pursue customized marketing.

When is a Niche Market likely to be Most Effective?

- A niche strategy can be effective when there is minimal competition. For instance, if the market is riddled with sports car manufacturers the profit potential will be low.
- It is ideal if there is no speedy growth. If the growth rate is fast it may become an ideal option for big players like Vauxhall.
- A niche strategy is ideal if strategically similar segments can be identified across markets. For instance, sports drivers in the UK, Germany and USA.
- This can be effective if the niche is large enough to enable profits to be reaped.
- It can be effective if your company is specialized in the given field, for instance sports car manufacture.
- This niche strategy can be ideal if you have competitive advantages that suit the given niche over possible competitors.

Senior Examiner's Comments

This student answer obtained an A grade. It answered all aspects of the question and was in report format, which added to the clarity of the answer.

Question 6

In the business-to-business sector, discuss the areas of an organization s marketing strategy that are likely to be affected by the development of the Internet and related e-commerce capabilities.

(20 marks)

Outline Answer – Question 6

Context

Although this is potentially a broad question, candidates need to address the effects of these developments on strategy and customer management in the B2B sector.

Effects on Marketing Strategy

The following are areas of marketing strategy that these developments are likely to affect thinking on:

- **Products**: A whole new generation of information-based products/services could be developed.
- **Markets**: Can be exploited that are not related to geographic nearness or physical contact (i.e. face-to-face activity.) Customers' needs can be serviced remotely using the new technologies.
- **Investment would be needed in the technological infrastructure**: organizations may also have to become more service oriented if delivery of their product/service is built on a relationship marketing approach.
- **Promotional**: Both developments create new approaches to promotion. The Internet creates a new mass communication medium for marketers to use.
- **Brands**: In the service sector the Internet may allow customers access to service providers anywhere in the world, where previously the customer has been restricted to local providers. This could lead to the globalization of service brands.
- **Distribution channels:** The Internet would allow an organization to operate in the world market from a small and centralized base. It could change the whole nature of distribution in the service sector in particular as a result.
- **Managing customers**: These developments allow for a customer relationship to be built without direct face to face contact. In order to do this successfully, companies will need to develop sophisticated databases.

Answer – Question 6

Business-to-Business Strategies Affected by the Internet and E-commerce

Though the Internet seems heavily weighted towards business to consumer markets, it is also having an effect on the business-to-business (B2B) environment.

Product

B2B products are often commodities. These are easily showcased and sold on-line, where the end-user already has a very good concept of the benefits and uses of such goods. Having a web site to sell them through is ideal.

Feedback from B2B consumers from the web site is also speeding up the idea generation stage of new product development. It is also ensuring that this remains customer-focused.

Price

As with web sites like shopsmart.com for the consumer markets, virtual marketplaces or B2B exchanges are changing the way businesses set prices.

It is now quicker and easier for potential buyers to compare prices of competing products on-line.

Place

As the Internet is an international tool, it breaks down previous barriers to entry. Customers from around the world can buy direct without having to use agents or distributors as intermediaries. An organization will have to ensure it has distribution mechanisms in place to cope with this need to buy direct.

Internets or Extranets can include order processing, order taking and distribution data available directly to customers. An organization's sales force will have to adapt to the competition from within the organization.

Promotion

The Internet is an expressive, interactive communications tool and should be an integral part of any B2B marketing communications plan.

Together with email marketing it is also set to become a key feature in B2B customer relationship programmes. Business contacts can be emailed at work with the latest product offerings or promotional campaigns.

Research

New developments in tracking software can generate a huge amount of rich data to be fed into an MkIS. A B2B organization needs to ensure this is possible. The Internet will alter the way data on the market, competitors and customers are gathered, processed and interpreted. Rather than weekly statistical reports, these can be run from web site data each minute if needed. Processes will therefore have to adapt, to maximize the potential that all this information has to offer.

Senior Examiner's Comments

This student answer obtained a B grade. The answer covers some interesting issues and ideas but failed to gain an A grade because its main focus was at a tactical rather than strategic level.

Question 7

A large UK grocery retailer has announced it is entering into a co-operation agreement with two other retailers based elsewhere in Europe. Explain the strategic rationale for building such an alliance.

(20 marks)

Outline Answer – Question 7

Motivations for an Alliance

- Globalization.
- Gaining access to additional assets and competencies.
- Sharing risk.
- Acquiring learning and innovation.

There are Four Key Types of Marketing Alliances

- Product and/or service alliances.
- Logistics alliances.
- Promotional alliances.
- Pricing collaborations.

Success of any strategic alliances are dependent on:

- Strategic compatibility.
- A long-term focus.
- Flexibility.

These issues need to be discussed in the context of the organization in the question.

Answer – Question 7

Co-operation agreements, or strategic alliances as they are more commonly known, offer a variety of benefits for the parties concerned. This paper will seek to explain the strategic rationale underpinning the decision by PQR Supermarket to enter into a co-operation agreement with two European retailers.

A strategic alliance sees two or more organizations joining together to pursue common aims. While the organizations will not have formally merged they may well have equity in one another's companies and will certainly be bound by some form of legal agreement.

The number of strategic alliances has increased over the past decade as organizations seek to combine forces to meet an increasingly competitive environment.

Advantages of Alliances

PQR Supermarket's decision has undoubtedly been driven at least in part by the following advantages of an alliance or co-operative agreement.

Purchasing Power

By combining their buyer power the retailers are in a position to force down suppliers' margins and demand the lowest possible prices. This could be used to support a cost leadership strategy.

Economies of Scale

Combining distribution and warehousing could lead to significant economies of scale.

Expansion without Risk

PQR now has an opportunity to build knowledge and experience of the European retail market with the risk of establishing its own outlets.

This knowledge will serve PQR well should it decide to enter Europe more directly, either by more formally merging, taking over or going into direct competition with its partners.

Offset Weaknesses

The alliance allows PQR to offset some of the weaknesses of its product portfolios. PQR's value clothing range has not done very well. However both its partners have primary clothing product lines. There is an opportunity to share knowledge and expertise as well as marketing.

Offset Capital Investment

PQR is known to be struggling with the set-up cost of its 'just in time' stock control system. This is a pioneering system and its application is not limited to the groceries industry. Its European partners should be keen to contribute to the cost of this investment in return for access.

Sharing Customer Base

While PQR's customer base is geographically separate from its European partners, there is still a tremendous opportunity to share customer data. At least one of PQR's partners is known to have a significant clothing mail order business in France and has been looking to expand to the UK. Access to PQR's MkIS and databases will be invaluable.

Risks

Strategic alliances also entail risks as well as opportunity and PQR and its partners should be mindful of this.

Alliances can develop into takeovers or direct competition. The knowledge PQR will gain through this partnership of the European market, would certainly support more direct entry in these markets.

For the moment Asda works in partnership with Wal-Mart but the relative ease with which Asda could be taken over by the American giant should be remembered.

Alliance also puts brand value and identity at risk. Negative publicity affecting one partner could spread to the whole group.

Senior Examiner's Comments

This student answer obtained an A grade. The answer covers the key issue in a practical way and in the context of the scenario outlined in the question. The paper also uses sub-headings providing added clarity to the answer.

Syllabus

Aims and Objectives

The aim of the unit is to enable students to develop a sound theoretical and practical understanding of marketing planning and control.

The objectives are to:

- Enable students to understand the theoretical concepts, techniques and models that underpin the marketing planning process.
- Build practical skills associated with the management of the planning process.
- Enable students to justify their strategic decisions and recommendations.
- Develop an understanding of the barriers that exist to effective implementation of strategy.
- Appreciate the need to tailor marketing plans and process to allow for the specific sector and situational factors that apply to any given organization.
- Develop an awareness of the techniques that underpin innovation and creativity in organizations.

Learning Outcomes

Students will be able to:

- Understand and critically appraise a wide variety of marketing techniques, concepts and models.
- Conduct and evaluate a detailed marketing audit, both internally and externally.
- Identify the elements that can be used to create competitive advantage.
- Compare and contrast strategic options.
- Specify a clear rationale when choosing between strategic alternatives.
- Prepare effective and realistic marketing plans.
- Initiate control systems for marketing planning.
- Understand and evaluate the processes that can be used to overcome barriers to effective implementation of marketing strategies and plans.
- Evaluate a range of techniques that facilitate innovation in organizations.

Indicative Content and Weighting

3.1 market-led approach to planning (10%)

3.1.1 Adopting a market-led orientation

- Marketing orientation
- Role of marketing in market-led strategic management
- Drivers of change in the business environment

3.1.2 The Strategic marketing process

- Corporate strategy/marketing interface
- The basis of planning and control: the structure of planning and the cycle of control

- The nature of strategic, tactical and contingency planning.

3.2 Analysis (25%)

3.2.1 External analysis

- Environmental analysis
- Industry analysis
- Market analysis
- Competitor analysis
    1. Competitive intelligence
    2. The competitive intelligence cycle
    3. Sources of competitive information
- Customer analysis

3.2.2 Internal analysis

- Resource-based approach: organizational assets, capabilities and competencies
    1. Technical resources
    2. Financial standing
    3. Managerial skills
    4. Organization
    5. Information systems
- Asset-based approach:
    1. Customer-based assets
    2. Distribution-based assets
    3. Alliance-based asset
    4. Internal assets
- Marketing Activities Audit:
    1. Marketing strategy audit
    2. Marketing structures audit
    3. Marketing systems audit
    4. Productivity audit
    5. Marketing functions audit
- Innovation audit:
    1. The organizational climate
    2. Rate of new product development
    3. Customer satisfaction ratings
    4. The innovation/value matrix
    5. The balance of cognitive styles of the senior management team

3.3 Techniques for analysis and strategy development (20%)

3.3.1 Techniques for developing a future orientation

- Trend extrapolation
- Modelling
- Intuitive forecasting

    Individual or genius forecasting

- Consensus forecasting
    1. Jury forecasting
    2. Delphi forecasts
- Scenario planning

- Market sensing
- War gaming
- Synthesis reports

3.3.2 Auditing tools

- Portfolio analysis
- Value chain
- PIMS
- Experience curves
- Financial
    1. Ratio analysis
    2. Productivity analysis
    3. Segmental analysis
    4. Balance sheet evaluation
    5. Profit and loss accounts
- SWOT analysis
- GAP analysis

3.4 Strategy formulation and selection (30%)

3.4.1 The Strategic Intent

- Mission
- Objectives
- Stakeholders
- Customer/competitor orientation
- Evaluation of balanced score card

3.4.2 Approaches to creating strategic advantage

- Generic strategies
- Developing sustainable advantage
    1.
    2. Superior product or service
    3. Perceived advantage
    4. Global skills
    5. Low-cost operator
    6. Superior competencies
    7. Superior assets
    8. Scale advantages
    9. Attitude advantages
    10. Legal advantages
    11. Superior relationships
- Alliances and networks
- Offensive/defensive strategies
- Competitive positions and strategy
    1. Strategies for market leaders
    2. Strategies for market challengers
    3. Strategies market followers
    4. Strategies for market nichers
- Product/market strategy
    1. Product/market matrix
    2. PLC

272

3. PIMS
4. Portfolio analysis
- Strategies for declining and hostile markets
- Strategic wear-out and renewal

3.4.3 Developing a specific competitive position

- Strategic alignment process

  Assets/competencies

- Segmentation and targeting
    1. Evaluation of balanced score card
- Positioning
- Branding strategy
    1. Brand equity
    2. Brand evaluation
    3. Brand name strategy
    4. Brand extension
    5. Brand stretching
    6. Brand revitalisation
    7. Brand repositioning
- Innovation and product development
- Building customer relationships

3.4.4 Strategic marketing plans

- Process and structure of marketing planning
- Strategic and tactical marketing decisions

3.5 Implementation and control (15%)

3.5.1 Key elements of implementation

- Leadership
- Internal marketing
- Project management
    1. Systems
    2. Skills
- Management of change

3.5.2 Key elements of control

- The dimensions of effective marketing feedback and control systems
- Basic control concepts and their application throughout the planning and implementation process.
- Financial control
    1. Budgets
    2. Ratios
- Benchmarking

Further study

Students are encouraged to read as widely as time permits to gain different perspectives on the syllabus. It is essential that students keep up-to-date particularly in the area of information technology by reading broadsheet newspapers and appropriate magazines.

The Financial Times has regular features on information and communications technologies relevant to marketing applications that you may find useful. If you want to find out more on a specific topic then use electronic databases available in many libraries e.g. MINTEL, FT Profile, McCarthy etc.

Reading list

- G Drummond, J Ensor; *Strategic Marketing: Planning and Control*, Butterworth-Heinemann, 2001, Essential reading
- G Hooley; J Saunders; N Piercy; *Marketing Strategy & Competitive Positioning,* Prentice Hall, 1998, Essential reading
- DA Aaker; *Strategic Market Management (5th Edition),* Wiley, 1998, Essential reading
- H. Meek, R Meek, J Ensor*; Strategic Marketing Management*, CIM/Butterworth-Heinemann, 2001, Workbook
- *Planning and Control*, BPP, 2001, Study Text
- N Piercy; *market-led Strategic Change.* Heinemann (2nd Ed), CIM/Butterworth-Heinemann, 2000, Additional Reading/Resources
- H Davidson; *Even More Offensive Marketing,* Penguin, 1997, Additional Reading/Resources
- M McDonald; *Marketing Plans (4th Edition),* CIM/Butterworth-Heinemann, 1999, Additional Reading/Resources
- D Mercer; *Marketing Strategy: The Challenge of the External Environment,* Sage, 1998, Additional Reading/Resources
- H Pringle; M Thompson; *Brand Spirit*, Wiley, 1999, Additional Reading/Resources
- S Adkins; *Cause Related Marketing: Who Cares Wins,* Butterworth-Heinemann, 1999
- F Janszen; *The Age of Innovation*, FT/Prentice Hall, 2000, Additional Reading/Resources
- D Jobber; *Principles and Practice of Marketing*, McGraw Hill, 2001, Additional Reading/Resources
- *Planning & Control Practice & Revision Kits,* BPP, 2001, Additional Reading/Resources
- *Learning Cassettes*, BPP, 2001,

Appendix 5
Answers and debriefing

Debriefing Activity 1.1

You should have had few difficulties in finding a range of different marketing definitions. They are probably all quite different but will have common characteristics. In general terms the definitions focus on two aspect of marketing. Firstly, that marketing is a functional activity that is concerned with the operational aspects of marketing such as market research, promotion, pricing and product development. Secondly, that marketing is more than just a functional activity. It is a business philosophy that permeates the whole organization and puts the customer at the centre of its activity.

Debriefing Activity 1.2

The questionnaire focuses on five aspects of market orientation – customer orientation, competitor orientation, long-term perspectives, interfunctional co-ordination and organizational culture.

By undertaking an assessment of your own organization you will be able to assess its level of market orientation. In particular you will be able to identify areas of strengths and weaknesses. The results may confirm your existing thoughts or else they may identify areas that you had not necessarily paid great attention to in the past.

The questionnaire is not designed to produce a definitive judgment about the level of market orientation, instead it provides a framework for discussing the key issues relating to market orientation.

You would probably find that if different individuals from different departments and backgrounds completed the questionnaire you would have different results. This is not a deficiency of the questionnaire, rather it relates to personal experiences and attitudes.

Debriefing Activity 1.3

All organizations will have their own personal planning processes. The nature of their planning and control cycles will vary according to a number of factors such as organizational size, culture, nature of the business (fast moving of slow moving), number of staff involved, top down or bottom up approach, responsibility for planning etc. Types of planning may include corporate planning, marketing planning, marketing mix planning, other functional types of planning such as HRM, Research and Development, and contingency planning. Time frames for planning will also be influenced by the type of industry in which an organization is working. Planning cycles may be monthly, six monthly, annually, five yearly or even longer in some situations. In some organizations planning is highly mechanized, in others it can often be ad hoc without formal planning cycles. Refer to unit nine for further information on control mechanisms and how the planning process can be improved.

Debriefing Activity 1.4

Organizational structure can have a major influence on the effectiveness of planning and communication and also the corporate culture. Highly hierarchical structures often result in effective vertical communication and planning. However, they can inhibit cross-departmental communication and develop a culture of competition between departments or different business units. In contrast, flatter organizations can aid communication across the company and can reduce the layers of bureaucracy often associated with highly hierarchical organizations. Matrix structures can be effective in breaking down departmental barriers but problems can sometimes arise because teams are faced with conflicting messages from two different managers.

Debriefing Activity 2.1

In an exam situation you often find your mind goes blank when asked for examples. This activity will provide you with a wealth of examples that you can refer to in the Planning and Control exam.

Debriefing Activity 2.2

All organizations approach environmental scanning in different ways. There are those organizations that have a rigorous and formal approach whilst others adopt more of an *ad hoc* and informal approach. There is no one 'best' method. The important aspect is how organizations translate the information they collect into action. Your recommendations may relate to a number of issues such as the way in which the information is collected, the means by which it is processed and the method by which it is disseminated.

Debriefing Activity 2.3

It is not enough to just identify the trends in the macroenvironment. Companies must be ready and able to take action in order to take advantage of opportunities or to deflect the threats created by changes in the external environment. This activity will highlight your company's ability to monitor and respond to these changes.

Debriefing Activity 2.4

This model can prove very helpful in understanding the dynamics of the industry within which you are operating. It will help to identify where the balance of power lies and will highlight the threat of new entrants and substitute products.

Debriefing Activity 2.5

This activity will help you to understand the structure of your industry and also identify those companies with whom you are competing directly.

Debriefing Activity 2.6

This activity will provide a structured approach to competitive analysis. It is helpful to consider different strategic business units or products in turn because it is likely that you will be competing with different companies in different markets. This framework will help to identify your key competitors, also those companies that are worth attacking and those to avoid.

Debriefing Activity 2.7

Lager/beer

Lager/beer Culture/subculture will influence whether consumers will drink lager or beer in the first place. For example, Muslims do not drink alcohol. Social class may be important because higher social class drinkers may choose 'premium' brands that might be seen as less 'vulgar' than ordinary brands.

Social factors will be important in this instance because lagers/beers are often consumed in social settings. Reference groups can be a powerful influence. The consumer may choose a brand that matches their reference group or may want to be seen to be as different. The drinker may also select a brand that they think an aspirant group might choose.

Personal influences such as age and life cycle stage may influence choice of lager/beer. A particular brand may be selected to reflect a particular lifestyle. Disposable income may influence which brands a drinker can afford to buy. A consumer may purchase a brand to match their personality – outgoing and individualistic or conservative and wanting to blend in with the crowd.

Psychological factors such as perception relates to how the drinker interprets advertisements and how the consumer's understanding of the brand may enhance their self-image. Attitudes towards various brands and beliefs about the kind of people who buy them will vary, as will attitudes to product attributes such as country of origin, strength or ingredients.

Financial services

Financial services are going to be less influenced by social factors because they are not consumed in public and are not necessarily perceived as status symbols.

Cultural factors will be important because some cultures/subcultures value financial services to a greater degree than others. Social class may influence peoples' attitudes to financial services. For example, higher social classes often seek delayed gratification whilst lower social classes look for immediate gratification and are therefore less likely to purchase pensions or life assurance.

Social factors such as the family may play an important role. Purchasers may seek advice of friends or colleagues. It is likely that the purchase will be made by a decision-making unit.

Personal influences such as age, stage in the life cycle, occupation and economic circumstances will be highly influential.

Psychological factors such as perception relate to the purchaser's interpretation of promotional campaigns.

There are enormous implications for marketing managers for both of these products. They will have to be marketed differently because they are influenced by very different factors.

Debriefing Activity 2.8

- *Repetitive buying behaviour* – may include products such as washing powder, baked beans, rice, pasta, milk, eggs.
- *Variety seeking* – may include products such as shampoos, books, CDs.
- *Buyer dissonance reduction* – may include products such as life assurance and pensions.
- *Complex buying behaviour* – may include products such as holidays, cars, house extensions.

Debriefing Activity 4.1

This portfolio of articles will ensure that in the exam you are armed with a number of current examples to exemplify your points.

Debriefing Question 4.2

The PLC is one of the best-known models in marketing and is arguably capable of providing a broad framework for strategic thinking. This question requires you to:

- Focus upon the strategies that are suited to the decline stage
- Identify the criteria that should be used in choosing between alternatives.

A good answer would include the following components:

- **Introduction** – a brief explanation of the PLC and its characteristics.
- **Reasons for decline** – technological advances, changing customer needs, increase in competition, etc.
- **Options** – Non-deletion, eliminate overnight (divest), increase price or reduce promotion (milk) or stay and attract competitor's customers.
- **Evaluation of alternatives** – could include inventory level, notification of customers, resource implications, legal implications, impact on associated products and services, entry barriers, industry attractiveness, competitor activity, marketing objectives, substitute products, overall product portfolio, number of replacement products, nature of market, market exist costs, degree of customer loyalty, importance of product to distributors.
- **Conclusions.**

Debriefing Activity 4.2

Examples of products that have been adopted rapidly are mobile phones, digital TV, Internet access. Examples of products that have been slowly adopted (or not at all) are Sinclair C5, some financial service products, electric cars.

The reasons as to why there are differences in rate of adoption relate to factors such as level of newness, ability to trial the product, the relative cost, additional costs that may be incurred and the complexity of the product.

Debriefing Activity 4.3

Below is a worked example for a hypothetical financial services company.

Table 1

Market Attractiveness	Product/ SBU 1 Pensions			Product/ SBU 2 Current Accounts			Product/ SBU 3 Insurance		
	Weighting	Score	Rating	Weighting	Score	Rating	Weighting	Score	Rating
1 Market growth rate	3	10	30	3	1	3	3	3	9
2 Market size	3	8	24	3	6	18	3	7	21
3 Profit opportunity	2	7	14	2	2	4	2	4	8
4 Strength of competition	2	6	12	2	1	2	2	3	6
Total	10		78	10		27	10		44

Table 2

Competitive Strength	Product/ SBU 1 Pensions			Product/ SBU 2 Current Accounts			Product/ SBU 3 Insurance		
	Weighting	Score	Rating	Weighting	Score	Rating	Weighting	Score	Rating
1 Market share	4	8	32	4	3	12	4	7	28
2 Cost advantages	1	7	7	1	5	5	1	5	5
3 Relationships	2	8	16	2	1	2	2	5	10
4 Distribution capabilities	3	8	24	3	2	6	3	4	12
Total	10		79	10		25	10		55

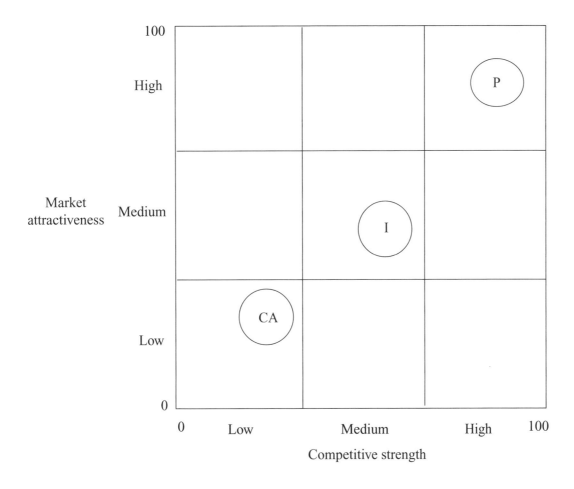

CA: Current Accounts   I: Insurance   P: Pensions

Debriefing Activity 5.1

Ratio calculations of topline financial variables more commonly used in strategic planning

Type of ratio

Example topline ratios

1. Profitability ratios

- gross profit margin = (GP/Sales) × 100

$$\frac{408,000}{1,160,000} \times 100 = 35\%$$

Fundamental strength of the business

- net profit margin = (NP/Sales) × 100

$$\frac{40,800}{1,160,000} \times 100 = 3.5\%$$

2. Capital structure ratios, also termed 'gearing' ratios

- debt ratio = total debt/total assets

  where:

  total debt = current liabilities (96,000) + long-term liabilities (60,000)

  total assets = fixed assets (729,000) + current assets = (190,400)

  = 1 : 5.9

3. Liquidity

- current ratio = current assets/ current liabilities

  190,400 / 96,900 = 1 : 1.96

- liquid ratio = (current assets – stock)/current liabilities

  (190,400 – 85,000)/96,900 = 1 : 1.09

4. Asset utilization

Operational efficiency of the business

- stock turnover ratio = cost of goods sold/stock at cost on balance sheet

  (752,000/85,000) = 1 : 8.85

- debtor turnover = sales turnover/debtors

  (1,160,000/64,600) = 1 : 18

- credit turnover ratios = cost of goods sold/Trade creditors from the balance sheet

  (752,000/51,000) = 1 : 14.7

5. Investment performance ratios

Investment performance

- Price to earnings ratio (P/E ratio) = market price per share[1]/earnings per share[2]

  165p/5.7p = 29

[1]From stock market (assumed to be 165p)

[2] Declared annually or twice per year by the company.

Detailed information as follows:

- Dividend payments (taken from profit and loss account) total £38,000 (i.e. 10p per share preference shareholders = £4,000, and £34,000 ordinary shareholders).
- Number of shareholders (taken from Balance Sheet) = 670,000
- Earnings per share = £38,000/670,000 = 5.7p

Debriefing Activity 6.1

This exercise will not provide definitive answers about the appropriateness of your selected mission statements. However, what it does do is to focus your mind on the important elements of a mission statement. Too often mission statements consist of bland generalizations that could be applied to any company. It is not an easy task to develop an appropriate and motivating mission statement but at least Piercy's framework provides a starting point.

Debriefing Activity 6.2

This activity will force you to consider the different types of objectives that exist and the relationship between the various levels of objectives within the organizational hierarchy. It will also illustrate the difficulties in writing appropriate SMART objectives. This will prove particularly helpful when you come to preparing for the Analysis and Decision case study exam.

Debriefing Activity 6.3

This activity should highlight the number of different stakeholders that your organization has. The number and diversity of the groups may surprise you. It is now possible to appreciate the difficulties facing organizations when they have to try to meet the needs of these diverse groups of people. Different organizations will give greater emphasis to the needs of some groups rather than others.

Debriefing Activity 7.1

This exercise will provide you with the opportunity to apply this theoretical framework to a practical example. You will probably find that many companies do not fall conveniently into one of the three categories. Instead they will probably use a combination of the three strategies. This model is helpful in focusing your mind on the generic strategies that companies may use to gain competitive advantage and the dangers of failing to have a clear and consistent strategy. The activity will also provide you with examples that you may be able to use in the exam.

Debriefing Activity 7.2

Davidson's approach provides a useful framework in which to identify various means of attaining a sustainable competitive advantage. This activity will encourage you to collect examples that you may be able to refer to in the exam.

Debriefing Activity 7.3

You may have selected companies such as Coca-Cola and Pepsi, Tesco and Sainsburys, McDonalds and Burger King, Caterpillar and Komatsu, Unilever and Proctor and Gamble (to name but a few). Research has shown that it can often be very expensive attack a market leader, and may end in disaster. For example Laker Airways attacked the major airlines in the 1970's on a low-price platform. The other airlines reacted by cutting their prices. This forced Laker out of business because the company did not have a lower cost structure than their competitors.

Debriefing Activity 7.4

This model should not be new to you and it is likely that you have had to apply it to practical situations before. The purpose of this activity is to revise the model and to ensure that you understand the practical implications of the model. It is a useful model for identifying the various growth strategies open to an organization. However, it does not really address the issue of what competitive advantage an organization should pursue.

Debriefing Activity 7.5

You should have no problems sourcing articles on strategic alliances. There appears to be an abundance of companies that have recognized that to sustain their competitive advantage they will have to join forces with other firms. The motivations for these alliances will vary considerably but will probably relate to the factors identified in this unit.

Debriefing Activity 7.6

This activity will provide you with contemporary examples that you may be able to use in the exam.

Debriefing Activity 8.1

This website obviously provides you with a snapshot of the types of questions that are used to build up the VALS profiles. Consider the extent to which you match the characteristics of your category – fulfilleds, experiencers, believers, strivers, makers or strugglers. You have probably concluded that some of the characteristics are relevant to yourself and others are not. This is likely to be true of all lifestyle segmentation methods because they are looking for common characteristics (which is challenging given that we are all individuals). The key question relating to segmentation is 'do those individuals in a particular segment behave in a similar manner?' It is likely that this method of segmentation will be more appropriate in some markets than others – for example, financial services, cars and holidays (i.e. those that relate to a person's lifestyle). There are obvious limitations of this type of framework due to the generalizations that are made. The questionnaire is more appropriate for Americans than for European citizens, which has implications for companies that are operating internationally. It is likely they will encounter problems relating to cultural differences when trying to develop cross-cultural segmentation bases.

Debriefing Activity 8.2

Virgin is operating in a diverse range of market sectors ranging from trains, planes, mobile phones, weddings, financial services, health clubs, wines, cars and car hire. The ability of Virgin to stretch its brand into so many unrelated markets is probably related to the brand values of the Virgin brand. Brands such as Coca-Cola and Guinness have very strong brand images that relate directly to the product itself, whereas the Virgin brand is not tied strongly to one product and is often regarded as the 'people's brand' (as an alternative to conventional brands) and particularly relates to Richard Branson himself. This has enabled Virgin to stretch into many unrelated markets.

It is difficult to judge the impact that the problems of Virgin Trains has had on the Virgin brand. Many of the problems associated with Virgin Trains are not in fact due to Virgin itself but to problems with Railtrack. Some customers appreciate this and feel that Richard Branson has a huge task ahead and as a result see Virgin Trains as a completely separate entity. However, it is undeniable that for some people the performance of Virgin Trains has had a negative umbrella affect on the overall Virgin brand.

Debriefing Activity 9.1

This activity will identify whether your organization can effectively implement the strategies it has developed. Many organizations find the implementation stage the most challenging and often find it difficult to translate plans into actions. The reason for your choice of quadrant will be influenced by factors such as organizational culture, effectiveness of communication, staff motivation, abilities of managers, sufficient resources (human, time and physical), planning process, staff rewards.

Debriefing Activity 9.2

The internal barriers that you have identified will probably resemble those factors identified in the Unit 'Implementation and control'. The challenge facing many organizations is how to overcome these barriers. Unit 'Implementation and control' identifies a number of strategies that companies can adopt to try to improve implementation of plans such as internal marketing, project management and change management.

Debriefing Activity 9.3

This model provides a representation of the stages people move through when faced with change. Different individuals will progress through the stages at different paces and some may not pass through all the stages in a linear manner. This model will highlight the need for managers to help staff to accept as rapidly as possible, for example by promoting the benefits of the change and offering incentives to adapt. It is inevitable that some people will continue to resist change and may in fact choose to leave the organization, rather than accept changes.

planning, 10, 11, 12, 275
strategy, 1, 10, 11, 22, 118, 179, 246, 260
Cost
    advantages, 64
    Efficiency Analysis, 233
    focus, 131
    leadership, 130, 131, 151
Counter-defence, 136
Creating strategic advantage, 128
Criteria, 186
Cultural context, 117
Cultural fit, 143
Culture, 17, 19, 20, 143
    clash, 143
Customer-based assets, 51
Customer-focused, 5
Customers, 1, 2, 3, 4, 5, 6, 7, 9, 10, 11, 12,
    22, 24, 27, 30, 31, 32, 36, 39, 46, 51, 53,
    63, 64, 65, 66, 67, 68, 70, 72, 73, 76, 87,
    99, 100, 115, 117, 119, 120, 123, 124, 126,
    129, 130, 131, 134, 139, 140, 148, 154,
    156, 157, 161, 165, 169, 170, 171, 173,
    174, 176, 178, 182, 183, 184, 185, 187,
    188, 189, 195, 196, 198, 211, 227, 234,
    239, 241, 242, 243, 250, 251, 255, 266,
    267, 277, 282
      retention, 182
    analysis, 24
    Analysis
      positioning, 39
      segmentation, 39
      targetting, 39
    behaviour, 47
    buying behaviour, 47
    complaints, 198
    databases, 10
    expectations, 142
    loyalty, 83, 182, 243
    needs, 1, 2, 3, 5, 8, 11, 12, 145, 149, 150,
      154, 155, 156, 213, 239, 277
    orientation, 6
    profitability, 10
    satisfaction, 57, 123, 198, 201
    segments, 39
Customized, 154
Cycle of control, 1
Cyclical variation, 99
Davidson's, 133, 134, 135
Decision-making
    process, 46
    pyramid, 108
    unit, 43, 45, 47
Decline stage, 69
Declining and hostile markets, 145

    strategic withdrawal, 145
Declining markets
    changes in the external environment, 145
Decomposition of data, 99
Defensive strategies, 138, 225
Delphi
    forecasting, 104
    forecasting techniques, 104
    forecasts, 103
Determining organizational strengths, 166
Developing, 97
    relationships, 183
Differentiated marketing, 168
Differentiation, 131, 151
    focus, 131
    strategy, 131
Diffusion of innovation, 72, 73, 87
    model, 87
Distribution, 198
    based assets, 51
    channels, 39
Distribution-based assets, 52
Diversification, 139, 140, 151
    growth strategies, 140
Divest, 145, 147
DMU, 43, 45
Driver of change, 29
Drivers of change, 8, 27
Economies of scale, 82, 83, 131, 134, 137,
    142, 173, 187, 227, 268
Effective Control Systems, 201
Effectiveness, 202
Efficiency, 202
    control, 207
Electronic
    commerce, 10
    marketing, 8
Encirclement attack, 137
Environmental
    analysis, 26
    monitoring systems, 47
    scanning, 25, 27, 47, 276
    Scanning, 25, 27
Establishing an alliance, 142
Ethical
    issues, 3
    products, 3
Ethical investment, 3
Evaluating market segments, 165
Evaluating mission statements, 115
Evaluation
    of performance, 200
    pressure, 59
Experience